BOGART

STEPHEN HUMPHREY BOGART

BOGART

In Search of My Father

A DUTTON BOOK

DUTTON
Published by the Penguin Group
Penguin Books USA Inc., 375 Hudson Street, New York, New York 10014, U.S.A.
Penguin Books Ltd, 27 Wrights Lane, London W8 5TZ, England
Penguin Books Australia Ltd, Ringwood, Victoria, Australia
Penguin Books Canada Ltd, 10 Alcorn Avenue, Toronto, Ontario, Canada M4V 3B2
Penguin Books (N.Z.) Ltd, 182–190 Wairau Road, Auckland 10, New Zealand

Penguin Books Ltd, Registered Offices:
Harmondsworth, Middlesex, England

First published by Dutton, an imprint of Dutton Signet,
a division of Penguin Books USA Inc.
Distributed in Canada by McClelland & Stewart Inc.

ISBN 0-525-93987-3

Printed in the United States of America

For my father

And in memory of
Gary Provost
1944–1995

Foreword

It is a long road he has travelled since that day on January 6, 1949, when Stephen Humphrey Bogart entered the world. Having firsthand and intimate knowledge of that time, I would say his first eight years of being Humphrey Bogart's son were happy years. After that, with the death of his father, he learned too soon about endings. Growing up as the son of Humphrey Bogart, with all the curiosity of others that would bring, and his yearning to somehow emerge with an identity of his own, was quite a different matter. Having had to cope with the indescribable pain of loss, the confusion and anger that accompanies it, the sense of isolation from his two-parent peers—all throughout his most impressionable, formative, and needy years—must have presented obstacles and miseries beyond comprehension. He did not have the good fortune of time spent with his father or that most precious thing—memories—happy memories—to comfort him.

Added to that came the rebirth of Humphrey Bogart;

the discovery of him by new generations elevated Bogie to an icon, to cult status (a status, incidentally, that now encompasses the world).

But it began while Steve was in his teens.

So it is no surprise that Steve dropped the curtain—not only to forget the pain of loss—but to try to find a place for himself.

For many years I have been hoping and praying he would find a way to come to terms with being his father's son, would get to know him, and perhaps begin to understand the rare qualities that Bogie had as a man—why he represents the kind of character and integrity so hard to find in today's world, and why he has become such an important figure to so many.

It cannot have been easy for Steve to face the unearthing of the past, to face for the first time the reality of his denial, to face himself. But he has done it. These are his words, his feelings, his discovery.

Though I cannot say I fully agree with each of his conclusions, I am happy and proud that he has taken the time and made this extraordinary effort. I am filled with admiration for his accomplishment. And for me, perhaps, what is most satisfying in these pages is that I think he is now ready to be Humphrey Bogart's son, with pride, and to pass on all that he has learned and feels to his children.

I respect him, love him, and am proud to be his mother. I am thankful that he has opened his heart and mind to what must have been a terribly painful—though I hope enlightening and rewarding—time.

Lauren Bacall

BOGART

Introduction

When I was a kid I had it all. Just like Bogie and Bacall. In fact, I had them, too. Humphrey Bogart and Lauren Bacall. They were my parents.

In the early 1950s we lived in a beautiful fourteen-room house at 232 South Mapleton Drive in Holmby Hills, which is a pricey little slice of real estate between Bel Air and Beverly Hills. It was a great house, two stories of whitewashed brick, hidden from the street by hedges and trees. At the entrance to the driveway there was a two-foot brick wall. On it my father had hung a sign: DANGER, CHILDREN AT PLAY.

For years the house was only partially furnished. The living room, especially, always looked incomplete, as if the family had just moved in. I'm not sure why, exactly. I think it was because my mother had promised Dad that if he came up with the money for the house she would furnish it slowly. Dad really wasn't interested in having a big house. He was the kind of guy who could be happy with two rooms, as long as one of them had a bar in it.

We also had a tennis court, a four-car garage, a lanai with wrought-iron tables and chairs, and an expansive lawn where my little sister, Leslie, and I used to do somersaults and play on the jungle gym that my father had bought us. After we moved in, Mother installed a swimming pool, where even today you can see the footprints that Leslie and I left in the concrete.

Along with the two movie stars and the two kids, there were three dogs named Harvey, Baby, and George. To serve us all there was a maid, a butler, a gardener, and a cook. Just as well. My mother was no cook, and my father was no handyman.

I must have thought that everybody lived this way. Sybil Christopher, who was Mrs. Richard Burton when I was a kid, says she took me to see *Hans Christian Andersen* when I was six years old and she remembers that when we walked up to the balcony of one of the huge old opulent movie theaters in Los Angeles, I asked her, "Whose house is this?"

The early fifties were an idyllic time and I have many fond memories of Mapleton Drive. But when I think of the house, I think, too, of my greatest regret, the fact that I had so little time there with my father. It is a regret made more poignant in recent years by the fact that I ignored his memory for most of my life. I resented Humphrey Bogart for reasons I only now understand, and for almost four decades I avoided learning about him, talking about him, and thinking about him. It was only with the marriage to my second wife, Barbara, in 1984, and with the birth of our two children, Richard and Brooke, that I began to pull from my shoulder a chip the size of Idaho that had been there since the death of my dad when I was eight.

I think in the early days of our marriage Barbara was shocked when she began to realize that I knew less about my father than many of his fans. Here I was, telling my new wife that the most important thing to me was family, and I couldn't even score well on a Bogie trivia test at the back of a magazine.

It's not as though nobody had ever urged me to find out about my father. Mother had been doing it for years. But you know how it is when your mother tells you that you should do something. It's practically a guarantee that you won't do it.

I might have gone on forever, fleeing my father's ghost at every turn. But Barbara wouldn't let me. She understood how I was feeling about it, understood certainly better than I did, and she didn't try to change my feelings. She simply showed me how important it was to know who my father was if I really wanted to understand who I was. She let me see that just because I didn't want to glorify my father, that didn't mean I had to ignore him.

"Find out about your father," she said. "Talk to your mother. Talk to his friends. I want our children to know about their grandfather."

And so I began to read about my father. I delved, reluctantly at first, back into my memories of him. And I visited people who knew him. I talked to people he did business with, like Sam Jaffe, his agent, and Jess Morgan, one of his business managers. I talked to people who had played in movies with him, like Katharine Hepburn and Rod Steiger. I talked to some of his writer friends, like Alistair Cooke and Art Buchwald. And I talked to family friends, like Carolyn Morris, and people who had known him briefly, like Dominick Dunne, and friends who had written about him, like Joe Hyams.

Perhaps if I were not Humphrey Bogart's son, but just some guy writing about Bogie, I would have spent more time with Lauren Bacall than with anyone else. But she's my mother. I already know her opinions on the subject. She helped me a great deal, but ultimately she wanted me to do this without having her as a crutch. But I think Mom is pleased. My father has become a character of folklore, and there are so many contradictory stories about him, that I needed to hear what a lot more people other than my mother had to say. Also, Bogart lived more than three-quarters of his life before he met Bacall. So if there are mistakes in this book, and I'm sure there are, don't blame Mom.

And don't blame the other people I spoke to. It is the nature of a legend like Bogie that the stories about him get embellished, relocated, even folded in with other stories. The precise truth is always elusive. But there are many people who took the time to tell me the truth about my father as they knew it, and I want to thank them:

Dominick Dunne, Carolyn Morris, Alistair Cooke, Adolph Green, Rod Steiger, Katharine Hepburn, Phil Gersh, Jess Morgan, Sam Jaffe, George Axelrod, Art Buchwald, Joe Hyams, Sybil (Burton) Christopher, Gloria Stuart, Julius Epstein, Bruce Davison, William Wellman, Jr., Joe Hayes, my sister, Leslie Bogart, and, of course, my mother.

I want to thank, too, the many celebrities and writers whose written words have led me to greater knowledge of my father. Special thanks go to Joe Hyams for *Bogie* and Nate Benchley for *Humphrey Bogart*. Thanks go also to Katharine Hepburn for *The Making of* The African Queen, Janet Leigh for *There Really Was A Hollywood*, Richard Schickel for *Legends:*

Humphrey Bogart, Melvyn Bragg and Sally Burton for *Richard Burton: A Life, 1925–1984,* John Huston for *An Open Book,* Gerold Frank for *Judy,* Bob Thomas for *Golden Boy,* Charles Higham for *Audrey: The Life of Audrey Hepburn,* Vera Thompson for *Bogie and Me,* Edward G. Robinson for *All My Yesterdays,* and Lawrence J. Quirk for *The Passionate Life of Bette Davis.*

And thanks also to the writers, too numerous to name, who wrote about my dad in a number of publications over the years. Among the most helpful ones were the *New York Times,* the *London Daily Mirror,* the *San Francisco Chronicle,* the *Hollywood Reporter,* the *Los Angeles Times,* the *Saturday Evening Post,* the *Chicago Tribune,* the *Hollywood Citizen News,* the Associated Press, *American Film, Esquire, Playboy,* the *New York Post, Atlantic Monthly,* and the *New York Herald.*

Also for their help in various ways in making this book possible I want to thank Chris Keane, Leslie Epstein, Nushka Resnikoff, Ted Eden, Bill Baer, Jeff Alan, Bob Pronvost, Warner Brothers, and the library staffs at the American Film Institute and the Academy of Motion Picture Arts and Sciences.

I want to thank my agent, Susan Crawford, of the Crawford Literary Agency for putting me with the right people at the right time.

And a special thanks to Audrey LaFehr at Dutton for having faith in the book, for her support along the way, and for her editorial wisdom in the final stages.

It is summer of 1993. I am in California.

I have been thinking about my father, Humphrey Bogart, for some time now. I want to write a book about him, but the words have been coming to me only with great difficulty. I have learned about my father, but, unaccountably, I am still reluctant to speak about him, and about what it is like to be his son.

My mother, Lauren Bacall, is in California, too. We have made arrangements to tour the house in Holmby Hills where we lived when I was a kid. The house now is the home of producer Ray Stark and he has graciously agreed to let my mother and I visit.

But now it is a few days before that scheduled tour with my mother. I am alone. I feel compelled to get up early and drive my rental car around the streets of Los Angeles. Inevitably, I drive to the house at 232 South Mapleton Drive. I know that returning to that house will be a powerful experience and I want it to be private. The truth is I want to see the house without my mother. I don't want her explaining things to me, altering my perceptions.

It is still early morning when I pull up beside the house. My first sight of it is more powerful than I expect. Almost immediately, I feel myself shaking. Though we lived in that house for some months after Bogie died, I feel now as if my father, the house, and my childhood were all wrenched away from me in a single violent moment. I do not cry, but I am overcome with emotion. I know that what fills my heart is sorrow, but it feels like fear. It is not a fear that I want to run from. It is something that I want to face. I want to rush out of my car, rap on the back door of the house, tell the people who live there that I am Bogie's son, and beg them to let me run from room to room.

But I don't really want to bother the people who live there. So I sit in my car for a long time, feeling the waves of emotion sweep over me. As I feel the feelings, I also watch myself have the emotions. I have always been able to detach myself from my feelings this way, playing both the patient and the therapist. I think my father did this, too.

"What are you feeling, Steve?" I ask myself.

"Oh, just a little afraid and sad."

"You want to talk about it?"

"No, it's no big deal. It was thirty-seven years ago, for God's sake."

"I see."

Ten minutes later my hands are still gripping the steering wheel. I stare out at the house, as if it, or I, could do something about the past. From where I am parked I can see the patio where Bacall sometimes served drinks. The pool, where I used to float in a yellow tube that was shaped like a duck. The door from the garage into the kitchen, where my friends waited for me. Soon I became self-conscious, thinking someone will call the police and report a stranger casing one of the expensive houses of Holmby Hills. I decide to leave. Still feeling shaky and scared, I drive off, thinking, God, that's the place, that's where my happy childhood ended on January 14, 1957.

1

Mr. Bogart said, "Listen, kid, there are twelve commandments," and then he ordered a drink.

—BOGIE'S GODSON

My mother is a woman who usually gets what she wants. And, in the late 1940s, she was resolved that her husband, Humphrey Bogart, would be a father. So Bogie and Bacall went to work on getting Bacall pregnant. They visited the doctor to see if all the plumbing was in good working order. The equipment was all functional, but the sperm count was a bit low. So Dad started taking vitamins, and his body had to be upgraded a bit because, though he had been a fine athlete at one time, he was now close to fifty and had made a mess of his body with cigarettes and alcohol. The doctor also told Bogie and Bacall to relax, everything would work out.

Though my father was not as oversexed as many well-known movie actors of his time, all indications are that he did enjoy sex. He once said that sex was the most fun you could have without laughing. And I don't think he really wanted his sex life complicated by talk of ovulation and uteral linings, and all the other unromantic considerations that arise when couples are trying to have a baby. Still, except for a small amount of grumbling, he went along with the idea of being a daddy. This would be a first for him. Dad had been married three times before, to Helen Menken, Mary Philips, and Mayo Methot. All three of them had careers as actresses, and neither Dad nor his wives had ever insisted on procreation. So it is not surprising that when my mother told Bogie that she was pregnant, in the summer of 1948, he had second thoughts.

My parents lived in a farmhouse in Benedict Canyon at the time, away from the Hollywood scene and all the "phonies" that my father abhorred. My mother says that when Dad came home from the studio that day, she met him outside the house and told him the glorious news. Dad got very quiet. Then he put his arm around her gently and led her into the house. He remained quiet through dinner. After dinner they had a terrible fight.

Mother says, "It was the worst fight we ever had. Bogie was very upset. He was afraid that the baby would come between us, that our lives would not be the same. He said he didn't marry me just so he could lose me to a child. It was horrid."

Like many Bogie stories, this one has two versions. There is no reason to think he would tell the press the real story, of course, but here is what he did tell a reporter some months later: "The day came when my spouse walked in the door with the words, 'Well, the doctor says you'll never forgive me, but I'm going to have a baby.' I made the proper sounds of elation. Frankly, I think I did them pretty well, considering it was my first take. Then I asked her, 'Why am I never going to forgive you? To me a baby is a baby.' 'Summer is coming, isn't it,' she said. 'Well, I'm not going to be able to do much sailing, you know.' I said, 'Oh.' "

He doesn't mention the fight, but the next morning, he apologized to my mother. He told her that he was shocked at his own behavior. He had been scared, more than anything else. He said he didn't want to lose all the happiness he had found in being married to her. He was afraid of being a lousy father, he said, and he didn't know how he would handle a kid.

I'm sure Bogie had all the birth defect fears that I had when I was an expectant father. Would his kid have all the fingers, toes, and ears that a kid is supposed to have? These fears probably loom even larger when you are almost fifty and expecting your first baby. Dad was full of anxiety about it all, but he also said that he *did* want a baby, more than anything in the world.

After his initial panic, Bogie started to get into this baby thing. His male pals gave him a baby shower, if you can imagine that. Frank Sinatra, Paul Douglas, Mike Romanoff, and others brought diapers and rattles and even little baby dresses, because in those days you didn't know if you would have a boy or a girl. "His shower was bigger than the one I had," Mother says.

Mother spent much of her pregnancy making home improvements in the middle of the night, and reading books about gadgets. Already she was lobbying for a bigger house because she wanted more children. Bogie told his friend

Mike Romanoff, "When other wives are pregnant they're supposed to demand pickles, ice cream, or strawberries out of season. Mine just wants houses."

I became known in the papers as "The most discussed baby-to-be in Hollywood." Hollywood columnists Hedda Hopper and Sheilah Graham called often. Did the baby move? Had they decided on a name?

Throughout the pregnancy Bogie was edgy. He paced. He ran his fingers through his thinning hair. At times he must have looked like one of those death row prisoners he had portrayed, waiting for a phone call from the governor. Bogie had no experience with kids so he started trying to get to know the children of his friends. But he tried too hard, it seems, and was often rebuffed, which made him all the more insecure about what sort of father he would be.

"I can't say that I truly ever wanted a child before I married Betty," he later said. (Betty is my mother. She was born Betty Perske. She took her mother's name of Bacall when she was a kid and her father ran away. Producer Howard Hawks made her Lauren, a name she has never felt comfortable with.) "For one thing, in the past, my life never seemed settled enough to wish it on a minor. I was in the theater in New York, or going on tour around the countryside. And in Hollywood, I was either trying to consolidate my foothold in pictures or was preoccupied by something else. But Betty wanted a child very much, and as she talked about it, I did, too. For one reason, which may seem a little grisly, but true, nonetheless. I wanted to leave a part of me with her when I died. There is quite a difference in our ages, you know, and I am realistic enough to be aware that I shall probably leave this sphere before she does. I wanted a child, therefore, to stay with her, to remind her of me."

* * *

On the day of my birth Bogie was a wreck. This was in the days when guys stayed out of the delivery room and felt pretty helpless. I know how Bogie felt, because I was not allowed in the delivery room when my first son, Jamie, was born. But I know what my father missed, too, because a decade later I watched Richard and Brooke being born and those births were easily the most deeply felt moments of my life.

In the labor room Bogie did not do well. He turned white and felt sick. My father had a great tolerance for pain, but he had almost no tolerance for the pain of people he cared about. (Several people recall that a few years later Bogie got sick when a doctor came to the house to stick a needle in *me*. And a few years after that, when I had my hernia operation, Bogie got sick. Later he bragged to Nunnally Johnson that I had been braver than a soldier.) At 11:22 P.M. on January 6, 1949, I came along. I was named Stephen Humphrey Bogart. I was named Stephen after the character my father played in *To Have and Have Not*, the film that brought my mother and father together. I weighed six pounds, six ounces, and I was twenty inches long. After the birth, Dad was well enough to yank a flask full of scotch out of his coat pocket and pour drinks for all the other fathers-to-be.

The press was notified and soon presents for me arrived from Bogie fans all over the world. Among them were several toy submachine guns, which Dad sent back.

The first present I ever got from my father was a snowman. Incredibly, it had snowed in Beverly Hills on the day I was born. Three inches covered the ground, a rarity in southern California, and when my mother brought me home my father had built a snowman on the lawn to welcome us back. When Mom saw the snowman she felt a lot better about the whole idea of Bogie and fatherhood.

A few days later she felt even better. My parents had set up an intercom between the bedroom and the nursery, so they could hear me if I started crying. One morning, on his way to work, Dad stopped in and began cooing all sorts of baby talk to me, completely unaware that Mother was listening to him through the intercom. Then she heard him speaking to me, somewhat shyly and awkwardly because he didn't know what you were supposed to say to babies. She heard him say, "Hello, son. You're a little fellow, aren't you? I'm Father. Welcome home." He would have been embarrassed if he'd known he was overheard.

Bogie was a proud father, and in family photos you can see him doting over me. In one famous photo you can even see him changing my diapers. But the photo is a fraud. It is, says my mother, the only time in recorded history that Bogie changed a diaper.

Whether my father avoided baby doo because he wanted to, or because he felt left out, is debatable. It seems that Bogie did suffer the feeling of isolation and abandonment that afflicts many new fathers.

"Betty gave me a son when I had given up hope of having a son," he said. "She is everything I wanted and now, Stephen, my son, completes the picture. I don't know what constitutes being a good father. I think I'm a good one, but only time, of course, can tell. At this stage in a child's life the father is packed away, put aside, and sat upon. The physical aspects—feeding, burping, changing, training—are matters before the Bogart committee, which is, as of now, a committee of one . . . Betty. So I won't take over for a while yet.

When I do I'll handle the boy as I would any human being in my orbit. That is, I'll let him be himself. I won't push him into anything or try to influence him."

In any case, Humphrey Bogart was by no means the diaper-changing, new-and-improved sensitive daddy of the 1990s, the one you see these days at the changing table in airport men's rooms. And if he had been, it would not have been a matter of sharing chores to reduce the burden on his wife. We had servants for that.

When I was born, Bogie was already forty-nine years old. He was on his fourth marriage, this time to a beautiful actress who was twenty-five years younger than him. Bogie was a man set in his ways. He was a man with one rule: I'm going to live my life the way I want to. That's the way he was, and he had been that way long before I came along. Even when he married my mother, Bogie kept his butler and cook, and his gardener, Aurelio. So Bogie was not about to make major changes in his life just for a baby.

Besides, he didn't *know how* to change his life for a kid. I've talked to a lot of his friends about this, and they all say the same thing. Bogie was awkward with children. He didn't know exactly what to do with kids. He was in awe of them.

What his agent, Sam Jaffe, said to me is typical. Sam said, "I am the father of three, the grandfather of four, and the great-grandfather of three, so I notice children and I have always noticed how other people deal with them. When I was in the house with Bogie and you kids for the first time, I paid attention. And I will never forget that when you and your sister came down the stairs his look was so . . . quizzical. He was looking at you children as objects of curiosity, as if he had never seen children. It was as if to say 'Who are these people?

What are you?' I'll never forget that. Fatherhood was an unknown thing to him. He came to it late in life. He didn't caress children, didn't do any of the things that I did as a father, because it was strange to him. He was not the sentimental type that gushed, though he did cry easily. I'm not saying he was not a good father, just that he had this look of curiosity around children. He was not ready to be a father. I don't think, until he married Betty, that he ever thought he would have children."

(This Sam, by the way, is not Sam Jaffe the actor, who played in the movie *Gunga Din* and later in the TV show *Ben Casey.*)

Because Dad was uncomfortable with kids, there are not many stories about Bogie and children before I came along. But one of them is that when Bogie was married to Mary Philips, he was godfather to the son of his friends John and Eleanor Halliday. Bogie once offered to take the boy to lunch. When the day came, he said to Eleanor Halliday, "For God's sake, what do you talk to a thirteen-year-old boy about?"

"Well," she said, "you're his godfather. That means you're supposed to be in charge of his religious instruction."

Later, when the boy returned from lunch his mother asked him, "What did you and Mr. Bogart talk about?"

"Not much," the boy told her. "Mr. Bogart said, 'Listen, kid, there are twelve commandments,' and then he ordered a drink."

Adolph Green, who got to know my father when Green and Betty Comden were in Hollywood writing the screenplays for *Singin' In the Rain* and *The Band Wagon*, remembers an incident at Mapleton Drive one day when the pool was being filled.

"They had been fixing the pool, and now they were

pouring new water into it," he says. "You and me and Bogie were there. You were four or five years old. You were watching them fill the pool. There was a hose pouring water into it, and suddenly you got hysterical. You were shrieking. You thought the pool was going to overflow and you were going to drown. I said, 'Don't be silly, Steve, it's okay.' But you kept getting more and more upset. What I remember most, though, is your father. He didn't know what to do. He had no idea how to handle it. He was just shaking his head. I asked him about you, and he said that something else had overflowed recently, a tub or something, so your hysteria had some valid reason behind it. I think your mother must have come out and taken care of you, I don't really remember. But I do remember Bogie shaking his head, helplessly. He had no idea how to handle a hysterical child."

When my sister, Leslie, came along a few years after me Dad fared only slightly better. Because she was a girl he was probably even more afraid of her. But he was also much more affectionate with her. He bounced her on his knee often, though he had done that rarely with me. He played on the seesaw with her. She was Daddy's little girl, the baby as well as the female, and he gave to her a quality of love that he never gave to me. He didn't know any better, of course, didn't understand that a boy needs to be hugged by his father, too. But sometimes when I am lonely, when I feel that life has cheated me out of something important, I wish for the memory of one of those hugs that went to my sister.

My father liked the idea of having kids. He was proud to have Leslie and me, and he would never hurt us or neglect our basic needs. But he was not about to integrate us into his life. Kids had to fit into his life where it was comfortable for him. My father, for example, didn't want to eat dinner with the kids. Which I can understand now, having often endured the torture of eating dinner with a two-year-old.

After I was born, my father's schedule was pretty much the same as it had been before I was born. He worked every day at the studio, making, on average, two movies a year. He got home at five-thirty. Then he liked to be alone for a while, which is why he didn't eat supper with us. On many weekends he went sailing. On days off he went to Romanoff's for lunch. Sometimes he played with us, but not much. He said, "What do you do with a kid? They don't drink."

He would appear, be with us for a little while, and then vanish and do his thing. As a result, I idolized my father, which may come as a surprise to the people who have heard me grumble about him over the years.

In fairness to my father, the pain of losing him seems to have wiped out most of my memories of him, and he might have spent much more time with me than I think. I have learned about many moments with him that I don't remember. When I was six, for example, he told a reporter, "The only thing I'm trying to impress on Steve right now is not to steal and not to squeal. When he comes home with some imaginary or real slight suffered at the hands of neighbor kids, I let him know right now that he's on his own. The other day he started telling me about getting clobbered by a kid up the street. I told him to knock it off. 'Hit him back,' I said. 'I did,' Steve said, 'I got him a beauty.' And that, for the time being, was the end of that."

I have no memory of this. I only know about it because I have the newspaper article. In that same interview, Dad said he looked forward to the day when I could take my place alongside him and help him tack the *Santana* down the Newport Channel. The reporter wrote, "That will be the day, no doubt, when Bogart figures his cup is filled."

Though my father did not make great changes in his daily life, there is little doubt that he was affected by fatherhood. He bragged about the fact that I looked like him. He told one friend, "I've finally begun to understand why men carry pictures of their children with them. They're proud of them." Another friend, Nathaniel Benchley, says, "When Bogie remarried and settled down to raise a family, there came a drastic change. Gentle and sentimental, devoted to his wife and children, he was the antithesis of everything he'd been before and the reconciling of the two sides was like the clashing of gears." And my mother remembers that Bogie cried the first time he saw me in a school room. She says, "I think the impact of fatherhood caught up with him."

It's understandable, I guess, that my father, who had never spent much time around children, would be uncomfortable with kids. But I wonder if it doesn't go deeper than that. I wonder if Bogie might have been unprepared to bond with children because of his own parents. Certainly, I have learned that being the child of famous people, or even just highly successful people, can take its toll. My father was also the child of well-known and very successful people and that, it seems, took its toll on him.

Contrary to the image many have of my father, derived largely from his early films, Humphrey Bogart did not fight his way up from the streets with fists ablaze. He came from wealth and privilege. He was born on Christmas Day in 1899, a circumstance which did not please him as a kid. Once, on my birthday, he said, "Steve, I hope you enjoy it. I never had a birthday of my own to celebrate. I got cheated out of a birthday."

He was the son of a prominent Manhattan surgeon, Belmont DeForest Bogart, and a nationally known magazine illustrator, Maud Humphrey, who had studied in Paris under Whistler.

Dr. Bogart and Maud were a fine-looking couple. He was tall and athletic, a good-looking guy whose tongue could be as sharp as a stiletto. Dr. Bogart could choose the right words and say them in just the right tone to sting people, tickle them, or just make them look ridiculous. This ability to needle was a trait that my father would adopt, and one for which he would be known his entire life. Though my grandfather was strong, handsome, and wealthy, he was less fortunate in other ways. When he was a young intern, a horse-drawn ambulance tumbled on him, and he was never in perfect health after that. In later life, he invested in many businesses that failed, and, because of the pain from the accident, he became addicted to morphine. Maud, my grandmother, was an elegant redhead who drew men to her like beagles to bones. She was a snob who had grown up in the Tory tradition in upper-class Rochester, New York. Bogie often referred to her as "a laboring Tory, if there is such a thing." She was an Episcopalian who cared deeply about the women's suffrage movement, and was a worthy adversary for her husband's debating skills.

Mrs. Bogart was known by everybody, including her kids, as simply Maud.

Bogie once said of his mother, "It was always easier for my two sisters and me to call her 'Maud' than 'Mother.' 'Mother' was somehow sentimental. 'Maud' was direct and impersonal, businesslike. She loved work, to the exclusion of everything else. I doubt that she read very much. I know that she never played any games. She went to no parties, gave none. Actually I can't remember that she even had a friend until she was a very old woman, and then she had only one. She had a few acquaintances who were mostly male artists, and she knew the people in her office well. But she never had a confidante, never was truly intimate with anyone and, I am certain, never wanted to be."

In the early 1900s, Bogie's parents were not super-rich, like the so-called robber barons of the time, but Dr. Bogart's practice raked in twenty thousand dollars a year, which was added to an inheritance he'd gotten from my great-grandfather, who had invented a kind of lithographing process. And Maud, who was in charge of all artistic work for *The Delineator* magazine, was one of the highest-paid illustrators in the country. So there was no danger of the Bogarts running out of oats. The family, which included my dad's two sisters, Frances and Catherine, lived comfortably in a four-story limestone house on 103rd Street and West End Avenue, near Riverside Drive in New York, which is where a lot of fat cats of the time lived.

Like me, my father grew up in a world of fine furniture, expensive rugs, polished silver, servants, celebrities, and modern conveniences, which in his case meant that the Bogarts had a gramophone and a telephone.

If Bogie had a childhood that was materially secure, I don't think it was emotionally satisfying. For one thing, his mother and father did not get along well. "My parents fought," Bogie once said. "We kids would pull the covers over our ears to keep out the sound of fighting. Our home was kept together for the sake of the children as well as for the sake of propriety."

His mother, who was plagued by migraine headaches, used to work at her office all day, then at night she'd put in many more hours in her upstairs studio. Maud was not one to let motherhood interfere with her work. Bogie was, of course, well taken care of by his Irish nurse. But I was taken care of by nurses, too, so I think I know something of what he might have felt. I think he was probably a lonely kid much of the time.

When Bogie's mother did take charge of him, she often took him to the park in his high-wheeled carriage. It was there one day that she sketched the first likeness of Humphrey Bogart. Maud's sketch of her baby was bought by Mellins Baby Food Company, and, before he could even talk, my father became famous as the "Original Maud Humphrey Baby." In fact, he was the most famous baby in the world. The watercolor drawings, with lines so fine that they looked like etchings, were published in magazines and books. They were even framed and sold as individual portraits. In these drawings my father has long curls and he's ridiculously overdressed, which was the stylish thing to do with babies back then.

When Humphrey got pneumonia, Maud got it into her head that he was a sickly child. "He is manly," she once wrote of the future tough guy, "but too delicate in health." That's about as weepy as Maud got over her son. The fact is that Maud Humphrey was not exactly a candidate for Mom of the Year.

"I was brought up very unsentimentally, but very straightforward," my father once said. "A kiss in our family was an event. Our mother and father didn't fawn over my two sisters and me. They had too many things to do, and so did we. Anyway, we were mainly the responsibility of the servants."

He once told a *Time* reporter, "I can't say that I loved my mother. I admired her and respected her. Ours was not the kind of affection that spills over or makes pretty pictures. If, when I was grown up, I sent my mother one of those Mother's Day telegrams or said it with flowers, she would have returned the wire and flowers to me collect."

Some of Bogie's friends have told me that this "I never loved my mother" business is a polite understatement—that, in fact, he could not stand her. Nevertheless, he did take care of her in her declining years, and she was living with him and his third wife when she died of cancer at the age of seventy-five.

Maud, according to my father, was totally incapable of showing affection. "This might have stemmed from shyness," he said, "from a fear of being considered weak." Her caress, he said, was like a blow. "She clapped you on the shoulder, almost the way a man does. When she was proud of you there was no running down the stairs with arms outstretched, no 'My darling son.' Only, 'Good job, Humphrey,' or something like that."

My father's relationship with his father, while far from perfect, seems to have been less disappointing. Dr. Bogart liked to fish, hunt, and sail a hell of a lot more than he liked to poke around in people's abdomens with surgical instruments. This sometimes led to friction between himself and Maud, but it was good for father and son. Dr. Bogart loved the open air and he often took young Humphrey with him. Though Bogie would grow up having no stomach for the killing of animals ("Went fishing for ten years," he said in his pithy way. "Didn't catch anything."), his love of sailing was an abiding one and it was the love of his life. Except for Bacall, of course.

Still, despite what they shared, few words of affection

passed between my father and his father before September of 1934. It was then that my father was playing chess for a dollar a game at a chess parlor on Sixth Avenue in Manhattan, when he got word that his father was dying. He rushed home. Two days later Dr. Bogart passed away in Bogie's arms.

"It was only in that moment that I realized how much I really loved him and needed him and that I had never told him," Bogie said later. "Just before he died I said, 'I love you, Father.' He heard me, because he looked at me and smiled. Then he died. He was a real gentleman. I was always sorry he couldn't have lived long enough to see me make some kind of success."

My own regrets about my father's death are somewhat different than that. I don't think much about whether or not I said, "I love you, Father." If I never used those words I certainly showed my love in the ways a small child does, by climbing on his lap, by coming to him for good-night hugs and kisses, and by calling him such charming pet names as "blubberhead," and "slob." No, my regrets have less to do with how I felt about him, and more with how he felt about me. I regret that he didn't spend as much time with me as I would have liked, and that he died when it seemed that he was just starting to get the hang of this fatherhood thing. I wasn't always sure of it, but I am sure now that if my father had lived a full life we would have had the kind of relationship that fathers and sons dream of.

But, as it is, I still have a few memories. One of them concerns Romanoff's restaurant. Though my father had gone to Africa to make *The African Queen,* and Italy to make *Beat the Devil,* he generally stayed around Hollywood. And when he wasn't working he was often schmoozing at Romanoff's restaurant.

Phil Gersh, who was a partner of Sam Jaffe, remembers my father's Romanoff's days well.

"I'd meet your father at Romanoff's," Gersh says. "Bogie always had the same lunch. Two scotch and sodas, French toast, and a brandy. He never looked at a menu. And he never carried money. He'd say 'Phil, have you got a dollar for the valet kid?'"

Actually, my father stuck people with more than just the valet's tip money. It was a running gag for him to see how often he could con somebody else into paying the bill.

Mike Romanoff, who owned the restaurant, was a close friend of my father. He was known as Prince Michael. As far as anybody knows, no drop of royal blood ever flowed through Mike Romanoff's veins, but for years he insisted he was Prince Michael Alexandrovitch Dmitri Obolensky Romanoff, a nephew of Russian Czar Nicholas Romanoff. Phoney prince or not, Mike was much loved by the Hollywood crowd. He was a guy Hollywood turned to for advice, a regular Ann Landers, and his restaurant was a famous watering hole for movers and shakers. Mike was also one of the few people who could beat my father at chess. It was Mike Romanoff who summed up my father about as well as anybody could in one sentence. He said, "Bogart is a first-class person with an obsessive compulsion to behave like a second-class person."

My father had his own reserved table at Romanoff's. I remember it well. It was the second booth to the left from the entry way. There Bogie would eat his lunch, drink his scotch, and shoot the breeze with some of the best-known people in the world.

One day, when I was seven, Bogie decided that I should join the world of men. That is, I should be taken to Romanoff's restaurant and shown off. On this day he wanted to be Daddy. That morning my mother dressed me up in new long trousers and a spiffy new shirt, then she brought me up to the bedroom to be inspected by the man himself.

My father, wearing gray flannels, a black cashmere jacket, and a checked bow tie, looked long and hard at me. "You look good, kid," he said. Then off we went, me and Bogie, in the Jaguar.

Romanoff's was in Beverly Hills. Dad and I arrived in the Jag at 12:30, my father's usual time. When we pulled in, the valet took the car and we were led immediately to Bogie's regular booth. Dad waved to a few of the many Hollywood notables who were already dining, and I'm sure most of them thought it adorable that he had his little Stevie with him. We sat in the booth and Mike Romanoff came over to greet us.

"Good afternoon, your royal highness," my father said. His usual greeting to Mike.

"Good afternoon, Mr. Bogart," Mike said, in his carefully cultivated Oxford accent. "Are you going to be paying your bill today? I thought that might be a pleasant change."

"Are you going to be putting any alcohol in your overpriced drinks?" Bogie asked. "That also would be a nice change."

"You won't be needing a necktie today?" Romanoff said. "No."

Romanoff, you see, had a jacket and tie policy at the restaurant, and he always made Dad wear a tie. One time my father had baited Mike by showing up with a bow tie that was one inch wide and sat on a pin.

"I see you've brought your grandson," Mike said.

Mike liked to rib my father about his age. Bogie was a quarter of a century older than Bacall, so when my mother was with Bogie at the restaurant, Mike would say to her, "I see you are still dating the same aging actor."

It went on like that for a while. I guess it always went on like that for a while. My strongest memories of that day are the feel of the green leather upholstery of the booth, the taste of creamed spinach, a specialty of the house which I loved, and the steady parade of grown-ups, which I wasn't crazy about.

I don't know everyone who came by to talk on that particular day. But this schmoozing at Romanoff's was a ritual. It was common for David Niven to stop by at my father's booth and visit, and for Judy Garland and Sid Luft, and Richard Brooks. And sometimes Spencer Tracy. I'm sure that Swifty Lazar came by on this particular day. Swifty, whose real name was Irving, got his nickname from my father after making three big deals in one day. He died only a few years ago. In fact, the 1987 Chrysler half-wagon which I drive today is one I bought from Swifty. He was known as the first Hollywood superagent, but he was not my father's agent; he was his friend. Swifty was a small man, with a face like a cherub's, but built as solidly as a fire hydrant. And he was one of the dandiest dressers in Hollywood history. He was once described by my godfather, writer Quentin Reynolds, as "a new kind of beach toy turned out by an expensive sporting goods store."

So Swifty came by, and movie stars and singers, and studio heads, all of them smiling at the rare sight of Bogie with a child. They paid their dues to me: "How are you, Stephen?" and "My, don't you look grown-up!" But then into shop talk they would go . . . Stanley Kramer had just bought rights to such and such a book, Gary Cooper was filming this, Harry Cohn was pissed off about that, and so on. A lot of celebrities, a lot of fascinating talk.

Fascinating, that is, to grown-ups, but not to a person whose idea of fun was sliding down banisters and climbing trees with Diane Linkletter. I was not impressed. I was the son of two movie stars, and, more to the point, I was only seven years old. So I was, in a word, bored.

By the time Bogie was into the brandy, my boredom had begun to take physical form. I was rapping my water glass with a fork.

"Don't do that, kid," my father said.

I was banging my feet under the table.

"Cut it out, kid," my father said.

And, no doubt, I was making faces, tapping my fingers, fidgeting, and glancing around. Acting like a kid. But the behavior of children was a complete mystery to Humphrey Bogart and, though he was almost continually amused by life, he was now getting less and less amused.

By the time we left the restaurant that day, we were not speaking to each other. My father's knuckles were white on the wheel of his Jaguar as he drove, perhaps a little too fast, through the streets of Beverly Hills, anxious to deliver the demon son back to the arms of Bacall.

I guess my father sometimes thought I was a handful. Once, discussing me with a friend, he said, "One word from me and he does as he pleases." And my mother's friend, Carolyn Morris, remembers, "You were challenging. Like your father. You did things your way and if anybody told you how to do them, you would do them more your way. Your dad was like that, very much."

When we got home that day my mother was out by the

pool reading. Dad led me directly to her, as if I might try to make a run for it.

"Baby," he said. "Never again."

My mother said nothing. She put her book down and looked at me, as if to ask, *What is your side of the story?*

"Never again," I said, mimicking my father, and off I went to read my comic book.

In fact, Bogie did take me to Romanoff's again, a few times. I don't remember any conflict connected with those visits, so things must have gone better.

I only have one other memory of causing trouble for my father, and that is mostly because I was told the story years later by David Niven, one of my father's closest Hollywood friends. He told me about a time when I almost knocked out one of the world's most famous playwrights in our living room.

The playwright was Noël Coward. It seems that one night in 1955, Niven and Coward were sitting with Bogie. Noël Coward was visiting on his way to Las Vegas, where he was to make his first Vegas appearance, at the Sands Hotel. Coward wanted to discuss his material with Bogie and Niven. He was very worried about it. Would the Vegas nightclub crowd even understand the sophisticated humor of a British playwright? Bogie and Niven were in the two easy chairs, facing Coward, who sat on the sofa. I was behind the sofa. I don't know whether I was being ignored or just in a pissy mood, or had something against British comedy or what, but Niven says I began moving ominously behind Coward, eyeing his head as if it were some sort of animal to be stalked. And I was armed with a large brass serving tray. When I got close behind Noël Coward, I lifted the tray and smashed it down on top of his head. It must have stung something awful, even if it was being wielded by a six-year-old. But the famous playwright never turned to look at me. He just looked at my father and, in that clipped British accent, said, "Bogart dear, do you know what I am going to give darling little Stephen for Christmas? A chocolate-covered hand grenade."

It was unusual for us to use the living room. It was not fully furnished, but it did contain a few expensive antiques and paintings. When my mother and father brought guests into the house, which was often, my mother was inclined to steer them toward the wood-paneled study, the butternut room, where the furniture was less pricey and more comfortable. And where there was a bar. The butternut room was a cozy room with full bookcases, comfortable chairs, folding tables, and a pull-down screen for film viewing. These guests were famous people: Sinatra, Tracy, Garland, Benchley, Niven, Huston, on and on, and many were very wealthy. But most of them were drinkers. My father was not comfortable with people who didn't drink. "I don't trust anyone who doesn't drink," he once said. So my parents' friends could be rowdy at times and I don't think Mother wanted them bumping into her paintings and shattering vases.

Bacall certainly had good reason to worry. My father and his friends were capable of mischief. Once, after John Huston and his father, Walter, got Academy Awards for their work on *The Treasure of the Sierra Madre,* Dad, who also got an Oscar nomination for the movie, went back to John Huston's place where Bogie and the director, still wearing tuxedoes, played football in the mud against a movie executive and a screenwriter. They either didn't have a football or were too drunk to look for one, so, instead, they ran pass patterns with a grapefruit.

* * *

There are many reasons why I did not see a lot of my father when I was a kid. One reason was his work. Another was his boat, the *Santana.*

While most people know that Bogie and Bacall had a great love affair, probably fewer know about my father's other great love affair. It was with sailing. Specifically, it was with the *Santana,* a fifty-five-foot sailing yacht, which he had bought from Dick Powell and June Allyson. The sea was my father's sanctuary.

My father was not simply some movie star throwing money into a hole in the water. He was very serious about the boat and he was an excellent helmsman who earned the respect of the sailing fraternity, despite some well-entrenched prejudices they had about actors with boats.

My father once answered a question about his devotion to sailing this way: "An actor needs something to stabilize his personality, something to nail down what he really is, not what he is currently pretending to be."

Phil Gersh says that at one point my father used to go out on the boat thirty-five weekends a year. I'd like to say that my father took me most of the time, but that's not true. There was a long time when I wanted to go, but Dad would not let me on the boat until I could swim. Most of my life I've thought that was just his way of not having the kids on the boat, but Carolyn Morris, one of my mother's best friends, says, "No, I think he was genuinely concerned about your safety. He had respect for the sea."

Later, when I could swim, Dad took me on the boat now and then. Carolyn says, "I remember him taking just you on the boat, you and Pete. He didn't like to show his emotions, but his eyes would give him away. He was really excited about having a boy. He loved you an awful lot and it was important to him that you love the sea."

I do remember a trip with my father and Joe Hyams, and Joe's son, who was about my age. And I remember Pete, the skipper, who was known as "Pete BS" when there were ladies aboard, or "Bullshit Pete" when there were only males. The name Bullshit Pete always made me giggle.

My mother was prone to seasickness, and by the time I was born her trips on the *Santana* were rare. That was okay with Dad. He liked his boating weekends to be all male anyhow. "The trouble with having dames on board," he said, "is you can't pee over the side."

The *Santana* could sleep two in the master cabin. Four more could sleep in the main cabin. And there was sleeping space for two more ahead of the galley. On the boat my father was a regular Miss Manners. If you made a mess, you cleaned it up.

I can remember driving down to the harbor in Newport with him. There was a big iron shed there near the water, though I'm not sure what was in it. Pete would be waiting on the dock by the boat. His real name was Carl Petersen, but Dad always called him "Square Head."

There would usually be a couple of young actors on the boat, who worked as crew. Dad would start the engine, and the crew would pull in the lines, and off to Catalina we would go. The trip took about four hours, depending on the wind. Catalina itself was no big deal. It was a fairly barren island with hills, and a lot of goats. The only town was Avalon. The thing about Catalina was getting there. From southern California it was the only place to go farther west. Once there, Bogie would anchor in White's Landing, north of Avalon. The water was clear there, and there was a beach where I could play. This was a kind of gathering place for other sailing folk. My dad and his friends would set lobster traps, which was illegal. Instead of buoys they would tie liquor bottles to the lines. Sometimes they would get a few lobsters and Bogie and his pals would cook them on the boat.

On one trip when I was six or seven, I went along and brought an empty cricket cage, in which I usually kept a toy skunk. I'm not sure of just who else was on the trip, but I know that Nathaniel Benchley was, because he also remembered the incident. On this trip I was determined to catch a fish, which I can see now was silly, because a fish could swim through the spaces in the cage. So I propped open the cage with a stick, and for bait I put in some crabs I had found on shore. I hung the cage by a string over the stern of the boat, and every ten minutes I pulled it up to see if I had caught a fish. Even after dark I checked my cage with a flashlight until finally my flashlight fell into the water, and I went to bed, while the adults drank and played dominoes. I figured when I woke up there would be a fish in my cage. So the next morning I woke up early. I have a vivid memory of pulling up that cage, being so excited and filled with anticipation because it was very heavy. I finally yanked it aboard and I couldn't believe what I saw. I had caught a lobster. Or more accurately, I had caught a lobster with no tail. I was overjoyed. I went crazy with excitement.

"I caught a lobster, I caught a lobster," I shouted, waking everybody up. Soon all the guys were smiling and congratulating me on my big catch. It was one of the most exciting moments of my life. I was so proud of myself.

It wasn't until I was twenty and had become a father myself that somebody told me that my father had placed the lobster in the cage for me to catch. Bogie, it seemed, was being my daddy even when I didn't know it.

I'm sure that the way my father treated me, and the loss of my father at an early age, have influenced me in ways that I cannot totally understand. But the most lasting effect of being Bogie's son is obvious to me; it is the way in which I raise my children.

Even though I was barely an adult myself when my first wife Dale and I had our son, Jamie, I was determined to put him first in my life. Nothing would be more important. I would be for Jamie the kind of father I wished Bogie had been for me. And I think I was. I hugged my son. I kissed him. I read to him. I played ball with him. I coached his baseball teams all the way through high school. In many ways, I guess, I was being a father to myself, and I'm sure I was a better father to my son because my own father died when I was eight. Jamie is an adult now, but I still have Richard and Brooke at home, and nothing has changed my mind about the importance of putting the kids first. When my kids are my age they will have many memories of times spent with their father.

That's important to me, because even during all those years when I was angry about being Humphrey Bogart's son, I wished that I had more complete memories of my dad. There were some. But far more common were those fragments of memory which became whole only when fitted in to the stories I was told. I remember, for example, taking a train trip with my father. But only in retrospect do I know that the trip was to northern California where we visited my mother on the set of *Blood Alley.*

Joe Hyams went on that trip and he remembers the details. He remembers Bogie calling and asking him to come along:

"We'll go up on the evening train to see Betty," Bogie said, "and then, maybe on Saturday, we can go to the zoo."

"The zoo?" Hyams said.

"Sure," Bogie said. "You and me and Betty and Steve."

"Steve? You want me along as a baby-sitter?"

"Of course not," Bogie said. "I want you for your company. But you've got kids."

"So."

"So, I figure you'll know what to do when Steve acts up."

Before the trip, Hyams stopped and bought some toys at the five-and-ten. When Bogie saw the toys he thought Hyams was a genius.

"Toys, yes," he said. "Great idea! Kids like toys." He told Hyams, "This is the first time I've been alone with the kid. I hope it works out all right."

Hyams remembers that once we found our compartments and the train got going Bogie was all for "bedding down the kid" and getting a drink in the dining car. But I was six and I insisted on hearing a fairy tale.

"I don't know any fairy tales," Dad said. "Uncle Joe will tell you one."

But I wanted a fairy tale from my father, not Uncle Joe. So Hyams sat on the lower bunk beneath me, making up a fairy tale and whispering the words to Bogie, who would then repeat them to me. According to Hyams I fell asleep, and so did my father.

Hyams also remembers that quizzical look that Dad often had with me and Leslie, a look that several people have told me about. And Hyams remembers being on that train trip the next day and seeing that look and Bogie saying to him, "I guess maybe I had the kid too late in life. I just don't know what to do about him." Then adding, "But I love him. I hope he knows that."

It is two days after my first visit to the house. I am inside the house now. I am with my mother. Not quite seventy years old, Bacall is still the glamorous figure she was back then in her twenties, and as she sweeps through the house, narrating her own memories in that trademark husky voice of hers that so long ago said, "You know how to whistle, don't you." I try very hard to hear my father whistle. This, after all, was the place where Bogie and Bacall had it all.

But while the memories come full blown and in living color for my mother, they come for me in shards of black and white. It is as if I am looking at a series of photographs, some of friends, some of strangers. When my mother leads me into what had been the dining room, it is as if I am seeing it for the first time. It is the same with the living room. There is no shock of recognition. But at other moments, a turn in the hall, a glance at the baseboard, I am swept back again to the feeling of being seven years old. The nostalgia is most potent when we stand by the wide white stairway that leads up from the living room to the second floor. Now, almost forty years later, I can feel myself sliding down the banister, I can hear my father's voice warning me to quiet down. For whatever reason, it is those stairs that most vividly transport me back to those days when I was a tumbling boy and my father was alive.

Lost in memories, I now see that my mother has led me to the butternut room where Bogie and Bacall enter-

tained their friends. God, *I think,* the people who used to laugh in this room. Frank Sinatra, John Huston, Katharine Hepburn, Judy Garland . . .

2

Bogie was never wrong about people. If he thought a person was all right, the person was all right. And if he thought a person was a phony, the person was a phony.

—SAM JAFFE

Looking back, I can see that Mapleton Drive was an extraordinary street. It was a celebrity enclave, the kind of well-heeled and neatly manicured neighborhood that my father swore he would never inhabit, right up to the day that Bacall talked him into it. On Mapleton, I played with the children of famous people. I took piano lessons with Tina Sinatra at Frank Sinatra's house. And my closest friend was Scott Johnson, whose father, Nunnally Johnson, was a Bogie pal. Nunnally wrote dozens of screenplays including *The Grapes of Wrath*, *The Dirty Dozen*, and *The Three Faces of Eve*, which he also produced and directed.

Living across the street from me was Art Linkletter, who was one of TV's top daytime personalities in the 1950s, with *Art Linkletter's House Party*. His daughter, Diane, and I were like Tarzan and Jane, constantly climbing trees together. And next to Linkletter lived Sammy Cahn, the famous composer. His son, Steve, and I liked to hike back into the woods behind my house, where we had a little camp. Sometimes we'd make a fire and roast marshmallows on a stick. Down the street was Judy Garland. Her daughter, Liza Minnelli, was my other close female friend. Liza, of course, is now a superstar in her own right, but then she was, like me, the child of famous people. Her father was Vincente Minnelli, who directed *An American In Paris*, *Gigi*, and *Lust for Life*. By this time, though, Judy Garland was married to Sid Luft, the producer, and their daughter, Lorna, was my sister's pal. Judy Garland visited my mother often. Judy, as everybody in the world knows, was troubled, and she often came to my parents for comfort.

Bing Crosby lived down the street with his four sons, who used to cruise up and down Mapleton in their Corvettes. Gloria Grahame lived there, too. And Lana Turner. Liza used to hang out with Lana Turner's daughter, Cheryl Crane, who, you might remember, got into one of the 1950s' biggest show-biz scandals when she stabbed to death her mother's mobster boyfriend, Johnny Stompanato. The incident was more than a scandal to Cheryl, of course. It was a tragedy that propelled her onto the front pages of newspapers all over America.

I had many good friends on Mapleton, but after my father died, when I was eight, I gradually lost them. And for years afterward I did not make friends easily. One reason was that I always heard the fearful whisper in my ear: *he only likes you because you're Bogie's boy*. Not surprisingly, my closest friends today are the people who didn't know or didn't care that I was Humphrey Bogart's son.

It wasn't until after I got thrown out of Boston University and moved to Torrington, Connecticut, with Dale that I got reconnected, that I began to develop the kind of friendships I had always wanted.

I had been to Dale's home in Torrington before, and from the moment I saw it, I knew it was home. For me this small Connecticut town was as magical as Brigadoon. The people there couldn't have cared less that I was Humphrey Bogart's son. As I saw it, I could hide there and be what I wanted. In Torrington, my friends were not the sons of movie stars or bank presidents. They were guys who drove trucks or worked in factories, or ran auto repair shops. They didn't have any film projects in development; they didn't have private swimming pools. These were guys I played poker with, and pickup basketball at the school yard. It was there that I was first able to shed the skin of being the Bogart kid. What I learned then was that friendship is what I really needed and it was what mattered. I learned, too, that if you want to know the truth about a person you should look at his friendships. With his family, a man often acts out of guilt and a sense of responsibility. With women he might be trying too hard to impress, or he's conniving so he can get laid. And with coworkers, if he wants to get ahead, he's got to pretend to care about a lot of things that he doesn't really care about. But with friends, well there's nothing there but the friendship, and I think it is with his friends that a man ends up revealing who he really is.

So I knew, when I started asking about my father, that if this was true of ordinary men, it was even more true for Bogie. Though he had many good friends over the years, Bogie did not see it that way. "I have a few good, close friends, that's all," my father once said.

On Christmas Eve, the night before his forty-sixth birthday, my mother threw him a surprise birthday party. She gathered about twenty of their friends, and ordered them to stand in the Roman tub at the Bogart house in Hollywood. When my father came home, Mother handed him a drink, but told him not to get too comfortable.

"There's something wrong with the tub," she said. "Can you take a look at it?"

When my father went in to check on the tub, there were all the friends, Robert Benchley and Raymond Massey among them, absurdly crowded together in the Roman tub. "Surprise!" they shouted, and "Happy Birthday!" not "Merry Christmas."

A party followed, and my father, who had never had a surprise party in his life, was deeply touched, even more than my mother expected.

"I think he was genuinely surprised," she says. "Not just by the party, but by the fact that all these people cared enough about him to come on Christmas Eve. Despite all the success he'd had, he didn't really feel popular. I don't think he ever really knew how much he was loved."

The first of my father's good friends was Bill Brady, Jr. Brady's father, William Brady, Sr., was a fight promoter and theatrical producer who would eventually give Dad his first break in show business. It was as a teenager with Bill Brady that my father first saw Broadway shows and moving pictures. Sadly, young Brady died in a fire right around the time that my father was becoming famous in *The Petrified Forest*. Dad, who rarely displayed his emotions, wept openly over the death of his friend. Years later, he was hit hard again when his pal, Mark Hellinger, died of a heart attack at age forty-four when Hellinger and Dad were trying to get a production company going.

From early adulthood on, the main thing that Bogie did with his friends was drink. When he was in his twenties he drank with friends in New York's Greenwich Village. When he was on Broadway he drank with friends in Times Square. When he was a movie star he drank with friends at 21 in Manhattan, and drank with other friends at Romanoff's when he was home. Of course, heavy drinking was not the politically incorrect activity that it is today. There were no Mothers Against Drunk Driving, and such heavy drinking was considered manly, even a bit amusing. And he also played games. He was a chess expert and very good at card games. He played poker, too. In these games, friends remember that he was always very meticulous, carefully counting out his moves on a Parcheesi board, for example.

Though Bogie had more friends than he ever realized, he was, by no means, universally loved. "Everybody doesn't like me, and I don't like everybody," he once said.

One reason that some people did not like him was that he was a world-class needler. It was one more game with him. He liked to test people as soon as he met them, perhaps see if they were worthy opponents. When he first met Frank Sinatra, for example, he said, "They tell me you have a voice that makes girls faint. Make me faint." And when he met John Steinbeck he said, "Hemingway tells me you're not all that good a writer."

Bogie needled everybody, including Mother. He needled her often about leaving Leslie and me so that she could work. "Look," he'd say, "if you're not going to be another Sarah

Bernhardt, don't give up everything just to be an actress." Or he would find a hole in a sock and say, "You've got time to be an actress but no time to darn my socks." My father, you can see, would have had to make a few adjustments if he lived in this postfeminist era.

Though my father never used foul language around women and never told off-color stories in their presence, he did not exempt them from his needling. My mother's friend Carolyn Morris remembers an incident that occurred the first time she met Bogie. It was when she went with my mother to see him at the Beverly Hills Hotel. When my mother was first seeing Bogie, it was all very secret because even though he was separated from Mayo Methot at the time, they were still married. So Bacall had asked Carolyn to go with her, to make it more innocent.

When Carolyn got into the hotel room she could see right away that Bogie had been drinking and was not pleased to see her with Bacall. He'd expected to have Mom alone.

At the time Carolyn's future husband, Buddy, was in Florida, so she decided to give him a call from Bogie's suite.

"What's the deal?" Bogie said to Bacall. "You bring your girlfriends up here so they can make long-distance calls on my phone?"

Carolyn, who was for the first time meeting the man that her friend Betty had been swooning over, didn't know what to think. He seemed pretty obnoxious to her.

"Maybe I should put up a sign," Bogie said. "Public telephone for friends of Bacall."

He kept it up all through Carolyn's call to Buddy. By the time she hung up, Carolyn was steaming. She slammed down the phone and pulled a five-dollar bill out of her pocketbook.

"Here," she said. "For the phone call."

"I don't want it," he said.

"Take it," she said. "I don't want you saying that I'm running up your precious phone bills."

"I don't want it," he said.

"I insist."

Finally, Bogie took the five-dollar bill and tore it up. It was only later that he and Carolyn became good friends.

Another Bogie friend, George Axelrod, said to me, "Your father was full of life. He was a demon. When I first met him he liked to get me drunk. He had a great sense of humor, very dry, and he would never laugh at his own jokes. He would mutter, always with a cigarette and always with a drink. I think he was born with a scotch in his hand.

"But this guy Bogart was always making trouble for people and wouldn't let them off easy. He liked to shake up the world. He was trying for his own private revolution. He often said to Rock Hudson, 'What kind of a name is that, what the hell is Rock Hudson?' Here we had a man named Humphrey making fun of someone else's name. Actually, Rock and your father were friends. Rock's real name was Roy and he hated to be called Rock. So your father teased him by calling him Rock all the time. Bogie thought 'Rock Hudson' was a pretension, so he kept on it, wouldn't let up on him."

This, I've learned, was not the only time my father made fun of names. It was a regular thing with him. One time he met a young writer at a party named Ben Ray Redman. He said to Redman, "You know what's wrong with you? You're just another goddamned three-named writer." Then, I guess Dad was feeling very clever, because he started reeling off a list of three-named writers. "Stephen Vincent Benet," he said.

"Mary Roberts Rinehart, Harriet Beecher Stowe, Louisa May Alcott, Marjorie Kinnan Rawlings," and on he went.

Dad wanted to see if people would stand up to him, and sometimes that was a mistake. For example, he met Judy Garland's third husband, Sid Luft, for the first time at a Swifty Lazar party. Bogie was drinking and started getting on Luft right from the beginning. But Luft, a former test pilot, who was a pretty powerful guy, was having none of it. He picked Bogie off the floor and pinned him to a wall.

"Put me down, you son of a bitch," Bogie said.

Instead of putting him down, Luft kissed him on both cheeks.

"We're going to be good friends, you and I," Luft said.

"Oh yeah, and why's that?"

"Because we're not going to needle each other."

"Oh, we're not, huh?"

"That's right," Luft said. "And the reason we are not going to needle each other is because I'd have to split your head open." Then he put my father down. "Right, Bogie?"

There was a moment of tension, followed by a burst of laughter from my father. Then everything was fine. I think my father liked this sort of thing because he was an actor. This was dramatic. This was bigger than life.

My father liked to show off. And needling people like Luft was a way to do it. Nat Benchley said, "There are some people who will argue that Bogart was simply an exhibitionist who caused severe rectal pains to all around him, but this argument neglects the fact that he could, when he chose, be as quiet and thoughtful as a Talmudic scholar. If he acted up, there was usually a reason for it, and the reason could often be found in the company."

Dad's tendency to take on people before he knew who

he was dealing with got him in trouble one time early in his career when he was working for Twentieth Century-Fox, and still trying to get a foothold in Hollywood. He was a serious golfer, at least then. He was playing with a friend, behind a very slow foursome. When Bogie asked if he could play through, one of the guys in the foursome turned and glared at him.

"Certainly not," the guy said. "Who the hell do you think you are, asking such a thing?"

"My name is Humphrey Bogart," my father said. "I work at Fox. And what the hell are you doing, playing a gentleman's game at a gentleman's club?"

Unfortunately, the man that my father shouted at was a vice president at Fox. Maybe that's why Dad ended up making most of his movies at Warner Brothers.

Dad didn't fight just with strangers, though. He often got into it with friends. One night he was needling his agent, Sam Jaffe, at Romanoff's and Jaffe got fed up.

"Listen," Sam said, "I don't take that guff from you or anyone else. If you need to be that way, get a new agent, I'll give your contract back. I'm not taking that stuff."

Bogart thought it over, and decided to quit the needling, at least for the night. There was another incident concerning Jaffe, this one at the Jaffe house. For some reason, Bogie was annoyed at the modern paintings that hung on the Jaffes' walls. Dad probably thought there was something pretentious about the work.

"Goddamn phoney artists," he said.

"What did you say?" Sam asked him.

"The paintings on your walls," Bogie said. "They're a bunch of phoney crap."

"Really?"

"Yes, really. You know what I ought to do?"

"What's that?"

"I ought to throw them all out."

It was then that Mrs. Jaffe entered the conversation.

"Get out," she said.

"Huh?"

"Get out, Mr. Bogart. Leave my house. You are not behaving properly."

Bogie left and never criticized the Jaffes' taste in paintings again.

John Huston is another close friend whom Bogie fought with. Kate Hepburn told me that Bogie and Huston exchanged words while making *The African Queen*. And Jess Morgan, who was a friend to both men, says that Bogie and Huston were two strongminded men who fought often. But Huston, apparently, didn't think of their disagreements as fights because he said that it was during the filming of *The Treasure of the Sierra Madre* that he and Bogie had "our one and only quarrel."

As Huston told the story, Bogie was getting impatient for shooting on *Sierra* to end because he wanted to get the *Santana* into a race to Honolulu. Bogie was afraid that the picture would run over schedule and he would miss out. Huston said my father "sulked and became progressively less cooperative."

One day they were shooting a scene between Bogie and Tim Holt.

"Okay," Huston said after they cut. "Let's do one more."

"Why?" Bogie asked.

"Why what?" Huston asked.

"Why another take?"

"Because I need another," Huston said.

"I thought I was good," Bogie said.

"You were," the director said. "It has nothing to do with you, Bogie. I'd just like to shoot it again."

"Well, I don't see why you have to shoot it again. I thought it was pretty good," my father said.

"Please," Huston asked. Now he was getting annoyed. "Just do it."

Bogie did the new take, but he wasn't happy about it. Later that evening, when Bogie and Huston and my mother sat down to supper, Dad started grumbling again.

"Too goddamn many takes," he said. "Don't need them all."

"What's that, Bogie?"

"You're taking too goddamn long to shoot this movie," Bogie said. He leaned across the table, poking an accusing finger at his friend. "The way we're going, I'll miss my race."

That's when Huston reached out and grabbed Dad's nose between two fingers and started squeezing.

"John, you're hurting him," my mother said.

"Yes, I know," Huston said. "I mean to." He gave Dad's nose one more solid twist and let it go.

Later my father felt bad, because he had fought with his friend. He came to Huston. "What the hell are we doing?" Bogie said. "Let's have things be the way they have always been with us." They made up and sealed it with a drink. Bogie, by the way, did miss the race.

Richard Burton also remembers that Bogie could be rough on his friends. Burton recalls one Catalina night out on the boat with Bogie, David Niven, and Frank Sinatra, who crooned all night long for dozens of other sailing people who floated around the *Santana* in their dinghies.

Burton says, "Frankie did sing all through the night, it's

true, and a lot of people sat around in boats and got drunk. Bogie and I went out lobster potting and Frankie got really pissed off with Bogie. David Niv was trying to set fire to the *Santana* at one point, because nobody could stop Francis from going on and on and on. I was drinking boilermakers with Bogie—rye whiskey with canned beer chasers—so the night is pretty vague, but I seem to remember a girl having a fight with her husband or boyfriend in a rowing dinghy and being thrown in the water by her irate mate. I don't know why, but I would guess that she wanted to stay and listen to Frankie, and he wanted to go. And Bogie and Frankie nearly came to blows the next day about the singing the night before and I drove Betty home because she was so angry with Bogie's cracks about Frankie's singing. At that time Frankie was out of work and was peculiarly vulnerable and Bogie was unnecessarily cruel."

Several people have mentioned the fact that Bogie sometimes went too far with his needling, and sometimes hurt people with his cutting remarks. But it was not out of meanness. Sometimes he just got carried away with his own cuteness and misjudged his target. Not everybody has thick skin, and even those who do sometimes shed it in moments of weakness. But I think if Dad pushed Frank Sinatra too hard at this particular time, it was probably because he felt that Sinatra was not being the person he could be, either personally or professionally. Bogie and Sinatra had a kind of father-son relationship, and Dad had often gotten on Sinatra for not taking his acting seriously enough. I think Dad saw Sinatra as a great talent that sometimes was wasted. My father had a philosophy about this, and it came from a valuable lesson he had learned years earlier in a producer's office.

Bogie had come into the producer's office while the producer was talking to a writer about his script. The producer told the writer that his script had some merit, that there were many good things in it, despite its shortcomings. After the writer left, the producer told Bogie that the script was lousy. Bogie asked him why he hadn't just said so. The producer told Bogie, "When you see that a person has done his best and it's no good, you cannot be cruel. If you know he can do better, then you say it stinks and he should fix it. But when you know this is his best, then be gentle."

I think that Bogie might have been telling Sinatra that if his life stinks he should fix it. I think that if Bogie felt Sinatra had really been doing his best, Bogie would have been gentle.

Though Bogie had some close actor friends, like Niven, Tracy, Burton, Sinatra, Peter Lorre, and Raymond Massey, most of Bogie's friends were writers: Nunnally Johnson, Louis Bromfield, Nathaniel Benchley, and even Huston, who started out as a screenwriter. He surrounded himself with writers because he admired them and he understood that without them, he would have no words to speak as an actor. Another reason he hung around with few actors was that he didn't have much respect for what he called "Hollywood types."

The trouble with many of them was that they had small vocabularies, he said. "They get my goat," he said. Of course, Dad's goat was easily gotten. "They get up there like stoops and say, 'Gosh, it's wonderful to be here. It's a wonderful night and I hear this is a wonderful picture. I know Willie Wyler did a wonderful job and I'm looking forward to a wonderful evening.' The word *wonderful* should be outlawed."

From the viewpoint of the Hollywood establishment, my

father was widely regarded as a social misfit, and I think he liked it that way. He didn't go to premieres. In fact, he didn't go to see his own pictures.

"I am not socially acceptable," he said. "People are afraid to invite me to their homes. They're afraid that I will say something to Darryl Zanuck or Louis B. Mayer, which, of course, I will. I don't really fit in with the Hollywood crowd. Why can't you be yourself, do your job, be your role at the studio and yourself at home, and not have to belong to the glitter-and-glamor group? Actors are always publicized as having a beautiful courtesy. I haven't. I'm the most impolite person in the world. It's thoughtlessness. If I start to be polite you can hear it for forty miles. I never think to light a lady's cigarette. Sometimes I rise when a lady leaves the room. If I open a door for a lady, my arm always gets in the way so that she either has to duck under or get hit in the nose. It's an effort for me to do things people believe should be done. I don't see why I should conform to Mrs. Emily Post, not because I'm an actor and believe that being an actor gives me special dispensations to be different, but because I'm a human being with a pattern of my own and the right to work out my pattern in my own way. I'm not a respecter of tradition, of the kind that makes people kowtow to some young pipsqueak because he is the descendant of a long line."

Comments like these spewed forth from Bogie almost every day. He loved to argue. When he and Mom lived in the farmhouse in Benedict Canyon she put up a sign that said:

DANGER: BOGART AT WORK. DO NOT DISCUSS POLITICS, RELIGION, WOMEN, MEN, PICTURES, THEATRE, OR ANYTHING ELSE.

Bogie seemed to bask in his role as troublemaker. Benchley says, "There was apparently some streak within him, some imp that was loosed by a variety of factors."

There really was an odd sort of puritanism about my father. He once bawled out Ingrid Bergman for throwing away her career in the scandal of having a baby out of wedlock.

"You were a great star," he said. "What are you now?"

Bergman replied, "A happy woman."

Dad was capable of obscenities but they were not common. While many people say that my father abhorred vulgarity, there are also people who recall him being vulgar. Conrad Nagel, for example, remembers Bogie saying of Bette Davis, "That dame is too uptight. What she needs is a good screw from a man who knows how to do it." Others recall that when my father had a dark room he used to make double exposures with his friend the writer Eric Hatch. They called them "trick photos," and one of them was of a skier skiing down a woman's bare breast.

I think Bogie's idea of vulgarity depended on who was present to hear it. Ruth Gordon said that one time Bogie told her that he was reading a script by "some college type."

"What's a college type?" she asked him.

"People who say 'fuck' in front of the children," Bogie replied.

Though my father poked fun at people he also poked fun at himself. He joked about the lifts he sometimes wore in his shoes to make him taller. And he made fun of the toupee he had to wear later in life, after a disease, called alopecia areata, caused much of his hair to fall out. He was extremely well-read in American history and Greek mythology, and could quote from Emerson, Pope, Plato, and over a thousand lines of Shakespeare, but he liked to play the dullard. "Henry the Fourth, part two, what's that?" he would ask. When someone gave him a compliment on his intellect or anything else, he would combat it with a wisecrack.

He wasn't any more comfortable giving compliments than he was with getting them. When he was very impressed by an actor's performance, for example, he would send a note instead of praising the actor to his face. He approached gift giving the same way. He hated birthdays and Christmas because on those days you were supposed to give a present. Typically, he would wait until the day had passed, then he would give a gift. Even then he would sabotage any possibility of sentiment with a zinger, such as giving someone a new watch and saying, "I'm sick of looking at the piece of junk you've been wearing on your wrist."

Another seeming contradiction for my father is that he was a guy who supposedly wanted nothing to do with Hollywood "in" groups and yet he was the leader of the most in group of all, the Holmby Hills Rat Pack. People my age and younger probably think of the Rat Pack as being Frank Sinatra, Dean Martin, Sammy Davis, Jr., Joey Bishop, Angie Dickinson, and others. But, except for Sinatra, those are not the original members.

My mother is the person who gave the pack its name. The story is that Frank Sinatra had flown Bogie and Bacall and a bunch of other friends over to Las Vegas for Noël Coward's opening there. (Now that I think of it, maybe this explains why I banged Coward over the head with a tray. I must have known that my parents and all their friends were going to see him in Vegas and not taking me with them.) In Vegas the group debauched for about four days straight, drinking, dancing, partying, and gambling. Apparently they didn't get much sleep, and after a while they all looked like hell. On the fourth day my mother said, "You look like a goddamn rat pack." The name stuck.

"We had a dinner later at Romanoff's," my mother says, "and we elected officers."

The first official notice of the Rat Pack appeared the next day in Joe Hyams's column in the *New York Herald Tribune.*

The Holmby Hills Rat Pack held its first annual meeting last night at Romanoff's restaurant in Beverly Hills and elected officers for the coming year. Named to executive positions were: Frank Sinatra, pack master; Judy Garland, first vice president; Lauren Bacall, den mother; Sid Luft, cage master; Humphrey Bogart, rat in charge of public relations; Irving Lazar, recording secretary and treasurer; Nathaniel Benchley, historian.

The only members of the organization not voted into office are David Niven, Michael Romanoff, and James Van Heusen. Mr. Niven, an Englishman, Mr. Romanoff, a Russian, and Mr. Van Heusen, an American, protested that they were discriminated against because of their national origins. Mr. Sinatra, who was acting chairman of the meeting, refused to enter their protests on the minutes.

A coat of arms designed by Mr. Benchley was unanimously approved as the official insignia of the Holmby Hills Rat Pack for use on letterheads and membership pins. The escutcheon features a rat gnawing on a human hand with a legend, "Never Rat on a Rat."

Mr. Bogart, who was spokesman, said the organization has no specific function other than "the relief of boredom and the perpetuation of independence. We admire ourselves and don't care for anyone else."

He said that membership is open to free-minded, successful individuals who don't care what anyone thinks about them.

A motion concerning the admittance of Claudette Colbert was tabled at the insistence of Miss Bacall, who said that Miss Colbert "is a nice person but not a rat."

My mother says that Spencer Tracy was only an honorary member because this was not really his scene. Tracy led a quieter life.

"You had to be a nonconformist," she says, "and you had to stay up late and drink and laugh a lot and not care what anybody said about you or thought about you."

Bogie came up with the motto, *Never Rat on a Rat*. They made rules, such as they were. One was that no new member could come in without the unanimous vote of the charter members.

Though my father was elected as director of public relations, people I talk to seem to feel that he was the spiritual leader of the group. Of course when Bogie died, the real leadership of the Rat Pack went to Frank Sinatra and its center moved from Hollywood to Las Vegas.

The press made a big deal of the Rat Pack, of course,

and even today when a group of celebrities hang out together they often get labeled with some version of the title, such as the Brat Pack of a few years ago.

You wouldn't think that forming a group of friends to have fun would be controversial, but it sometimes was. William Holden, who had already had a few run-ins with my father, didn't care for the Rat Pack. Holden said, "It's terribly important for people to realize that their conduct reflects the way a nation is represented in the eyes of the world. That's why the rat-pack idea makes our job so tough. If you were to go to Japan or India or France and represent an entire industry, which has made an artistic contribution to the entire world, and were faced then with the problem of someone asking, 'Do they really have a Rat Pack in Holmby Hills?' what would you say? It makes your job doubly tough.

"In every barrel there's bound to be a rotten apple. Not all actors are bad. It may sound stuffy and dull, but it is quite possible for people to have social intercourse without resorting to a Rat Pack."

I never met William Holden, but I can understand why he wasn't a favorite of my father's.

There are many stories that make my father sound like a wiseguy and a show-off. But there are also stories that portray him as a generous man. For example, he once got three friends together to pitch in $10,000 for his writer friend Eric Hatch, who was down on his luck. And there are stories that show that Bogie treated people kindly, regardless of where they stood in the Hollywood pecking order. He was never a snob.

Adolph Green remembers running into Bogie in a hotel

in England one time. This was just after Bogie had finished filming *The African Queen.*

Green was alone and lonely at the time, and he didn't know Bogie very well. Bogie sat and talked with him in the lobby of the hotel, and after awhile Dad seemed to catch on that Green had no one to talk to.

"Look," Bogie said, "I'm having a few friends over later. Why don't you come by and join us?"

Green, delighted to have some company, accepted. He was excited and flattered. Here he was, being invited over to Bogie's suite. When he got there, he realized he'd been invited to a very small gathering. There were only two other people there.

"Adolph, I want you to meet my friends," Bogie said. "Laurence Olivier and Vivien Leigh."

Green was thrilled, and it was a moment he never forgot. For the rest of his stay in England, Bogie checked on Green from time to time to make sure that he was getting along okay, and was not lonely.

"Your father was thoughtful that way," Green told me. "And it wasn't just me. Your father was very kind to a lot of people, like Judy Garland. Judy was always getting herself in trouble, she was a sick girl and spoiled in a way, and he would always be nice to her, though sometimes he would lose his temper with her."

Nat Benchley tells a story about the first time Benchley's wife, Marjorie, came to Hollywood. It was around Christmas of 1955. She was going to meet Bogart for the first time, and she was scared to death, because of Dad's reputation as a needler.

"What do I do if he starts picking on me?" she asked her husband.

"If he picks on you, pick right back," Benchley told his wife. "Tell him you don't take any crap from bald men. Tell him to put on his wig and then you'll talk."

When Mrs. Benchley did meet my father it was at a party, after which they decided they would all go on to Mapleton Drive. Benchley had to return home first to pick up something and my father insisted on driving Mrs. Benchley to our house in his black Thunderbird.

Marjorie was, of course, a wreck. Would this lunatic insult her, would he smash up the car? She had heard terrible things. Dad, of course, was charming beyond words. He told her how happy he was that she had come, he told her that if she needed help or advice, to call him immediately. The next day he took her on his boat. He told her his philosophy of life and talked to her about bringing up kids. By the end of her stay, Marjorie Benchley was, says her husband, "more than a little in love with him."

The next time Benchley saw Bogie, after Marjorie had gone back east, Benchley said, "I think I should report that my wife has a thing for you."

Bogie got embarrassed. "Tell her I'm really a shit," he mumbled. "Tell her I was nice only because she's new out here."

Janet Leigh is another woman who was afraid to meet Bogie, even though she was already well on her way to stardom when she did.

"We were guests at one of Rocky and Gary Cooper's dinner parties, a star-studded evening," she says. "I felt we were in the company of royalty. Actually, we were—Hollywood royalty. In that context we met a king, Humphrey Bogart. Rumor had it that Bogart took delight in verbally attacking a vulnerable victim with the zest of a witch doctor sticking pins in the proverbial doll. I had no desire to be the recipient, so I kept my distance."

After supper, Leigh was standing in a group that had gathered around the piano. Bogie walked in and stood next to her. Feeling intimidated, but fascinated at the same time, Leigh kept silent. When she was certain that Bogie was not looking, she stole a glance at the legend. She saw that Bogie wore, of all things, a little gold earring. I have no idea why my father was wearing an earring, except maybe to create controversy. An earring on a man was rare in those days, so Leigh tried to look at it, without actually staring. She was mesmerized. Suddenly Bogie turned and caught her looking at him.

"Oh," he said, "admiring my earring?"

"Well . . . yes, I guess."

"Don't get any ideas," Bogie said. "I'm all man, sweetheart. Who are you?"

Leigh was too flabbergasted to reply. She stuttered.

"What's the matter with you?" Bogie said. "You afraid of me? I won't bite you."

Leigh says, "And he didn't, perceptively realizing that I was no opponent."

The stories I like best about my father are those that show me he was not on a star trip. My mother, I think, sometimes takes her celebrity status seriously, and actually believes that she deserves to be treated better than waiters and barbers. But my father, it seems, had no such pretensions. It's true, he did divide the world into phonies and non-phonies, but never on the basis of how much money they made or what they did for a living.

Dominick Dunne, for example, is now one of our leading novelists and journalists, but he knew Bogie at a time
when Dunne was an unknown and Bogie was one of the biggest movie stars in the world.

He says, "Bogie was extremely kind to me. It was 1955
when he and Lauren Bacall were doing *The Petrified Forest* on
television. This was part of a series called *Producers Showcase.*
It was a big deal, an hour and a half of live TV. I was working
for NBC as a stage manager. The show was to be televised
from Burbank and I was sent out to California. We rehearsed
for three weeks, and performed it once. During this time
Bogart took a great interest in me and was incredibly nice to
me. I had a similar background to his, having gone to prep
school. I think he got a big kick out of that.

"I had lunch with him one day and I told him how much
I loved movie stars. So he invited me to a party at the
Mapleton Drive house one Saturday night. At that party Mr.
Bogart introduced me to Judy Garland and Lana Turner, who
lived nearby, and Katharine Hepburn and Spencer Tracy
were there. Everybody was there. I can hardly convey what
heady stuff this was to a starstruck young man in his twenties,
as I was. I think Bogart really got off on how thrilled I was to
be there meeting these people.

"Perhaps I didn't realize it at the time. But since then I
lived for twenty-five years in Hollywood and I understand
now that Hollywood has a pecking order and a caste system
as much as India, and I realize it was incredible for me, the
stage manager, to be at that party. For me to be invited was
really quite something. That was a great kindness your father
did me.

"I have always been a very shy person, but after I went

back to New York, I sometimes called Mr. Bogart up just to say hello. And he was so gracious. This man was a major fucking star and yet he was always so goddamn nice to me."

My mother walks around the first floor of the house on Mapleton, telling me where pieces of furniture were. But I stare out a window at the trees in the yard and I remember something else:

It is a few days after my father's funeral. I am alone in the yard looking at the tree where Diane Linkletter and I often play Swiss Family Robinson. I go up into the tree alone. I am a skinny boy, all arms and legs, but now my limbs feel as heavy as the limbs on the tree. I reach my favorite branch. And there, as lost as I have ever been, I scream at God. "Why did my father have to die?" I scream. "Why did you give him cancer? Why did you kill him? Why did you do this to me?" I am hysterical. My heart is broken.

I scream until my throat hurts. Then I sob.

"Stephen," I hear.

It is May, the big black woman who is our cook, and part of our family.

"Stephen, what are you doing up there?" she asks. I stare down at her. I don't answer.

"Stephen," she says softly.

I understand that she is trying to make me feel better. I know that she is sad, too, because she knew my father for a long time. We stare at each other. She is crying, too.

Finally, she says, "You be careful coming down, Stephen." She walks back to the house, shaking her head.

I've lived with celebrities and with stars, great people, great directors, and I can tell you that the children always have to suffer. You
just cannot live up to the reputation of a parent who becomes
successful. To have to follow in those footsteps is a very
big handicap.

—SAM JAFFE

The heaviest thing I have ever had to carry is my father's fame.

Bogie's reputation has often made normal conversation
difficult. It has brought me attention that I didn't want. And
often it has deprived me of attention that I did want. It has
made me sometimes distrustful of friendly people. It has, I
am the first to admit, placed that big chip on my shoulder. It
is a subject that, until now, I haven't wanted to talk about.

I am not the sole owner of this problem. I have talked to

the sons and daughters of many celebrities, and always it is the same. The fame of the celebrity exerts some strange gravitational pull on the children, and makes it difficult for them to simply break free.

Perhaps if I had been the son of some famous actor who fell from fame when the lights went out, it might not have been so bad. But I had the luck to be fathered by a man who became even more famous after he died. Humphrey Bogart, whether I like it or not, is our most enduring Hollywood legend. In 1993, *Entertainment Weekly* crowned Bogie the number-one movie legend of all time. (Number two, by the way, was his friend Katharine Hepburn.)

So Bogie is very big stuff. And, as a consequence, I have gone through life accompanied by what I call "The Bogie Thing." This is the big, red-lettered label that hangs from me. It doesn't say "Steve." It says, HUMPHREY BOGART'S SON.

"Jack, I want you to meet my friend, Steve Bogart. He's Humphrey Bogart's son."

"No kidding? You're really Bogie's boy?"

"Yes."

"God, I loved your father."

"Really?"

"Oh yeah, my first date with my wife was when we went to see *Sabrina*. Bogie! Now there was a man's man. God, this is so weird! Just the other night we rented *The Maltese Falcon*. That's the one where he plays Sam Spade."

"Right."

"It's really nice to meet you. Hey, this could be the start of a beautiful friendship. Get it, huh, a beautiful friendship?"

"I get it."

"*Casablanca*! What a great movie."

I have had this conversation, or some version of it, more

than a million times. At least it seems that way. This, of course, pisses me off.

I deal with these encounters in many ways. Usually I am polite and patient. I know that people don't mean to rob me of my identity. Besides, they are just meeting Bogart's son *once*. They're excited to have some connection to the screen legend. They're not thinking about the fact that every day I have to listen to strangers tell me what a great guy my dad was.

There are other times when I amuse myself to keep from getting angry. For example, one time a guy said to me, "Are you Humphrey Bogart's son? I heard he had a son named Steve."

"He did," I said.

"And you're him?"

"No," I said. "My parents named me after Humphrey Bogart's son."

And many times I simply deny it.

"Are you Humphrey Bogart's son?"

"No, but a lot of people ask me that."

Often, when I worked as a producer at ESPN and later at NBC and Court TV, I would see one of my coworkers giving some people a tour of the studio. At some point the tour guide would point to me. Then I would see the visitors smile and they would gaze at me for a little too long. *He told them,* I would think. It always made me angry and uncomfortable.

But let's get real for a minute. There are crack-addicted babies being born every day, while I was born in the affluence and safety of Beverly Hills. There are children being beaten, while I spent my early childhood with two parents who loved me. And there are cancer wards filled with kids who will never get to be teenagers, while my greatest health problems as a kid were a hernia operation at age three, and a gashed chin from a bicycling mishap. So, yes, I gripe about my problems like everybody else, but I try to keep some perspective. Carrying the burden of being Humphrey Bogart's son is not actually the worst thing that can happen to a person, and the only reason we are talking about it at all is that the public remains fascinated by anything to do with Humphrey Bogart.

For me, the Bogie thing began at my father's funeral at All Saints Episcopal Church.

The days just before the funeral are not clear to me. I remember little. But there are others who have memories of how I reacted in those unreal days following my father's death from cancer at age fifty-seven. My mother remembers that on the day after Dad died I stood at the top of the stairs, clutching a small notebook in my hand, and asked her, "What day is yesterday?"

"January fourteenth," she said.

Then I sat on the top stair and wrote in my notebook, "January 14, Daddy died."

And Sam Jaffe remembers talking to me on the same day.

I said to him, "I'm glad I sat on my father's bed with him."

"Why are you glad?" Sam asked me.

"Because of what he did yesterday," I said, meaning in my own eight-year-old way that I was glad I said good-bye to my father before he died.

It is the funeral that begins the time when my father's fame was a weight upon me.

I went to my father's funeral in a limousine. We were the

first car in a long row, and my mother sat between me and Leslie, holding us in her arms. John Huston was also with us. I remember that he said little, and that was unusual.

When the driver pulled up to the church I peered through the window of the limousine. A huge crowd had gathered. Hundreds of people lined the sidewalks outside the church. Though none of the women were crying, many of them carried handkerchiefs, as if they knew they soon would be. The people were very quiet, respectful, some had flowers. But still, I was scared.

"Who are all those people?" I asked my mother.

"They're fans, Stephen," my mother said. "They are people who went to see your father's movies, and they are sad that he is dead."

"What do they want?"

"They are going to hear the service for your father."

"They're coming to our church?"

"No," she said. "They will hear it outside. Over the loudspeaker."

"I hate them," I said.

"No, you don't, Stephen. You don't hate them."

"He's my father, not theirs. They don't even know him."

I was sad, I was hurt, I was angry. What right did these people have to invade my life that way and gawk at my father's death? I was there to say good-bye to Daddy—that's what I'd been told—and I didn't want to share it with thousands of strangers.

Six years later, when John Kennedy died, I would be fourteen years old, and I would understand the sense of personal loss that people feel when a public figure passes. But then I was not at all understanding. I was enraged. Somehow it felt to me that if thousands of people could cry at my father's funeral, then I had no special relationship with him. At some level I think I have always felt that way, and still do.

She took one of my hands, and one of Leslie's. Holding us tightly, she led us out of the limo. As I climbed from the car I heard a woman say, "That's his son." I wanted to punch her. I felt as if I was being forced to perform. I was being thrust into the spotlight, which is not where an eight-year-old who has just lost his father wants to be.

Mother led us into the church. Huston stayed close, as if he could somehow protect us from the fans.

In addition to the bereaved fans on the street, eight hundred of Bogie's Hollywood friends and associates had come to attend the service. The fans had come, of course, not just to say good-bye to Bogie, but to gawk at the movie stars who would be there. Gary Cooper came, and so did Charles Boyer, Dick Powell, Tony Martin, Gregory Peck, Marlene Dietrich, Ida Lupino, Howard Duff, Danny Kaye, and of course Kate Hepburn and Spencer Tracy. (Frank Sinatra wanted to come to Dad's funeral, of course, but if he had, it would have created great hardship for the club where he was performing in New York. My mother told him it was okay to stay in New York.)

We moved slowly down to the front of the church and took a pew. All eyes were on us, probably my mother mostly, but I felt as if they were all watching me. I remember that the priest, a man named Kermit Castellanos, who everyone called K.C., talked for a while about my father.

Then John Huston spoke. He was such a big, impressive-looking man and he had an incredible voice. He gave the eulogy, though I didn't yet know that word. I've since learned that Huston was actually my mother's second choice. She had first asked Spencer Tracy, but Tracy was so devastated by Bogie's death that he told my mother he was afraid he could not speak about his friend without falling apart.

There was no body at my father's funeral service. Bogie had expressed his wishes to my mother long before, at the funeral of his friend Mark Hellinger.

"Once you're gone, you're gone," he said. "I hate funerals. They aren't for the one who's dead, but for the ones who are left and enjoy mourning. When I die I want no funeral. Cremation, which is clean and final, and my ashes strewn over the Pacific. My friends can raise a glass and exchange stories about me if they like. No mourning, I don't believe in it. The Irish have the right idea, a wake."

Unfortunately, when Jess Morgan, who was then the young associate of my father's business manager, Morgan Maree, went to make arrangements for the cremation he was told that such a scattering was illegal. My mother was very upset. She had wanted Bogie to go back to the sea, which he loved. So Dad was cremated. Mother had arranged for the cremation to take place at the same time as the service, and after the service the ashes were placed in an urn in the Gardens of Memory at Forest Lawn Cemetery. Included with the ashes was the gold whistle my mother had used in their first film together, *To Have and Have Not*. On the whistle were inscribed the initials B & B—Bogie and Baby. And at 12:30 that day, a moment of silence was observed at both Warner Brothers and Twentieth Century-Fox.

Most of that day I've forgotten. They played music. I know now that it was from the works of Bach and Debussy, Bogie's favorite composers. Leslie and I kneeled when we were supposed to. I remember the crowds. I remember the familiar smell of magnolias, cut from our front yard, and the white roses that surrounded the altar. And on the altar there was Bogie's treasured glass-encased model of the *Santana*. I remember thinking my father should be there to see it. But mostly I remember just being stunned by it all, being in a kind of daze.

When it was over, people rose from the pews, began to mill around, shaking hands with old friends, clapping each other sympathetically on the back. I felt lost for a moment and then John Huston leaned down to me. He put his big hands gently on my shoulders and he whispered, "You know, Stephen, there are going to be many photographers out there trying to take your picture."

I guess if Huston was warning me, he must have understood how angry and scared the photographers had already made me feel.

Between the day my father died and the day of the funeral there had been two school days. My mother, thinking that it was best to keep things as close to normal for us as she could, had sent Leslie and me to school on those mornings. But normalcy was not to be had. Incredibly, when I was dropped off at school that first day there was a group of photographers waiting for me. They just came at me, like a gang of big kids, taking my picture without even asking. I hated it. I didn't want my picture taken anymore. But now at the church after the funeral, I knew how to stop them, I thought. I would simply put my hand over my face so they couldn't see me and they would not take my picture. That's what I believed. So as we filed out of the church, I stood next to my mother and John Huston and I held my hand up over my face. We moved through the crowd of people who were being kept behind ropes. Suddenly it seemed as if everybody in the world had a camera. *They were taking my picture.* I couldn't believe it. It didn't matter that I had my hand over my face.

They still took pictures, one after the other. I was scared. I felt as if I was being jumped on or called names. By the time we got into the car I was bawling.

The next morning the front page of the newspaper featured a big picture of me coming out of my father's funeral with my hand over my face. I was mortified. I felt as if somehow everybody had lied to me.

After the funeral dozens of people gathered at the house on Mapleton. There were many celebrities there. But there were neighbors, too, and studio executives, makeup men, sailing people, hairdressers, all people who loved Bogart. As long as there were people around, and things to do, Mother was able to hold herself together. Even before the funeral she had been able to keep busy constantly by answering some of the thousands of telegrams that came in from sympathetic friends and strangers.

It was a telegram that made for one light moment on the afternoon of Dad's funeral. My mother had asked that no flowers be sent for my father, that instead, donations be made to the American Cancer Society. Then she got a telegram from the American Floral Association, which she read to the gathering. It said, "Do we say don't go to see Lauren Bacall movies?"

So it was not a totally somber afternoon. People chatted and gossiped and exchanged Bogie stories. Mother was happy to have the house filled with people. But the friends had to leave sometime, and when they did we were alone again, Mother, me, and Leslie, in a home with no father. That's when the problems began.

If I was uncommonly quiet in the weeks that followed, my little sister was the opposite. Leslie was full of questions.

"Why did Daddy go to heaven?" she asked my grandmother, Mom's mother, Natalie, who had been living with us through much of my father's illness. Our other grandmother, Maud, had died of cancer more than a decade earlier.

"Because God needed him," my grandmother answered.

"But we needed him, too," Leslie said. "Did God think he needed him more than his kids?"

She was four years old and an expert at asking the unanswerable questions.

Leslie was going through her own awful time. She had been Daddy's little girl and Bogie had doted on her. Now he wasn't there to scoop her into his lap, or ride on the seesaw with her. Now was the time when Leslie needed her mother the most, but Mom couldn't give her enough. I was the reason. Because I was so troubled, my mother gave me a lot of attention and in the process, they both agree, neglected some of Leslie's emotional needs. It has been, as you can imagine, a sore spot between mother and daughter over the years.

However, I was the one who was most obviously in need of special attention.

Not so long ago I told my wife about a bicycle accident that I'd had about a year after my father died. I had cut open my jaw and been taken to the hospital for stitches. There was no lasting injury from that accident, but all my life I had been unaccountably angry about the fact that my mother was at work when it occurred.

Barbara said, "Well, perhaps you were angry because you felt there was no one to protect you." And it struck home. Yes, that was it, exactly. That's how I felt, that nobody was there to protect me. My mother was gone, and my father was gone, too.

In a strange way, this idea that I was unprotected was a

comforting thought. Because for so many years I had felt that I didn't think enough about my father, that I didn't feel enough about him. I had always believed that, while Humphrey Bogart's fame has tainted every single minute of my life, he, personally, never really had much impact on my life. But now I realize that if his absence made me feel so damn vulnerable and unprotected, then his presence, his being alive, must have made me feel safe. When he died my world was shattered. And it took me many years to put it all back together.

It was a few days after the funeral that I climbed that tree in the backyard and started screaming at God. When May, the cook, came out and heard me, she must have sensed that I was about to become a major headache for my mother. For several days in a row I sat in that tree and screamed for my father and cried for hours on end.

The hours I spent in that tree, feeling the pain and frustration of losing my father, mark the end of my belief in a personal God. My mother was a lapsed Jew, and my father a lapsed Episcopalian. Neither of my parents had any strong belief in God, but, like many parents, they sent their children to Sunday school, out of a vague sense that religion was a good thing for a kid. We were being raised Episcopalian rather than Jewish because my mother felt that would make life easier for Leslie and me during those post–World War II years.

In any case, when I was eight years old I still believed in the God that adults told me about. But I have always been a very logical person, even then, and during the days when I sat in that tree bawling my eyes out, the equation became very simple for me: *My father is dead. God wouldn't let that happen. Therefore, there is no God.* In that tree I gave up a belief in

God, and nothing I have seen in the last thirty-seven years has changed my mind on that point.

Though my mother didn't know at the time about the tree screaming, she had plenty of evidence that things were not right with me.

One night just before Valentine's Day, Mother, Leslie, and I were eating supper in the dining room.

"I know how we can surprise Daddy," I said.

"How is that?" my mother asked.

"We can all shoot ourselves, and then we can be with him for Valentine's Day."

This comment, understandably, made my mother worry. She began talking to doctors about me. They assured her that my behavior was normal. They said it was natural for me to be full of resentment because my father had died. They said I was probably feeling that I had done something wrong to make him leave.

Apparently, it was common for me to make announcements about my father at the dinner table. Adolph Green says, "I remember one night having dinner on Mapleton Drive, shortly after your father died, and you looked up and said, 'There's Daddy flying over the dining room table.' You were not hysterical, you just said it very calmly."

At the Warner Avenue School, where all of my friends went, I was not so calm. I had been getting good grades. But now, with the onset of the Bogie thing, I began working on a one-way ticket out the door.

Looking back I realize that the main thing was that it infuriated me that all my friends knew that my father was dead. I hated the fact that they all had fathers and I didn't, and they all knew that I didn't. They knew I was fatherless because they had seen it on television, or their parents had read it in the newspaper. People were not pointing at me in the corridors and laughing, but that's how it felt. It was as if everybody was in on some joke except me. I felt no sense of privacy.

One day a kid said to me, "Too bad about your father," and I slugged him.

A few days later it happened again. "Sorry about your dad." Pow, right in the face.

For a while I was getting in fights every day with kids who hadn't done anything except mention my father.

In school it wasn't only the fighting that got me into trouble. I also had a habit of standing on my desk and screaming. When the mood possessed me, I would suddenly climb on top of my small wooden desk, wave my hands in the air, and shriek hysterically. The kids just stared at me and the teachers wrung their hands. Nobody knew quite what to make of it except that, obviously, I was trying to get attention. I don't think I was screaming for my father as I had in the tree, I was just screaming so that somebody would notice that I was in pain.

The principal called my mother into his office. He was a tall, carrot-haired man.

"There's a problem with Stephen," he said.

"A problem?"

"He seems very withdrawn most of the time."

"That's understandable," my mother said.

"But he's also getting in fights."

"Fights?"

"He gave one boy a bloody nose. And he stands on his desk, shrieking. Are there difficulties at home?"

"Well, of course there are difficulties at home," my mother said. "He's lost his father."

"Yes, and we are all very sympathetic," Carrot Head said. "But he's become a disruption in class. If this continues, we'll have to ask you to take your son out of the school."

A few days later I climbed onto my desk again and screamed. They couldn't handle me. Warner Avenue became the first school I was "asked to leave." It would not be the last.

So, still reeling from the blow of losing my father, I was yanked out of Warner Avenue School, where all my friends were. I had no idea what was going on. My marks were good, so why was I being put into another school? I felt as if I were being punished. I knew that all of this was, in some mysterious way, linked up with my father's death. Beginning in September, 1958, I went to the Carl Curtis School. I remember that they had a swimming pool.

Adding to my sense of loss during this period, we also moved out of the Mapleton Drive house and away from everything I had grown up with. It was partly thanks to Frank Sinatra. Several months after my father died my mother entered into a rather volatile romance with Frank Sinatra, which I guess is the only kind of romance Sinatra had. During my father's illness, Frank, as devoted as a son to my father, had come over to see Dad often, so it's not as though Leslie and I were suddenly being confronted with a new man in the house when he and Mother started dating. We already knew Frank as a guy who would come to the house a lot, and sometimes play with us for a few minutes before going off to talk with the grown-ups.

Back in 1957, if anyone had told my mother that her romance with Sinatra was an attempt to forget Bogie, she would have said that was absurd. But that is how she sees it now. Frank was an anesthetic to the pain of losing Bogie.

Frank was good for my mother in many ways. She had always been close to him as a friend, and after the long ordeal of Bogie's declining health in the last year, she needed to get out and dance a bit. But Frank was a bit screwed up, and the romance brought with it a quantity of pain, as a number of women have discovered over the years. My mother says Sinatra was incredibly charming and handsome and talented, but also incredibly juvenile and insecure. One week Frank would be courting her like a prince, taking her to parties and premieres and concerts. And then suddenly he would go as cold as stone on her. He would avoid calling. He would act as if she did not exist. And when he finally did call again he'd act as if nothing had happened. This is an aspect of Sinatra's personality which has exasperated people close to him for years. It was especially trying for my mother because, as she says, "I had been married to a grown-up."

Everybody who cared about my mother, including Frank's friends, prayed that she would not marry him. The opinion seemed to be universal that any woman who married Sinatra might as well take a knife and stab herself in the heart.

After one of his cold and silent absences, Frank did ask Bacall to marry him. Mom accepted. She was in heaven. She would have a life again. Leslie and I would have Sinatra for a father. All the pain would be gone.

The plans for the marriage were supposed to be kept secret for a while. But when Swifty Lazar spilled the beans to Louella Parsons, the "Bacall–Sinatra marriage plans" hit the papers. Frank went ballistic. He went into his iceman routine and broke off the relationship, except he forgot to tell my mother that he was breaking it off. All he did was ignore her and humiliate her. There were times when he was actually in the same room with my mother and acted as if he didn't know her. Though the passing of years has put my mother in a forgiving mood, she doesn't discuss their relationship anymore.

It was during Mother's romance with Sinatra that we moved out of the Mapleton Drive house, and Sinatra was one of the main reasons.

"I don't think Frank was comfortable in that house," my mother says. "The ghost of your father was always there, and I knew that Frank would feel better if I moved."

So Mother, believing that she would never have a future with Frank unless she moved, jettisoned her silver and much of her furniture and sold the house in which my father had died. We moved into a rented house on Bellagio Road in Bel Air. The house belonged to William Powell, the actor.

By this time, then, I had lost my father, lost my school, and lost my house. And through it all I was losing my friends.

Most of my friends had gone to Warner Avenue School, and when I was taken out of that school I was cut out of their lives. I felt it happening gradually, I guess, but it all seemed to come down on me one afternoon when I was at a birthday party for Steve Cahn, who had been my closest friend on Mapleton.

Steve's father, Sammy, was one of the most famous lyricists of the time. Sammy had worked with composers like Jules Styne and Jimmy Van Heusen, doing film work. He had already won an Academy Award for the song "Three Coins in the Fountain," and it was around this time that he won another Academy Award for "All the Way," which was from Sinatra's film *The Joker Is Wild*. He would eventually win two more Academy Awards.

Anyhow, at that birthday party I felt incredibly out of place. It was as if everybody else was a person and I was a goat or a donkey or something. This "outsider" feeling had been growing in me ever since my father's death. It had started with the strange awareness that all my friends knew about my father. And it had gotten worse after I was pulled out of the Warner Avenue School. At the end of that birthday party I stood in the hallway with no one to talk to, like some unwanted vagrant who had wandered in. The kids were all saying good-bye to each other, and talking about what they would do tomorrow in school. Even though I was among all my friends, I felt a terrible pang of loneliness. Now I went to Curtis School and they still went to Warner and they lived together in a world that I was no longer part of.

After we moved to Bellagio Road, of course, it got worse. If the death of my father had not already broken my heart, this surely did. I was devastated by the loss of my friends and the gradual realization that their lives went on as usual.

This cycle of loss, which I'm sure was during the most important formative time of my life, was completed in January of 1959, just short of two years after Bogie's death. My mother had gone on a trip to London looking for a job, leaving Leslie and me in our nurse's care. There she had wined and dined with Laurence Olivier and Vivien Leigh and Richard and Sybil Burton. She had also been offered work in a film, which was to be shot throughout Europe. She had accepted the job. As a result, we moved to London for six months and, as it turned out, away from California forever.

Now I was down one father, one school, one house, dozens of friends, and an entire state and country.

In London there were more photographers, first at the airport and later at the school. By now I had developed an almost pathological hatred of cameras and I would turn my head any time I saw one, even if it was just hanging over the neck of a tourist. I was enrolled in the American School in London, one of the few schools, by the way, that I have not been thrown out of. Apparently, I pretty much kept to myself. But everywhere I went somebody knew me because of who my father had been. I never perceived any jealousy from other kids, but that's what I was always afraid of. More than anything, I just wanted to blend into the woodwork. I remember at school that there was a girl who kept passing me a piece of paper. She wanted my autograph because I was Humphrey Bogart's son. I didn't want that kind of notice. And there was a guy there, Jeff Eaton. I remember that he intercepted the paper every time, and signed his name to it and sent it back to her. I remember Jeff fondly because he knew how self-conscious I felt about being the Bogie boy, and he deflected the attention away from me and on to him. And he made me laugh, too.

The message I got from all this moving, each time farther away from where we'd lived with Bogie, was clear: your father is no longer a part of your life, forget about him. And that's what I tried to do for most of my life.

Of course, all this has created conflict over the years between me and Mom. I didn't want to think of myself as "the son of Humphrey Bogart." I have always wanted to be just plain Steve. I didn't want any kind of spotlight on me for being Bogie's son, and I didn't want the responsibility of meeting some expectation that people might have for the child of Bogie.

You might think that I would want to stay in the world of celebrities who are so much a part of my mother's life. After all, celebrities aren't going to be impressed by my being the son of a celebrity. But by the time I was a teenager I had met a few celebrities and, believe it or not, it was exactly the same.

"Oh, I knew your father. I loved him. He was great."

It was always your father this, and your father that. Nobody ever said to me, "Tell me Steve, how do you make a gasket, exactly?" which is something I did once.

There was never anything specific that my mother wanted me to *do* about my father's fame. It was just that she wanted me to somehow dedicate my life to keeping his spirit alive, something that Bogie has managed to do just fine without me.

At a minimum my mother would have liked me to talk a lot about Bogie. To her, Bogie was, and remains, perfect. She always wanted me to ask her what he was like. I seldom did that because she was always telling me anyhow, and to hear her tell it, he *was* perfect. It was bad enough that I was constantly besieged by strangers telling me what a great guy my dad was. I wanted somebody to say to me, "Bogie was great, but sometimes he was a prick, you know . . ." and maybe show that the guy had some shortcomings so that I wouldn't have to live up to a legend. But my mother could never bring herself to say anything that might reflect negatively on him.

"Stephen," she would say, "why do you always want to know the bad stuff?"

"Because that's what would make him real to me," I would say.

I realize now that perfect is Mom's perception of my father, and that she was just trying to make him perfect for me. But the effect of all this, for years, was that I simply did not learn much about my father. So when I began to take more interest in my father's life, I was especially curious about the nature of his fame. After all, his fame has caused me so much trouble that I wanted to understand it. Where did it come from? Why is it so durable when the fame of others has faded? The truth is if you had asked me to recite a filmography of Humphrey Bogart a few years ago, I would not have done any better than the average movie fan. But now I'm much more familiar with this shadow in my life known as Humphrey Bogart and I know a little more, though I suspect no one will ever completely understand the lasting impression of Bogie.

My father was not the most famous movie star of his time. Certainly Clark Gable surpassed him, and you could make a case for James Cagney and others. But today, for reasons which have been discussed many times, my father is the one that the older generation remembers and the younger generation idolizes. He is generally conceded to be the number-one movie star of all time. Stories about my father almost invariably describe him as a "legend," a man who has a "mystique," and the center of the "Bogart cult." There are many reasons why my father is more famous today than when he died thirty-eight years ago. One of them is simply the fact that he was the first of his generation of movie greats to die prematurely. Clark Gable and Gary Cooper also died in their fifties, but they died after Bogie. Dying young is no guarantee of immortality, but it helps. Do you think the names Marilyn Monroe, James Dean, and Elvis Presley would mean quite what they do today if they had died in their eighties? Likewise, Bogie.

If there is a year marking the beginning of my father's fame it is 1935, fourteen years before I was born. By that time he had been in dozens of Broadway plays and even a few really awful movies. In one of them, *Up the River,* he made his only screen appearance with Spencer Tracy. For years, Bogie had shuttled back and forth between Hollywood and Broadway with a notable lack of film success. "I wasn't Gable and I flopped," he said.

But in 1935, Bogie got the role of a psychopathic gangster by the name of Duke Mantee, in Robert Sherwood's Broadway play *The Petrified Forest.* Over the years a lot of people have told me that when my father walked on stage as Duke Mantee you could hear a gasp from the audience, and that happened every single night. Somehow Dad created the shuffling gait of a convict who might have had his legs manacled, and his hands dangled as if they might have been recently handcuffed together. His voice was cold, his eyes heartless. At the time of the play, John Dillinger was king of the tabloids, and Bogie, they say, looked a lot like Dillinger. For years people talked about that nightly gasp in the audience and how it always seemed that John Dillinger had just walked onto the stage.

The play, with Leslie Howard as the star, was a big hit. Bogie got the best reviews of his stage career. He was hopeful that repeating the role on film would finally make him a Hollywood star. But when Warner Brothers bought the rights to film the play they announced that Mantee would be played by Edward G. Robinson. Robinson was already a major movie star, mostly playing gangsters. Bogie was pissed off. He sent a cable to Leslie Howard, because Howard (who, incidentally, was my mother's screen idol, though she never got to meet him) had promised to help Bogie get the Mantee movie role. Howard, true to his word, told Warner Brothers that they could shove their movie if they didn't cast Dad as Mantee, though I suppose Howard used more genteel language. The studio caved in. Bogie got the part and he was a sensation. And that is why my sister is named Leslie; she was named after Leslie Howard.

The Petrified Forest, however, did not make Bogie a movie star. Warner Brothers signed him to one of their so-called slave contracts, and they plugged him into a whole series of roles that they thought suited his "type." During the next five years my father appeared in twenty-eight films, playing so many gangsters you would have thought he was born with a .38 in his hand. The titles say it all: *Racket Busters, San Quentin, You Can't Get Away With Murder,* and so on. But Bogie never even got to be the top gangster in these flicks, because Warner Brothers already had big gangster-role stars like Robinson, James Cagney, and George Raft. Bogie did get to play a cowboy on occasion, and he had top billing from time to time, such as in *Dead End,* notable because it was the first film featuring the Dead End Kids.

Bogie was not great in these films—but then, the films weren't great either. In some he was good, in others lousy. He did, however, get good at dramatic death scenes because he had lots of practice. In these gangster films, he was always getting knocked off at the end by Robinson or Cagney. He joked about how absurd it was that he, brought up in wealth and culture, was known to the public as a tough street guy. But he was not happy playing these parts. He really cared about acting, and he wanted to make something of himself as an actor.

Still, if these films do not represent Bogie at his best, they do show that he was sometimes able to make the most of roles that were as common as lice. Raymond Chandler said, "Bogart can be tough without a gun. Also, he has a sense of humor that contains that grating undertone of contempt. Alan Ladd is hard, bitter, and occasionally charming, but he is after all a small boy's idea of a tough guy. Bogart is the genuine article."

It wasn't until 1941 and *High Sierra* that Bogie began to emerge as someone who would make his mark on film history. He got the role because he fought for it after George Raft turned it down. Raft did not want to die at the end. This would not be the last time that Bogie benefited from Raft's fussiness.

In that movie, Bogie played Roy Earle, another Dillinger-like character. Earle was ruthless and cold-blooded. But somehow Bogie created sympathy for the guy, developing the Earle character as a last-of-a-dying-breed type. Audiences responded. When Earle was killed at the end of the movie, as bad guys always were in those days, the moviegoers felt sympathy instead of glee. It was probably my father's best performance to date. The movie was a hit.

The screenwriter on *High Sierra,* along with W. R. Burnett, was John Huston. Later that year, Huston got his first directing assignment. The movie was *The Maltese Falcon,* and it was to star George Raft. Raft said no. This time he was afraid of jeopardizing his career by working with a new director. Right. Anybody could see that Huston had no future as a director. So, Bogie got the role, and Huston was happy to have him.

In *The Maltese Falcon,* Bogie was on the right side of the law, more or less, as Dashiell Hammett's private eye Sam

Spade, another self-sufficient loner type. Bogie was still ruthless, but now it was ruthlessness in the name of principles.

The Maltese Falcon had been made twice before, but this time they did it right and the movie was a big success. My mother thinks it is the movie against which all other private-eye films are judged.

In one of his most famous scenes, Bogie tells Mary Astor that he is "sending her over," for killing his partner. They supposedly love each other, but Bogie says, "I don't care who loves you. I won't play the sap for you. You killed Miles and you're going over for it." He tells her, "I hope they don't hang you by your sweet neck. If you're a good girl you'll be out in twenty years and you'll come back to me. If they hang you, I'll always remember you."

This, I guess, is the beginning of Bogie as Mr. Cool. Richard Brooks, the director, says, "Finally, the film was done the way it was written. The whole purpose of the story was that his partner was killed and a woman who got him killed was trying to make love to Bogie on the couch. And she wanted to go free. And when he finally says to her, 'I have to send you over, somebody has to take the fall,' they loved him for it because he could do it and maybe we couldn't do it."

Alistair Cooke knew my father and he says that *The Maltese Falcon* was the film that finally isolated my father's character. "That was the quintessential Bogart," he says. "All that matters is what is going on in your father's mind. You could see everything in his face. The camera loved Bogie. He was born to be in films."

Richard Schickel, the movie critic for *Time,* says that *The Maltese Falcon* was the movie that put Bogie over the top as a star. "The public now had what it required of all movie stars in those days," Schickel says, "a firm sense of his character, a

ABOVE, LEFT: Dr. Belmont DeForest Bogart. *ABOVE, RIGHT:* Maud Humphrey holding her young son, Humphrey. (1900) *(COURTESY BALLIOL CORP.)* *BELOW:* Dad at 18 months old. (1900)

ABOVE: Dad, now 2 years old. (1901)

BELOW: Bogie, 7 years old. (1906)

LEFT: *In the navy during WWI.* (1917)

BELOW: *Back to civilian life.* (1918)

ABOVE: **Dad** *on one of his first sailboats.* *(1940)* *(COURTESY STEPHEN BOGART)*

Sam Spade with "the bird"—
The Maltese Falcon.

From left: my father,
Peter Lorre, Mary Astor,
Sidney Greenstreet
—The Maltese Falcon.
(1941) (WARNER/MPTV)

The Maltese Falcon:
Dad the tough guy.
With Peter Lorre.
(1941) (WARNER/MPTV)

ABOVE: A toast to a great movie—Dad and Bergman during Casablanca.
(1942) (WARNER/MPTV)

BELOW: A famous scene from Casablanca *with my father and Dooley Wilson.*
(WARNER/MPTV)

ABOVE: Casablanca — *Rick and Ilsa say goodbye at the airport.*
(WARNER/MPTV)

*BELOW: Bogart and Ingrid Bergman during
the shooting of* Casablanca. *(1942)* (WARNER/MPTV)

ABOVE AND BELOW: Bogie (as Steve, my namesake) and Bacall (as Marie) fall in love, in To Have and Have Not. *(1945) (WARNER/PHOTO BY MAC JULIAN/MPTV)*

ABOVE: Dad with third wife Mayo Methot in 1944.

BELOW: Dad and Mom with director John Huston
shooting Key Largo. *(1948)* (WARNER/PHOTO BY MAC JULIAN/MPTV)

ABOVE: Who loves ya, baby? Mom and me at Cedars of Lebanon Hospital. *(January 1949)* *(COURTESY STEPHEN BOGART)*

OPPOSITE PAGE: Mom and Dad on the Santana. *(1946)*
OPPOSITE, INSET: Dad and Mom in love, after the wedding.

BELOW: Granny visits us at the hospital. *(COURTESY STEPHEN BOGART)*

ABOVE: Mom, Dad and little me at the hospital. He is in awe and in love.

BELOW: Dad, with me, getting the hang of it. (1949)

ABOVE: Who's this guy holding me and smiling? Bogie and me. (1949)

RIGHT: Dad, Mom and me at home in Benedict Canyon. (1949)

ABOVE: Dad and Kate Hepburn during filming of The African Queen, *for which my father won the Oscar.* *(1951)* *(ROMULUS-HORIZON/MPTV)*

OPPOSITE PAGE: Benedict Canyon—I'm starting to get fed up with the cameras. *(1949)* *(COURTESY STEPHEN BOGART)*

BELOW: Remember the scene with the leeches! As Charlie Allnut in The African Queen. *(1951)* *(ROMULUS-HORIZON/MPTV)*

LEFT: Dad phones home during the shooting of The Enforcer. *(1951)*

RIGHT: Bogie with Judy Garland at Ciro's nightclub. (1955) (PHOTO COPYRIGHT © 1978 DAVID SUTTON/MPTV)

feeling that they knew what they were bargaining for when they paid their money to see a Bogart picture. And from this point onward, with his name fixed firmly above the title, in the first billing position he would never again be forced to relinquish, that is what he appeared in: Bogart pictures. He had become what a star had to be, a genre unto himself."

In 1943 came the next big magnification of the Bogart star. It was my father's forty-fifth movie, *Casablanca*, which, even though it won the Oscar for best picture, has been called "the best bad movie ever made." It is also, of my father's five most important films, the only one that was not written or directed by John Huston. Alistair Cooke says, "Bogie's continuing fame is a mystery but a lot of it is tied up in that film, *Casablanca*."

"*Casablanca* was never supposed to be anything special," Julius Epstein told me. Epstein, along with his twin brother, Philip, and Howard Koch, wrote the screenplay. "In those days the studios owned the theaters and each studio made a picture a week. *Casablanca* was just one more picture. It was corny and it was sentimental, and your father made a lot of better films that don't get as much attention. But somehow magic happened and it became a classic."

Epstein went on to say, "The first preview was not a howling success. The movie did not become the cult film it is now until after your father died."

Though *Casablanca* went on to win the Academy Award for Best Picture and Best Director, and my father got his first Best Actor nomination, the road to being a classic was not a smooth ride. "We were making changes in the script every day during shooting," Epstein says. "Your father didn't like that. He was a professional, always prepared, and he didn't like sloppiness. But that's what it was. We were handing in dialogue hours, even minutes, before it was to be shot."

No one really knew where the picture was going or how it was going to end. All of this, of course, raised havoc with characterizations. Ingrid Bergman recalls in her book, *My Story*, "Every morning we said, 'Well, who are we, what are we doing here?' And Michael Curtiz, the director, would say, 'We're not quite sure, but let's get through this scene today and we'll let you know tomorrow.' "

In fact, the famous ending of the movie where my father says to Claude Rains, "Louis, I think this is the beginning of a beautiful friendship," was not the only ending planned. Curtiz also planned to shoot an ending in which Bergman stays with Bogart. It was only after the "beautiful friendship" line was shot that Curtiz knew he had something perfect and decided to go with it.

It was a difficult movie for my father. He spent most of his time in his trailer. He was not happy with the part at first. He wanted to get the girl, but so did Paul Henreid, because that, to some extent, was the definition of stardom: the guy who got the girl was the star. But Bogie also worried that the public would not believe that a woman as beautiful as Ingrid Bergman could fall for a guy who looked like him. He was, after all, a five-foot-ten, 155-pound, forty-four-year-old, balding man who had spent most of his film life playing snarling triggermen.

Dad was also troubled by the fact that, in the original script, Rick Blaine was a bit of a whiner, and that Rick didn't actually *do* much of anything. So the role was beefed up.

The role became more challenging. Dad had to convince his audience that Rick was a man's man, a tough guy, but that he also could be brought close to tears by the sound of "As Time Goes By" played on the piano by Dooley Wilson as Sam. (By the way, Bogie never said, "Play it again, Sam.")

My father, I have learned, was not a ladies' man, in real life, or on film. In fact, his aloofness with women on screen, the ease with which he could turn a dame into the cops if she was bad, is one of the things that makes him attractive both to men and women. *Casablanca* was probably his most romantic role, and even then most of the romance is in the back story.

Bogie, with not a lot of experience in romantic parts, took advice on how to play it. His friend Mel Baker told him, "This is the first time you've ever played the romantic lead against a major star. You stand still, and always make her come to you. Mike [Curtiz, the director] probably won't notice it, and if she complains you can tell her it's tacit in the script. You've got something she wants, so she has to come to you."

Whatever my father did worked. *Casablanca* turned Bogie into a sex symbol. As Rick Blaine he represented one of what Ingrid Bergman called "the two poles of male attractiveness." Paul Henreid as Victor Laszlo was the other. Laszlo was honest, responsible, conservative, and fatherly. Bogie, as Rick, was sexy, romantic, irresponsible, and funny. In other words: dangerous. Women love rascals.

"I didn't do anything I've never done before," Bogie said, "but when the camera moves in on that Bergman face, and she's saying she loves you, it would make anybody look romantic."

In fact, the chemistry between my father and Bergman was so palpable that many people thought they must have had something going on off the screen. But the truth is they were practically strangers.

"I kissed him," Bergman says, "but I never knew him."

Bob Williams, who was the studio's publicist on the film, has said that he thinks my father was in love with Ingrid Bergman, and that a romance might have developed if he were not married to the fanatically jealous Mayo Methot at the time. "Bogie was kind of jealous if I would bring another man onto the set to see her," Williams says. "He would sulk. I think he was kind of smitten with her."

Perhaps. But my father was not the kind to flirt with his costars. He was more inclined to retire to his trailer and study his script or play chess, in this case with Howard Koch.

Nobody can say for sure why *Casablanca* has become the beloved film that it is, or why so many lines from it have become installed in our language. All I know is that I would be a very rich man if I got a quarter every time somebody said to me, "This could be the start of a beautiful friendship," or "We'll always have Paris," or "Here's looking at you, kid," or "Of all the gin joints in all the world," and on and on. Barely a day goes by that I don't see or hear some reference to Bogie on the news, and most commonly it is one of the *Casablanca* lines. Even Secretary of State Warren Christopher summed up his comments on the GATT Treaty: "This could be the start of a beautiful friendship."

Casablanca was truly a serendipitous combination of things. But if the soul of my father's fame is the merging of his real self with his screen image, as film historians have suggested, then *Casablanca* probably is the best example of that merging.

Perhaps this is the phenomenon that Bergman is talking about when she writes that she came to Hollywood troubled by the fact that in Hollywood you were expected to play some version of yourself in every film. She was from Sweden where actors played different ages, different ethnic groups, people very different from who they really were. She says that Michael Curtiz told her, "American audiences pay their money to see Gary Cooper being Gary Cooper, not the Hunchback of Notre Dame." Rick Blaine was not a clone of Humphrey Bogart, but he was a hell of a lot closer to being my father than any of those gun-toting gangsters ever had been.

Richard Schickel puts it this way: "What Bogart found in Rick Blaine was something more interesting than Tough Guy, no less complex than Existential Hero, but much more appealing—to some of us, at least—than both. For Rick was but a minor variation on the role Bogart had himself been playing most of his adult life. A role he had taken up with particular relish when he made his permanent residence in Hollywood. It was the role of Declassed Gentleman. A man of breeding and privilege who found himself far from his native haunts, among people of rather less quality, rather fewer standards morally, socially, intellectually, than he had been raised to expect to find among his acquaintances. Rick Blaine should not have ended up running a gin joint in *Casablanca,* and Humphrey Bogart should not have ended up being an actor in Hollywood."

I think Curtiz and Schickel are, at least partially, right. The movie stars who endure, including my father, often play a big part of themselves. Nonetheless, the next three important films in the Bogie cult were movies in which Dad played parts much further from himself than Rick Blaine or Sam Spade were.

* * *

In *The Treasure of the Sierra Madre,* which is my favorite, Dad was no confident, highly principled Sam Spade. He played a paranoid gold prospector. Huston directed and had a cameo part. Walter Huston, John's father, was in the film and he won the 1948 Academy Award for Best Supporting Actor while John was winning the Oscar for Best Director. My father got his second Oscar nomination for that film.

While this was one of my father's favorite roles, Sam Jaffe says that Bogie had some reservations at first.

"Your father came to me one day and said, 'Have you read the script for *The Treasure of the Sierra Madre*?' I said yes. He made a face. I said, 'Bogie, I can see that something's bothering you.' It seemed to me that he was concerned about the size of the part, since he had already done *The Maltese Falcon* and *Casablanca* by this point. I said to him, 'I don't know if you are considering not doing this, but you're a great friend of John Huston and you have great respect for Walter Huston. There is nothing wrong with being second in a movie that stars Walter Huston and is directed by John Huston. You may have some doubts, but let me say that if you don't do this picture, it won't get made because they won't make a picture with Walter and another actor. And what will happen to your relationship with John Huston? You will crush John. I want to relieve your mind that you will not be hurt by playing in this movie. You'll be good in the picture and people will not say, Oh, Bogie's not important anymore because he is being second to Walter Huston.' "

John Huston, of course, was a major force in my father's career. Perhaps *the* major force. It would be Huston, of course, who would later direct Bogie in *The African Queen,* the last of the five films which I think are mainly responsible for my father's fame.

Of course, these five films only make up one-fifteenth of my father's film work. Everybody I meet has a favorite. A lot of people like *The Big Sleep,* which I can't make heads or tails of. Some people favor the other Bogie and Bacall movies, like *To Have and Have Not* and *Key Largo,* the latter of which was also directed by Huston. And there are people who just love those old gangster movies, especially *The Roaring Twenties* and *They Drive By Night.* Still I think it was those five: *High Sierra, The Maltese Falcon, Casablanca, The Treasure of the Sierra Madre,* and *The African Queen,* which are most responsible for making my father the most famous movie star in the world.

Tracing the arc of my father's fame is a lot easier than understanding it. I see him kind of moving along from film to film like an airplane gaining speed, then finally lifting off into stardom. But then there is a moment when he seems to go into the stratosphere, breaking away from the pull of gravity which holds the rest of us on earth. We can, more or less, figure out when it happened, but nobody can say for sure why it happened.

Some film critics say that the first sign of Bogie's film immortality was in France in 1960. It was in the famous French movie *Breathless* that Jean-Paul Belmondo stood in front of a poster of my father smoking a cigarette and simply said, "Bogie." Critics disagree about just what Belmondo was trying to say, but the fact that they discuss it at all is the telling thing.

But other film historians will tell you that the Bogie cult was born in America, specifically in Cambridge, Massachusetts, at the Brattle Theatre in Harvard Square. In 1956, a year before he died, the Brattle booked *Beat the Devil*, which had come out in 1954. *Beat the Devil* was an offbeat comedy which starred, along with my father, Robert Morley and Gina Lollobrigida and Dad's friend Peter Lorre. Huston directed. It was another one of those movies where nobody was quite sure of what the movie was, even by the time they started shooting. It had not been a commercial success.

But in Cambridge in 1956 the students from Harvard and MIT loved the offbeat humor and they loved Bogie.

The following year, the Brattle booked *Casablanca* and the response was even greater. It turned into a Bogart film festival and the Bogie cult was born. In fact, in Harvard Square there is still a Bogie-themed restaurant.

Then the Bogart cult spread to the Bleecker Street Cinema in New York City's Greenwich Village and the Lyric in Lexington, Virginia, and all across the country, first in college towns and then art houses, and then everywhere. Posters went up on walls. Woody Allen wrote *Play It Again, Sam.* Eventually there was a hit record, *Key Largo.* Howard Koch, one of the cowriters on *Casablanca,* and one of Dad's chess partners, says that when he appeared at college showings of *Casablanca,* the kids would recite the dialogue along with the actors just as they did for the *Rocky Horror Picture Show.* He says he has met students who have seen the film dozens of times.

So over the years there has been a lot written about the appeal of Bogie. And there is little diversity in the opinions. Almost everybody who has written about the Bogart myth says that we love Bogart because he was his own man. He told the truth. He saw right through phonies. He was cynical, yet he could be idealistic when the time came.

The last family friend I talked to about this phenomenon was George Axelrod. Axelrod is the writer-producer-director who is probably best known for writing Broadway comedies like *The Seven Year Itch*. He was a friend of my father's and when I asked him why he thought Bogie has endured, he said, "Your father understood that the world was absurd. That's something that nobody understood. He didn't really take life seriously. He knew it was all bullshit. Steve, it's good to go through life knowing it is all bullshit. Bogie would have loved all this politically correct stuff today. Oh, what he would have done with this. When you understand that there's no purpose, that it's all an accident and there's no value and you still make a life for yourself, that's the trick of the thing. Once you understand that, you realize everything is delusion and illusion, then life is kind of existential, and Bogie understood that this existential quality is the kind of subtext that comes out in his performance and that is why he is an immortal figure. Bogie made that quality somehow come across on the screen, and he had it in real life, too. He was an existentialist. I don't know if he would use that word, because that would be too pretentious for him, but that's what he was."

Rod Steiger, who starred with my father in his last movie, *The Harder They Fall*, also had an interesting take on Bogart's lasting fame. He said, "I think Mr. Bogart—that's what I always called him—has endured because in our society the family unit has softened and gone to pieces. And here you had a guy about whom there was no doubt. There is no doubt that he is the leader. There is no doubt that he is the strong one. There is no doubt with this man that he can handle himself, that he can protect the family. This is all unconscious, of course, but with Bogart you are secure, you never doubt that he will take care of things."

I guess the real question is not, why do we like Bogart? It's which Bogie are we talking about—the Bogart movie image projected on film screens around the world through seventy-five films? Or my father, the wry, but somewhat insecure man, who I think was kind of lonely and did not tell everybody what was on his mind all the time? I think George Axelrod was telling me that the answer is both, and I think he's right.

One of the first things all Bogie historians like to point out is that Bogart was educated, well spoken, genteel, not at all like the gangsters he portrayed in most of his early films. This, they say, is the starting point for separating Bogie from his roles. But I think it might also be the ending point, because my father really was a somewhat cynical wisecracker who hated phonies. Aside from the fact that he had no background with real gangsters, and that he had the insecurities that come with being human, there is no big surprise in the real Bogart. Sure, he played chess and golf, and maybe you didn't know that. And maybe you didn't know he was an avid reader, or that he coined the phrase "Tennis, anyone?" But that's the end of the surprises. My father was not a child abuser, like Joan Crawford, and he did not have bad breath, like Clark Gable. He was not gay and he was not a Nazi spy, and if he had a secret life I think it was mostly a secret life of the mind. These days it seems like once a month we are shocked and disappointed by the gap between a star's real nature and his public image. So maybe my father has endured because there is no significant gap. Bogie, to a great extent, really was Bogie. He was the man John Huston described in his eulogy when he said:

Humphrey Bogart died early Monday morning. His wife was at his bedside, and his children were nearby. He had been unconscious for a day. He was not in any pain. It was a peaceful death. At no time during the months of his illness did he believe he was going to die, not that he refused to consider the thought—it simply never occurred to him. He loved life. Life meant his family, his friends, his work, his boat. He could not imagine leaving any of them, and so until the very last he planned what he would do when he got well. His boat was being repainted. Stephen, his son, was getting of an age when he could be taught to sail, and to learn his father's love of the seas. A few weeks sailing and Bogie would be all ready to go to work again. He was going to make fine pictures—only fine pictures—from here on in.

With the years he had become increasingly aware of the dignity of his profession . . . actor, not star. Actor. Himself, he never took too seriously—his work most seriously. He regarded the somewhat gaudy figure of Bogart, the star, with an amused cynicism; Bogart, the actor, he held in deep respect. Those who did not know him well, who never worked with him, who were not of the small circle of his close friends, had another completely different idea of the man than the few who were so privileged. I suppose the ones who knew him but slightly were at the greatest disadvantage, particularly if they were the least bit solemn about their own importance. Bigwigs have been known to stay away from the brilliant Hollywood occasions rather than expose their swelling neck muscles to Bogart's banderillas.

In each of the fountains at Versailles there is a pike which keeps all the carp active, otherwise they would grow overfat and die. Bogie took rare delight in performing a similar duty in the fountains of Hollywood. Yet his victims seldom bore him any malice, and when they did, not for long. His shafts were fashioned only to stick into the outer layer of complacency, and not to penetrate through to the regions of the spirit where real injuries are done.

The great houses of Beverly Hills, and for that matter of the world, were so many shooting galleries so far as Bogie was concerned. His own house was a sanctuary. Within those walls anyone, no matter how elevated his position, could breathe easy. Bogie's hospitality went far beyond food and drink. He fed a guest's spirit as well as his body, plied him with good will until he became drunk in the heart as well as in the legs.

Bogie was lucky at love and he was lucky at dice. To begin with he was endowed with the greatest gift a man can have: talent. The whole world came to recognize it. Through it all he was able to live in comfort and to provide well for his wife and children.

His life, though not a long one measured in years, was a rich, full life. Over all the other blessings were the two children, Stephen and Leslie, who gave a final lasting meaning to his life. Yes, Bogie wanted for nothing. He got all that he asked for out of life and more. We have no reason to feel any sorrow for him—only for ourselves for having lost him. He is quite irreplaceable. There will never be another like him.

I am on the floor watching television. I am straddled across Pandy, my giant stuffed panda, pretending that Pandy is a horse. My father comes in. "What you watching, Steve?" he asks.

"The Alone Ranger," I tell him.

"Good," he says. "Good."

"Wanna see me ride?" I say.

"Sure, pal. Go ahead, Steve, ride 'em cowboy."

I lift myself higher in my make-believe saddle. I make galloping noises with my mouth. I fire my cap pistol at the outlaws on the black-and-white television. I spank Pandy with my other hand to make him ride faster. I sway back and forth as if I might fall from my horse, and I start giggling.

"Go get 'em, cowboy," my father says. "Go get 'em." He watches me for a while longer, then he laughs and leaves the room. I think to call him back. I want to ask him if he wants to watch the Alone Ranger with me. But I don't. I stare at the door. He is gone. I hear him downstairs talking to my mother. I turn back to the TV screen and watch the rest of the Alone Ranger alone, riding my stuffed panda.

4

Bogart thought of himself as Scaramouch, the mischievous scamp who sets off the fireworks, then nips out.

—NUNNALLY JOHNSON

We left England when my mother finished making *Flame Over India*, which was a fast-paced action film set on the northern frontier of India. She plays the governess of an Indian prince, and she's trying to help British soldiers get the prince to safety from some bad guys. I thought Mom was excellent, and the movie did very well.

With the film in the can, Mom moved us from London back to the US. But we did not return to California where I had spent my childhood. We flew, instead, to New York, where we moved into an apartment that was being rented jointly by us and Richard and Sybil Burton.

My parents had met the Burtons in England in 1951. As

a toddler I had spent a lot of time on Richard Burton's knee. I think I might have vomited on his shoes once. (God, when I think of the voices I used to listen to as a kid: John Huston, Richard Burton, Humphrey Bogart, and of course, Lauren Bacall, who is known for her voice.) I know I used to confuse Burton with Richard Greene, who played Robin Hood on television, and I always pronounced Richard and Sybil, "Wretched and Simple."

When we moved to New York, May, the cook, was still with us, and a new nurse was hired to look after Leslie and me.

We were in New York because Mother had been offered a leading role in *Good-bye Charlie*, a Broadway play about a gangster who dies and comes back to earth as a woman. Mom was determined to have a career and not spend the rest of her life being described in newspaper articles as "Bogie's widow."

Good-bye Charlie was written and directed by my parents' friend George Axelrod. The actors, including my mother, got great reviews, but the play was panned by the critics. After only three months on Broadway it was good-bye to *Good-bye Charlie*. The story did, however, resurface in 1964 as a pretty pathetic excuse for a movie, starring Tony Curtis and Debbie Reynolds. Still, *Good-bye Charlie* was a shot of adrenaline for my mother's career, and she continued to get work on Broadway and in Hollywood.

On our first New Year's Eve in New York, Mother met Jason Robards, Jr. Jason was then, and still is, one of our best stage and screen actors. He is an enormous talent, regarded by a lot of people as the finest interpreter of the works of Eugene O'Neill. Now, we know, Jason has appeared in something like a million movies. But at the time his star was just rising. He had recently won the New York Drama Critics Award for *Long Day's Journey Into Night*. If there's one thing that turns my mother on it is excellence, and Jason was a brilliant actor. She fell for him quickly, and he fell for her. Unfortunately, he was an alcoholic.

My mother says that when Jason was sober, he was charming, thoughtful, kind, and gentle. When Jason was slightly drunk, he was still charming, though less thoughtful and kind, which he made up for by being eloquent, often reciting poetry or soliloquies in Greenwich Village bars. But when Jason was very drunk he was not charming, thoughtful, kind, or gentle. And Jason drank a lot.

So Mother married him.

Like a zillion women before her, Mother deluded herself that she could change a man by marrying him. This heavy drinking thing, she thought, was just a stage Jason was going through because of his recent divorce. This was a problem that would vanish after they were married. Yes, yes, the love of a good woman would cure him. Right. What Mother should have done was listen to Spencer Tracy, who said to her, "Betty, get it through your head. No alcoholic ever changes because somebody asks him to." Or her good friend, Adlai Stevenson, who told her, "It's not going to get better after you are married, it's going to get worse."

There are those who say that Jason Robards looks a lot like my father. By those I mean just about everybody who has eyes, except Lauren Bacall. Mom has never seen the resemblance, but I think it is quite striking. What it all means, if anything, is something a psychologist would have to figure out. But whether he looked like Bogie or not, Jason had to wrestle with the ghost of Humphrey Bogart. When word got to the press that Jason and Mother were a serious item, there were dozens of stories to the effect: *can he fill Bogie's shoes?* It's unfortunate for anyone to have to suffer those comparisons, but particularly unjust for Jason, who is such a towering talent in his own right.

By the time they got married in July, 1961, we had moved out of the rented apartment and into a fourteen-room apartment at the Dakota. The Dakota is a famous old building on Central Park West. You might remember it as the setting of *Rosemary's Baby*, where Mia Farrow's husband gets involved with a witch's coven right there in the building. The Dakota is also the place where, in real life, John Lennon was shot dead by Mark David Chapman. Of course, when we moved into the building the Beatles were just unknown teenagers in Liverpool, but years later on visits to my mother, I would see John Lennon walking in and out of the building, often standing on the very spot where he would be murdered.

The huge apartment at the Dakota allowed for a large family, which we suddenly had. That was the best thing about Mother's marriage to Jason. Jason had three kids by a previous marriage: Sarah, Jady, and David. Jady was my age. Sarah was around Leslie's age. And David became the baby of this extended family. Though the three Robards kids lived with their mother, we spent a lot of time together, and there was a period of about a year when Jady and Sarah lived with us at the Dakota. So we had our own Brady Bunch. Or maybe I should say *Eight Is Enough*, because within a year of the wedding my half-brother, Sam Robards, was born. Sam is now a successful movie actor. (If Sam seems a small part of this book it is only because there is a fourteen-year difference in our ages, and I was away from home through most of Sam's childhood. Sam, like me, had to live through the experience of having two famous parents. It took a lot of guts for him to become an actor, considering who his parents are, and the inevitable comparisons that would be made with his father. But he turned into quite a good actor. Sam and I remain very close. I love him, and I love his son, Jasper, my first nephew.)

On the whole, though, the Bacall–Robards marriage was lousy. My mother had fallen in love with an alcoholic, and after she married him, Jason continued to drink heavily, just as everybody in the universe, except my mother, knew he would.

Leslie and I, in the innocence of youth, didn't realize at the time how bad it really was. Sure, Jason sometimes came in late and slept all day, but Mother explained that that was because he worked late nights on Broadway. Sure, he seemed to be away a lot, but then, so was Mother when she was making a movie. Actually I liked Jason a lot, and he liked me. Jason and I got along great. I think that was because Jason was really a kid at heart. He didn't try to be a replacement father. He was more of a big brother who liked to goof off, not unlike the character he played in *A Thousand Clowns,* where he was kind of a social dropout who lived with his nephew.

Jason had been a top athlete at Hollywood High School, a swimmer and track man. He loved sports. After he married my mother, that was something he shared with me. He used to take me to the Sheeps Meadow in Central Park and pitch baseballs to me, and he would hit high flies so that I could practice my fielding. When we spent a summer in California, Jason taught me to bodysurf. I will always treasure these times with Jason because they were such traditional father-son things, and I never had a chance to do them with my father.

Many of the things Jason did with me were things I later did with my sons.

Jason sometimes took Jady and me to New York Mets games during their first season, when the Mets were known as the team that couldn't throw straight. Their most famous player then was Marvelous Marv Thronberry, known for his ineptitude at third base.

Like my father, Jason was more of a man's man than a ladies' man, and he liked to stay up all night, hanging out with the guys.

I remember one particular night at the Dakota, Jason coming into my room and shaking me.

"Stevie, you awake?"

I hadn't been, but I was now, with a slightly tipsy Jason Robards poking at me.

"What? What's up?"

"Nothing, pal," he said. "Just me and the guys having a few drinks and shooting the shit in the living room."

"So?"

"So, why don't you come in and join us."

I didn't really want to. I was half asleep. But Jason was insistent. So I got up and went into the living room where Jason was entertaining Peter O'Toole and a few other guys. We stayed up most of the night, the guys telling off-color jokes and getting loaded while I drank Cokes. It was a great, raucous night and I'll always remember that Jason made me feel like one of the boys.

So, now that I think about it, it seems that it was my mother's fate to be surrounded by bad boys. First there was Bogart. Then Jason. Then me.

* * *

Though I never participated in drive-by shootings or dealt crack in alleys, I did get into mischief often during the next ten years, and I think a lot of it had to do with anger over my father's death, and the continuing issue of his fame. Perhaps I inherited a mischief gene from my father, because it turns out he also was a handful at a young age.

When Bogie was thirteen he went to a private school in New York. It was the Trinity School, an old Episcopalian institute for young gentlemen. It was on 91st Street near Amsterdam Avenue in Manhattan.

Trinity was like a European school, with a lot of emphasis on Latin and other languages that never come up in real life unless you're a priest, and I think my father knew he would never need them. Trinity also made a big deal about memorization, which my father despised, though perhaps it was a discipline that he would later apply to movie scripts. He said, "At Trinity I wasn't taught right. They made you learn dates and that was all. They would tell you a war was fought in 1812. So what? They never told you why people decided to kill each other at just that moment."

The young Bogart boy at Trinity wore a blue serge suit, white vest, white shirts, and maybe a brass buttoned Chesterfield for good measure. My father was the properly dressed boy, all right, but he also wore a hat to school every day, apparently just to get attention. He did not fit in well, mostly because immediately after school every day he had to rush home to work as a model for his mother, the artist.

At Trinity he was called into the headmaster's office to be reprimanded on a regular basis. He describes one of his conversations with the headmaster this way:

"Herr Luther has reported you again," the headmaster said.

"Yes, sir," I replied.

"He complains that you started a riot in class this morning, and he's given you a failure in German."

"Yes, sir."

"Why?"

"I don't like German," I said.

"Nor Herr Luther?"

"No, sir."

"Since you don't like German and you don't like English or history or economics, will you tell me if there is anything that you do like, Master Bogart."

"I like math, sir. Algebra."

"Why?"

"Because there's nothing theoretical about it. It's simply fact. You can do a problem and get your answer and then you prove the answer's right."

"But these riots. This endless flouting of authority. Why do you do these things?"

I don't know what my father told the headmaster that day. But this flouting of authority was a Bogart trademark throughout his life.

"I always liked stirring things up, needling authority," he said. "Even in my childhood it gave me pleasure. I guess I inherited it from my parents. They needled everyone including each other."

He inherited it from his parents, and maybe I inherited it from him. Like my father, I went to a private school in New

York. I went to Buckley, a very exclusive school, where I was probably the only child of movie stars, but I was also probably from the poorest family. It seemed as if most of the kids were the sons of multimillionaire industrialists and bankers.

I got into a lot of mischief at Buckley, but somehow I got through it and went on to prep school in Massachusetts, which is the same thing my father had done.

Bogie had to repeat his third year at Trinity because of a bout with scarlet fever, but after that he went to Phillips Academy in Andover, where his father had gone to prep school.

"You will go on to Yale," his mother Maud told him.

It was a hope that my mother would later have for me. Both mothers were to be disappointed.

It was 1917 when Dad went into Phillips.

"Studying will be encouraged and hijinx will not be tolerated," he was told on his first day. So right away he didn't care for it. One classmate says, "The thing I remembered was his sullenness. I got the impression that he was a very spoiled boy. When things didn't go his way he didn't like it a bit."

"People in authority are so damn smug," Bogie said. "I can't show reverence when I don't feel it. So I was always testing my instructors to see if they were as bright or godlike as they seemed to be."

By Christmas of that year my father was flunking most of his courses, and he was thinking of burning his report card or maybe burying it under the campus green. But no, he brought it home, and when he did show it to Maud and Belmont, his folks told him to bring his marks up or he would be yanked out of school and put to work. His marks did not improve, however, and Humphrey's father, in a last ditch effort to keep the boy enrolled wrote to the headmaster, saying that Humphrey was basically a good kid who had just "lost the way."

Doctor Bogart wrote, "The whole problem seems to be that the boy has given up his mind to sports and continuous correspondence with his girl friends." This, I can relate to with ease. When I was that age I was also obsessed with sports and girls.

Bogie's father went on to say that, "the harder the screws are put on, the better it will be for my son."

This, I guess, was tough love for the times, but the fact is that tighter screws did not do the trick. On May 15, 1918, Dad was, in the politest possible language, thrown out of Phillips with a promise from the headmaster that he would probably "profit from this unfortunate occurrence."

Years later my father put his own spin on the dismissal. He attributed it to "high spirits" and "infractions of the rules." My father, apparently, would rather be thought of as a discipline case than an academic failure, and he bragged about a couple of pranks which probably never occurred. No discipline problems showed up on his report card, but failures in Chemistry, English, French, Geometry, the Bible, and even Algebra did.

Discipline problems did, however, show up on my report cards years later when I also went to a Massachusetts prep school. My school was Milton Academy in the town of Milton. I remember when I got suspended from Milton. They put me on a train back to New York. As the train rumbled through Connecticut and into New York, I rehearsed in my mind what I would say to my mother, how I would explain the terrible mistake that had been made by Milton. When I got home to the Dakota I went up to the door leading to the kitchen, as I always did. We have always been a kitchen family. Mother was in another part of the apartment, so for a long time I stood alone outside the apartment like a wounded pup, bracing myself for the terrible tongue-lashing I would get from my mother. I tried to work myself into a state of hysteria that would bring on a good crying jag so that I would get some sympathy.

Now, a digression about my famous mother, Betty Bacall. Don't call her Lauren and don't call her Baby. She's Betty to her friends, and Ms. Bacall to everybody else.

My mother is a woman who has dedicated her life to excellence. She adores excellence in art, in music, in everything. Unfortunately, Mom is a perfectionist. Which means she not only adores excellence, she expects it. And she expects it in people. So if you are one of my mother's children and you do something great, get A's on your report card, win a trophy, marry well, whatever, don't plan on getting congratulated or patted on the back. It is merely expected of you.

Having said this, I'm now going to tell you that I caught holy hell when my mother opened the back door and I had to tell her I had been suspended from Milton Academy, right? Wrong. I understand my mother better now than I did then, and I should have known she would not bawl me out.

When I told her what happened, she just held me in her arms. "It's all right, Stephen, it's all right."

My mother has always been a good mother, always loved us and worried about us. She has always put her children first. Though she might not have always shown the love, Leslie and I always knew it was there. This time she certainly showed it. It is when the chips are down that my mother is at her best. When the chips are down she is always there.

Unfortunately, it takes the chips being down for her to get to that point. She is not a fair-weather friend; she is a foul-weather friend.

So when things were bad for me, my mother was a hell of a lot more supportive than Bogie's mother was of him, and maybe that's why I eventually graduated from Milton, while he flunked out of Phillips. Bogie's mother tended to harass him for being a failure, which is why, after he was thrown out of Phillips, my father joined the navy.

The First World War was on, and Dad was assigned as the helmsman on the *Leviathan,* a troop transport ship which had once been a German passenger liner. My father's irreverence for authority figures continued, and it wasn't long before his low opinion of people in high places got him in hot water. An officer gave Bogie an order and he told the officer, "That's not my detail." As the story goes, the officer slugged my father, and Bogie never made that particular mistake again.

However, there were other incidents.

"One time he took an unauthorized leave," says Phil Gersh, who worked with Sam Jaffe, "so they posted him as a deserter. He got ten days in the brig. Bogie didn't care for the sentence so he gave his captain some lip about it, and they made it twenty days. He gave them more lip and they made it thirty days."

Dad also liked to shoot craps on the ship and on at least one occasion he lost his entire month's pay before reaching Paris and the French girls that he had so eagerly looked forward to.

Shortly after the armistice was signed my father pulled his final navy prank. His captain ordered him to make out the discharge papers for two hundred of the most deserving men. Dr. James Mitchell, who served with my father, and was later a physician for MGM, says, "Humphrey went below and made out his own discharge first. He was about to go over the side with seabag and hammock in hand when the captain spied him and asked where he was going. Humphrey answered that he had orders to discharge the most deserving men first, and he thought he was the most deserving man aboard ship. The captain insisted he go below and finish out his service time."

While my father was not exactly a model of navy excellence, he did look great in uniform. In photos from those days he looks handsome and dashing, a regular navy poster boy. And he finally did get his honorable discharge.

I often wonder about my father's life in the military. On the one hand, he was a patriot and I am sure he would have died for his country if it came to that. But he was an iconoclast, too, forever thumbing his nose at institutions like the military. He was perhaps amused by the very idea of himself in uniform. And I wonder, too, about the difference between two men, one who serves in the military and one who doesn't. Did the navy instill my father with a discipline that I never had? Did the navy "make a man out of him," as we are so often told that service does? If he had not served, would he still have had the work ethic that later characterized his career?

The questions I ask about my father are often disguised versions of questions I am asking about myself, and often I wonder how my life might be different if I had served in the military, if I had gone to war instead of getting a draft deferment.

After I left Milton in 1967, when I was about the age that Dad entered the navy, I went to the University of Pennsylvania in Philadelphia for a year and got into more mischief. That year in Philadelphia was my year as a lowlife. My mother was paying for college, so my normal living expenses were taken care of. But I had a steady girlfriend by this time, and the $100 a month that my mother sent didn't seem to go far enough. So I got a job at a record store, and did something that bothers me to this day. Something I'm not proud of. I gave away hundreds of record albums so that people would like me. My new friends would come in and say, "Hey Steve, can I take some records?" and I'd say, "Sure, help yourself." It got ridiculous. One time a guy I hardly even knew came in, and he must have walked off with twenty record albums. This was my way of making friends. My class at Milton had sixty-three boys, and when I got to this big school in Philly it was like being dropped off in the center of a huge city where I knew no one. I didn't really know how to make friends, except by giving them stuff. All I had to do was give them records that weren't mine. I think in some weird way it was part of the Bogie thing, a way of being popular for who I was. In Philadelphia, people didn't like me because I was Humphrey Bogart's son—they liked me because I would let them steal albums out of the record shop. At the time, crazy as it seems now, anything was better than being liked because of my father.

During this whole period I lost contact with my mother. It was the breakaway scenario, a time of rebellion, of trying to be anonymous. I never called home. Most of the time my mother didn't really know where I was. During that year I did a lot of things I'm ashamed of. For example, I stole money from my friend Jon Avnet, who was one of the people I moved in with after I got kicked out of my dormitory. When Avnet found I had robbed him of sixty bucks he came to me and said, "Why didn't you just ask?" I didn't have an answer. Then, I stole money from him a second time and that's when he stopped being my friend. Today Jon is a very successful Hollywood producer and director, with films like *Fried Green Tomatoes* and *Risky Business* to his credit. Maybe by now he has forgotten what I did, but I never have. Sorry, Jon.

For a while I was deep into fraternity life. I was in a fraternity of real jocks, guys like Chuck Mercene who would later play for the New York Giants, and Timmy Cutter, a brilliant hockey player. This was the period of time when I started smoking grass. And I did some drinking, too, though I've never really been much of a drinker.

When I got back from Christmas break that year, I returned to the record store and the woman who was the assistant manager said, "Steve, we did inventory."

"And?"

"Ronnie's looking for you," she said. Ronnie was the boss.

When Ronnie found me he said, "Steve, there are six hundred albums missing."

I said, "I think I'm fired."

He said, "Right."

I don't know when I really stopped getting into trouble. I guess it was in the early 1980s when I met Barbara, and she helped me get over my cocaine dependence.

It was Barbara, of course, who got me to think about my father and encouraged me to ask questions whenever I met someone who had known my father. Naturally, because of my own history, I asked a lot about his misbehavior. It seemed as if everybody had a story to tell about Bogie being a bad boy.

* * *

His defiance of authority, for example, is always there, all through his life.

If Dad wasn't going to kowtow to authority in prep school and the military he certainly wasn't going to do it years later in Hollywood. His irreverence for the icons of the movie world became one of his best-known characteristics.

In the 1930s when the studio public relations departments were trying to make every actor look like a model of gentility, Bogie refused to pose for the cornball photos they wanted of him patting dogs, smoking pipes, and riding horses. He thought that was phony. He hated phoniness. He just wanted to be himself. I understand how he felt. Sometimes when people ask me about being Bogart's son I feel as if I am being asked to, somehow, pose for something that is not really me.

"If I feel like going to the Trocadero wearing a pair of moccasins, that is the way I go to the Troc," Bogart said. "If I go to the Troc and want to make a jackass of myself in front of every producer in town, that's my business."

The biggest Hollywood authority figure for much of my father's career was Jack Warner, and Bogie's battles with Warner became a part of Hollywood lore.

Jack was one of the four Warner brothers. He was the production chief, the guy who ran the studio. He fought, not just with Bogie, but with Bette Davis, Olivia De Havilland, and James Cagney, among others. Warner was, my father once said in an interview, "a creep."

Warner called him up after that remark. "How can you call me a thing like that?" Warner asked. "A creep is a loathsome, crawling thing in my dictionary."

"But I spell it 'kreep,' with a k, not a c," Bogie said.

"But how can you do this to me?"

"I did it for the publicity, for the studio and you," Bogie told him.

I suspect that the Bogart–Warner battles were special because Jack Warner could be as tactless as Dad. Once when Warner was introduced to Madame Chiang Kai-shek, he allegedly muttered that he had forgotten to bring his laundry.

I asked Sam Jaffe what my father and Warner fought about.

"Scripts," Sam said. "Jack Warner knew your father was a good actor, but he would never consider him for better roles. I remember one time Bogart wouldn't do a certain picture. Warner said to me, 'Sam, you have no control of your client.' I said, 'Jack, I can't control Bogart's mind. He reads scripts and he knows what he wants to do. I can't tell him what to do.' This was when they had what were called slave contracts, and the studio could lay Bogie off if he rejected a story. So he was always getting suspended. Warner would hand Bogie a script and Bogie would read it and say, 'This is a piece of crap.' The Warners never bought a really good book or play for him. They would get some lousy script and give it to your father just so they could comply with the contract requirement that they offer him a script. But Bogie always said it was crap. He used that word, crap, a lot."

Talking about his conflicts with Warner, my father said, "I'd read a movie script and yell that it was not right for me. I'd be called for wardrobe and refuse to report. Jack Warner would phone and say, 'Be a good sport.' I'd say no. Then I'd get a letter from the Warner Brothers lawyers ordering me to report. I'd refuse. Then another wire from Warner saying that if I did not report he'd cut my throat. He'd always sign it, *Love to Mayo.*" (My father's wife during much of this haggling.)

I was happy to hear that my father fought with Warner about scripts. We are always hearing that everybody in Hollywood these days cares only about the deal, not the movie. My father, admittedly, played in a lot of stinkers, but he was always fighting for better movies and better scripts, never for bigger paychecks.

Jack Warner certainly was not the only Hollywood figure to get the Bogart needle. Bogie often slammed Hollywood figures in print. And he was annoyed and amused when people found this outrageous.

He said, "All over Hollywood they are continually advising me, 'Oh, you mustn't say that. That will get you in a lot of trouble,' when I remark that some picture or director or writer or producer is no good. I don't get it. If he isn't any good why can't you say so? If more people would mention it, pretty soon it might have some effect. The local idea that anyone making a thousand dollars a week is sacred and is beyond the realm of criticism never strikes me as particularly sound."

The press, of course, loved the fact that Bogie was outspoken and irreverent. They found him very quotable because he did not dish out the pablum they were used to.

"I believe in speaking my mind," Bogie said. "I don't believe in hiding anything. If you are ashamed of anything, correct it. There's nothing I won't talk about. I've never gone along with the social structure of this town and as a result I don't have many close friends among the actors."

My father was outspoken not just about Hollywood, but about everything. He loved to argue. This is certainly one area in which I am my father's son. I love to argue just for the fun of it. I'll take the opposite side on any issue just to watch the sparks fly. Dad was stimulated by the music of the words and the exchange of ideas. And he was amused by the positions people held on various topics. One of his favorite tricks was to say something outrageous in a group, get a debate going, and then sneak away while the others continued arguing.

Bogie said, "I can't even get in a mild discussion without turning it into an argument. There must be something in my tone of voice, or this arrogant face. Something that antagonizes everybody. Nobody likes me on sight. I suppose that's why I'm cast as the heavy.

"The thing is, I can't understand why people get mad. You can't live in a vacuum, and you can't have a discussion without two sides. If you don't agree with the other fellow, that's what makes it a discussion. I'd feel like a sap, starting things by throwing in with my opponent and saying, 'Well, of course, you may be right,' or 'You know more about it than I do,' and all the other half-baked compromises the tact and diplomacy boys use. My idea of an honest discussion is to begin by declaring my opinion. Then, when the other fellow says, 'Why you're nothing but a goddamned fool, Bogart,' things begin to move and we can get somewhere. Or, I'm the one that pulls that line on him. Anyway, it gets a lot of action."

Because my father was burdened with the screen image of being a tough guy, he was often confronted by jerks who wanted to test him so they could boast in the office the next day about how they had drawn down on Bogie the tough guy.

It was always a difficult spot for Dad. Usually his wit could win over these dolts, who often as not were drunk. But Bogie couldn't always wisecrack his way out of a sticky situation. Sometimes things got physical.

Because Dad was not well known during the time of his marriages to Mary Philips and Helen Menken, most of his physical fights occurred during his third marriage, to Mayo Methot, from 1938 to 1945. In fact, she was involved in many of them. One night, for example, he and Mayo were closing down a bar. Some guy came over to their table, leaned down real close to my father and said, "I hear you're a tough guy. But they must have been talking about somebody else, because you don't look so tough to me."

"You're probably right," my father said. "Why don't you sit down, pal, and have a drink on me."

The man accepted my father's offer. But soon he started getting belligerent again. "You know what I heard?" he said.

"No," Bogie said, "what did you hear?"

"I heard you won't sign autographs for kids. I heard you're too tough for that, you just brush them off."

Bogie could see that he wasn't going to charm this guy into submission, so he turned to Mayo and suggested it was time to quit for the night.

"Just what I thought," the stranger said. "You're trying to run out. Tough, huh? That's a laugh."

Suddenly, the man took a swing at my father. My father ducked and caught only a slight glancing blow. Then they started grappling and finally ended up on the floor of this New York night spot. Mayo yanked off one of her shoes and began banging the man with it. Finally the manager had to step in and break up the brawl.

"Darling," Mayo later said, "it must be wonderful to be a movie star and receive such recognition from your fans."

If Dad's being a movie star sometimes got him into trouble, there were other times when he used his screen persona to create trouble. One time at a restaurant a friend of his, knowing Bogie's love for pranks, came up behind my father and tapped him on the shoulder.

"All right," the friend said, "finish your drink and get out of here. We don't want you in this place."

Bogart turned slowly, looked carefully around the room, then took the cigarette out of his mouth and flipped it onto the floor, grinding it out. He narrowed his eyes, spat out the last of the cigarette smoke, and said, "Listen, pal, I'm staying here. If you don't like it you can move along. This is my territory and you know it. Or do I have to prove it to you?"

The people in the restaurant were getting nervous now and some of them started putting distance between themselves and Bogart. Bogie let the tension hang in the room for a moment, then he started laughing.

This was something he did a lot, and sometimes he would get into fake fights, pulling his punches the way he had to in the movies.

Many of my father's pranks would be big hits today on David Letterman. When Bogie was in Paris with Mother, Peter Viertel, and Joan Fontaine, he picked up a street wino and invited him to join them all for dinner. After dinner he gave the bum fifty bucks and a cigar. Also in Paris, he picked up a prostitute and introduced her around as his fiancée.

When I was eight months old, Bogie went back to New

York and his visit to the El Morocco club led to one of the most infamous stories of his mischief.

The story, as it appeared in newspapers the next day, was that Bogie and Bacall were in New York on vacation. They went out nightclubbing with Bogie's friend Bill Seeman and other friends. Around midnight my mother and the others went home, but Bogie and Seeman stayed out to continue carousing. They arrived at El Morocco after midnight, carrying two giant stuffed pandas, which my father had bought for me. They introduced the pandas all around as their "dates," and asked to be seated at a table for four, so their pandas could have chairs. They propped the pandas, which were over three feet high, in the chairs and proceeded to drink.

At a nearby table two young women, one a socialite, the other a well-known fashion model, were having drinks with their dates. At one point one of the young women came over and picked up one of the pandas. Bogie, offended, pushed her and she fell to the floor. When the other young woman picked up the other panda, Bogie said something insulting to her. At that point the second woman's boyfriend got into the act and started throwing dishes. This was followed by a melee, the details of which were not clear to anybody. My father, his friend, and their pandas were thrown out of El Morocco and banned from the club forever.

My father, admitting he was drunk at the time and that he was not completely clear on the sequence of events, tells a similar story but with important differences.

"My wife had some sense and went home to bed," he says, "which I guess is where I should have been. But Mr. Seeman and myself went on to make it a stag party. It seemed like a good idea to us to buy a couple of those huge pandas as a present for my son and it seemed like a very good idea to take them to El Morocco for a nightcap.

"Mr. Seeman and myself were sitting perfectly quietly around a table for four at about three forty-five A.M. when some Jane I never saw before tried to steal one of the pandas on a bet or something. I couldn't let that happen, could I?

"So I wrestled the panda away from the girl. I guess she did fall down. I'd never hit a lady. They're too dangerous. But those pandas were huge, almost as big as she was, and she must have gotten a little top heavy. Anyway, she looked as if she'd been drinking too many Coca-Colas."

Bogie denied that the other woman's date had assaulted him with plates. "Nobody threatened me," he says. "I would have pasted him. There was no slugging and nobody got hurt." In telling his story to the papers, he even managed to quote Shakespeare. "It was just a lot of sound and fury, signifying nothing," he said. "You know how it is at that hour of the morning when everybody's had quite a few drinks. Anyway, Mr. Seeman and myself and our two pandas left the club under our own steam."

A few days later my father was served with a summons in his suite at the St. Regis. The model was accusing him of assault, and claiming back and neck injuries. My uncle, Charlie Weinstein, was Bogie's lawyer.

"I thought this was a tempest in a teapot," Bogie said, "but it has grown into a full-size hurricane. Sure, I'll appear in court tomorrow. They tell me I'd better or else. They send policemen after you, put you in jail, and do other bad things. I think the girls are both very pretty. Too pretty to have to do anything like this for publicity. So I don't know what the score is. I'll tag along and see."

The model was also suing my father for twenty-five thousand bucks, but he didn't take it too seriously. In court he was asked, "Were you drunk at the time?" He replied, "Isn't everybody at three in the morning?" The case was dropped.

My mother tells me, "The funny thing about the pandas is that when Bogie took them home you wouldn't play with them and you didn't even look at them for three years. When you were four you used to ride them when you watched cowboy films on television."

It was the panda incident more than others that cemented my father's reputation as a carouser. A couple of months later he was quoted in a newspaper column as saying that New York was a fun town, implying that the city's clubs and restaurants closed their eyes to drunkenness and disorderly conduct. My father thought such carousing was becoming a lost art, at least among movie stars. "Errol Flynn and I are the only ones left who do any good old hell-raising," he said.

The head of New York's Society of Restaurateurs responded by saying that Bogart and Errol Flynn would get the "bum's rush" the next time they tried to "get stiff and raise hell."

"New York restaurant owners don't condone misbehavior by big movie stars, millionaires, or anyone else," he said. "This is a clean town. There isn't a public place here that wouldn't give Bogart, Flynn, or anyone else the boot if they carried on in a disturbing manner."

One prominent theatrical publicist at the time was sure

that this outrageous night life would ruin my father's career. "If that guy doesn't get wise to himself pretty soon and stop trying to make like he's in the movies all the time, he'll be finished," he said.

Of course, by the time of the panda incident my father was married to Bacall, and he was also fifty years old. Both of these things inhibited wild nightlife, and he was really not the party animal he once had been.

Still, he was concerned about the image of him that was being created. Just before he left to film *The African Queen* he said, "Some people think the only thing I've done is get involved in barroom bouts. Why, I've been in over forty plays. I've done some lasting things, too. What they are I can't think of at the moment, but there must have been some."

My father was a guy who had a lot to say about a lot of things, including celebrity reporting.

"People who live in glass houses need ear plugs and a sense of humor," he said. "If they hear everything that's said about them and are disturbed by everything they hear, they'll go through life in a constant state of hypertension and high blood pressure. By the nature of my profession I live in a glass house. When I chose to be an actor I knew I'd be working in the spotlight. I also knew that the higher a monkey climbs the more you can see of his tail. So I keep my sense of humor and go right along leading my life and enjoying it. I wouldn't trade places with anybody.

"Like many another honest burgher, my vices are reasonably modest and unspectacular. But some of the stories you should hear. I have an interesting, never dull, but hardly scandalous life. I am not going about slugging people in saloons, chasing starlets, smoking marijuana, or otherwise making headlines. Of course, I express an opinion now and then, but it's all in fun. So if people want to create a legend of a hell-raising Bogie, in keeping with some of my film roles, it is necessary that they invent little stories and pass them along as authentic."

Though my father eventually ran out of energy for late-night drinking, he never tired of pranks. There are many stories about my father's mischief and there is no reason to doubt most of them. However, I've learned that my father's impishness was so legendary that it has spawned a good many stories which are suspect.

One story that is true, though, concerns the time when my father made *Action in the North Atlantic* with Raymond Massey. There was a scene where he and Massey were supposed to jump from a burning tanker ship into a burning oil slick on the ocean. Of course, stunt doubles would be doing the jumping for the high-priced talent.

"My double is braver than your double," Bogie said to Massey.

"Like hell, he is," Massey said. "My double is twice as brave as your double."

Somehow this disagreement became a discussion of which actor was the braver and before long the men had ma-choed their way into doing the stunt themselves. Both of them got burned slightly, but not seriously, leaping into the water. The director, of course, was horrified that millions of Warner Brothers dollars had been put in jeopardy by the prank, which made it all the more enjoyable for my father.

On that same film, Bogie told Dane Clark, who then was waiting to be built up as "the new Bogart," that Warner's was going to change Clark's name to José O'Toole and make him into a new Irish-South American sensation. Clark apparently fell for it, and had a big blow-up with Jack Warner, until the two of them figured out that Bogie had tricked them.

Richard Brooks, the director, tells a Bogie story concerning chess. My father was a great chess player, but Mike Romanoff was better. Brooks says that one time Bogie and Romanoff were playing a series of games and Romanoff had to pay a hundred bucks to charity if my father won a certain number of them. During this series of games the prince had to go into the hospital for some minor surgery and they decided they would keep playing the chess match, by phone. But Bogie set it up so that he played in his booth at Romanoff's and he had two phones handy. Romanoff would call in with his move and Bogie would stall for time before making a counter move. Then he'd get on the other phone and call some big US chess champion who would tell him what moves to make.

Swifty Lazar told me about the time my father pushed him in the pool at Sinatra's house. When Swifty got even by pushing Bogie into the pool my father was really pissed off because he was wearing a very expensive watch that my mother had just bought him. "What the hell are you going to do about this?" he asked, handing Swifty the soaked watch. "I'm going to dry it off," Swifty said and he tossed the watch in the fireplace. The next day he bought my father a Mickey Mouse watch to replace it, but eventually he replaced the expensive one.

Inevitably, Dad became the target of pranksters, as well. Sybil Christopher, who used to be Sybil Burton, told me, "I remember one time Richard and Betty playing a trick. Bogie was working on a film and when he got home Richard was lying on the couch, wearing Bogie's pajamas. But Bogie outsmarted them; he just said hello, and pretended nothing was odd. Bogie would not admit that Richard was wearing his pajamas—he didn't react at all. The joke fell flat because Bogie outsmarted them."

I found out that my father was feisty. And he was combative. But his battles were not all fought to show off his wit, or to win an argument. He had, everybody says, an unmoving set of principles and he would rather raise hell than be silent when the events around him came in conflict with what he believed was right. This did not surprise me, but it pleased me to hear it from people who knew him. Did I, too, have an unmoving set of principles? Yes, I decided. Could some of my behavior be excused because I was fighting for what I believed in? No. But I heard stories about my father standing up for people, and I like to think that if Bogie could somehow be plucked from those stories and I could take his place, I would behave similarly.

"I didn't go on the set much," Sam Jaffe says, "but I remember one time I was on the set, visiting your father, and he was being directed in a film at Columbia. I don't remember who the director was, but at one point the producer was there and he was interfering, telling the director what to do. Finally, Bogie just stopped working and he said to the producer, 'Look, I can't be directed by you and him. He is the director. If you want to tell him something, do it at some other time. If you want to be a director I'll help you find a story and you can direct your own picture. But don't try to direct this man.' That's an example of what Bogie represented as a person."

And Phil Gersh remembers that my father was very affected by World War II, and that he put in a lot of time visiting wounded soldiers. Gersh remembers being with Bogie in 1942 during the Second World War when Bogie went overseas to do a show for the troops with Mayo Methot. Bogie stayed at a hotel that was there for generals and colonels. Phil stayed with the grunts. When Bogie realized that Phil was not at the hotel he went looking for him.

"Where are you sleeping?" Bogie asked.

"On the ground," Phil said.

"No," Bogie said, "I want you to stay in my room."

"But that's for officers," Phil said.

"I don't care," Bogie told him. "We'll get you a bed and you can stay in my room."

So Bogie went to some commanding general and told him he wanted an extra bed for his friend. When the brass turned him down, he said, "Fine. If you won't let me have a bed in my room for my friend, then you won't have a show."

So, of course, he got the bed, and Phil got a good night's sleep.

Gersh was one of many people who had stories to tell about Bogie ruffling feathers, needling people, even speaking unkindly and hurting feelings. But I also heard stories like this one, stories about Bogie speaking out for the little guy. I liked to hear those stories. Because the truth is my own mischief was not always cute at the time that it was happening. I had often behaved badly, and I often hurt the feelings of people who had been kind to me. A lot of my mischief made me feel crummy about myself. So it was reassuring to learn that my imperfect father must have felt crummy about himself from time to time, must have had his own regrets about shallow moments and thoughtless remarks.

And as I roamed from one Bogie friend to the next and

listened to the stories about my father's more admirable traits, I found that they, too, were deeply satisfying because I still had some growing up to do and my father, though dead these many years, was teaching me ways to do it.

I am in my room at the Mapleton Drive House. But it is not my room. It has not been my room for thirty-six years. It is someone else's room, and there is no evidence that I have ever been here before. I find that this room does not sweep me back to my childhood as easily as I'd thought it would. In fact, I remember little. What I do remember, oddly, is something that hung on the wall. A wooden frame, a square of glass, and in the middle is a check from the President of the United States.

In my memory I am a kid again, and one day I take the frame down from the wall and examine it. I expect the check to be somehow bigger than other checks, but it is ordinary looking. It is from Harry S Truman and it is made out to "Baby Bogart." I ask my father about it.

"Well," he says, "before you were born I made a bet with the president that you would be a girl. He said you would be a boy. He was right."

"So how come you didn't send him a check?"

"I did," my father says. "He wrote me a note. He said, 'It is a rare instance when I find a man who remembers his commitments and meets them on the dot.' Then he sent the money back, only he sent it to you."

These memories are just slivers, so frustratingly fleeting, and now I am awakened from this one. I look one last time around the room that once was mine. I try to remember exactly where the framed check hung on the wall. But

I can't. I smile. I still have that check at home. It's like winning a bet from my father.

5

It was not a good time to be a Democrat in the movie business, especially one partisan to me. But Bogie never seemed to give a damn for what people said or thought.

—ADLAI STEVENSON

My father and I both reached the age of military service during a war. The big difference was that his was a "good war," World War I, and mine was an unpopular war in Vietnam. Another difference: he enlisted, I was drafted.

That is, I got my draft notice. It came four weeks after I got thrown out of Boston University, which is where I went to school for a short time after I got thrown out of the University of Pennsylvania.

I tried heroically to get out of being drafted, but it seemed as if all the legal dodges were being snatched away from me faster than I could scheme up ways of using them.

First they dropped the student deferment. Then they dropped the deferment for being married. Then they dropped the deferment for being a father. It looked for a while there as if I was about to be dropped into South Vietnam, or at least to some godforsaken military base in South Carolina.

So I did the only rational thing. I applied for status as a conscientious objector. This conscientious objector thing was big in the 1960s. People who couldn't even spell *conscientious* were suddenly having pangs of conscience. Lots of guys like me had gotten the crazy idea that they didn't want to be shot to death in an Asian jungle, but you couldn't say that. What you could say was that you didn't want to shoot somebody *else* to death in an Asian jungle.

So I filled out this conscientious objector application and it was sent to some kind of three-man board that would decide whether or not I qualified. Amazingly, one guy on the board actually voted in my favor, which meant that my plea was sent on to Richard Nixon. Tricky Dick turned me down. Maybe that was because Nixon just didn't like conscientious objectors. Or maybe it was because he remembered that my father stumped for Helen Gahagan Douglas, when she ran against Nixon for the Senate in 1950. Anyhow, the president said, "You're next, Steve."

I went to some federal building in Hartford, Connecticut, and I took all the mental and physical tests. Unfortunately, I was healthy, hetero, and relatively sane. I was qualified to get shot in the jungle. So I figured I'd better check out the navy. After all, my father had been in the navy and he had lived.

At the navy recruiting office, I remember being in this harshly lit, bare-walled room and there was this big dog-faced navy guy behind a long table, and he looked very officious.

"Bogart?" he said. "Any relation to Humphrey?"

"I'm his son."

"No shit?" he said. "I didn't know he had kids."

So he went through the drill. He told me all his favorite Bogie movies, and then did his Bogie impression. We seemed to be getting along okay, so I said to him, "Hey, look, I'll sign up if you can take me after January 6, my birthday."

"Jesus, I'd love to do it," he said. "You know, for your father and all." He shuffled around a few papers and said, "The latest we can take you is December 24th."

I didn't want that, so I said, "Look, if I get drafted, can I come down here and sign up?"

He said yes.

So I resigned myself to the fact that I would get drafted and I'd go into the navy and probably drown in the South China Sea.

But, you know, every once in a while life acts like a movie, and gives you a last minute reprieve, like the scene in *The African Queen,* when the homemade torpedo exploded right on cue just as the Germans were about to hang my father and Katharine Hepburn. My lucky torpedo was that the draft lottery came in, and I got number 224, a high number. That first year the lottery picks went up to 218 so I was spared. The next year they started all over again, beginning with the new kids who had turned eighteen, so I was spared again. In this way, I never did have to go into the military.

But the thing was—and it's always kind of bothered me—I didn't have a strong political conscience. I just wanted to stay alive.

So naturally when I started exploring my father's life, I wondered just how politically involved my father was. Was he like me, a bit on the apathetic side? Or was he the kind of person who would carry banners and say that people like me were part of the problem?

When I started talking to his friends, I found out that Bogie certainly was less concerned about getting shot at than I was. He did not try to avoid combat, the way I did, but, of course, the wars were more noble in his day.

Bogie's pal Stuart Rose, who would later marry Bogie's sister Frances, known as Pat, had joined the army and had some colorful stories to tell. So joining the military seemed like a good idea to my father. He'd get to wear a uniform and meet beautiful French girls, and, as a bonus, he'd get the hell away from Maud, who was driving him nuts.

Consent came with some difficulty from his parents. But they must have sensed that he desperately needed to put a few thousand miles of saltwater between himself and them. I'm sure he didn't come right out and say, "Mother, I've got to get away from your constant harping about what a failure and troublemaker I am," but that's what it amounted to.

While the idea of dying in Vietnam was very real to me in the late 1960s—after all, I had seen it on television—the possibility of death in combat was not real to my father when he was eighteen. "Death was a big joke," he said. "Death? What does death mean to a kid of eighteen? The idea of death starts getting to you only when you're older, when you read obituaries of famous people whose accomplishments have touched you, and when people of your own generation die. At eighteen war was great stuff. Paris. French girls. Hot damn!"

There are two well-known but conflicting stories about his navy days. Only one of them, at most, is true.

The first story is that his boat, the *Leviathan,* was shelled by a German U-boat and one explosion caused a splinter of wood to pierce my father's upper lip. The injury damaged a nerve and left the lip partially paralyzed. The resulting tight-set lip would forever be associated with Humphrey Bogart and it would be the physical feature that three generations of impressionists would focus on when they tried to create their own Humphrey Bogart. The paralysis also affected my father's speech, leaving him with a slight lisp that doesn't seem to have hurt his movie career.

However, there is another story about how he got the stiff lip. In this one, Dad was not yet onboard. He was on shore duty and he was assigned to take a navy prisoner up to the Portsmouth Naval Prison in New Hampshire. The prisoner was handcuffed. When they changed trains in Boston the prisoner asked my father for a cigarette. Bogie (who, by the way, was not yet known as Bogie—that would come later in Hollywood) gave the guy a Lucky Strike and, while he was fishing around in his pea jacket for a match, the guy raised his manacled hands, smashed Dad across the mouth, and split. My father, with his lip damn near ripped from his face, whipped out his .45 and put the prisoner down with a couple of shots. The results were the same: my father was scarred for life.

Nathaniel Benchley says this second story is the true one. He says the shrapnel story is ridiculous because it is alleged to have happened sixteen days after the war was over and that even if there was delayed-action shrapnel, it could not have traveled in any direction which would have produced the scar.

Maybe. But the thing that bothers me about Benchley's conclusion is that he says the shrapnel story was made up by a studio publicity department. I don't get it. Why would a studio PR flack make up a story about Humphrey Bogart catching shrapnel in the lip if there was already a true story about how he plugged an escaping prisoner with his .45? If anything sounds like studio fiction it's the prisoner story. Anyhow, Dad got stitched up by a navy doctor in both stories, and the lip became part of the legend.

In talking to Bogie's friends I heard different versions of many stories and there is, at this point, no way to get the precise truth. That's what happens when you're a legend. Of course, it bothers me to hear stories about my father, never knowing for sure if they are true. And it bothers me to tell them, too. We all crave certainty in these things; we'd all like to say, "My father did this, he didn't do that." But the truth is that not only the sons of legends have to deal with it. We all do from time to time. We all have a colorful Uncle Jack or a Cousin Mertie whose exploits have been distorted over the years, and whose stories have been filtered down through different family lines in different ways. When I began to write about my father, people said to me, "You can't tell two different stories about the same event. You'll lose credibility." They seemed to think that Bogie's son should be the one who always knows the truth, though they certainly didn't know the whole truth about their own fathers or mothers. I disagree. I think credibility comes from owning up to uncertainty, from simply saying from time to time, "I don't know."

I do know that when his navy tour was over Bogie went back to his mother, who belittled him constantly about his lack of education.

The military, it seems, had not been a particularly formative experience.

"I'm sorry that the war had not touched me mentally," my father said. "When it was over I was still no nearer to an understanding of what I wanted to be or what I was."

* * *

Bogie, of course, was not done with the military after serving in World War I. Gloria Stuart, an actress who used to play card games with Bogie and Mayo Methot, remembers that when World War II came along, my father began a series of chess matches which he would play by mail with troops overseas.

My father wanted to do what he could for the troops, so during the Christmas season of 1943 he and Mayo went to North Africa for a twelve-week tour of army rest camps. It's a humorous image, Humphrey Bogart doing a soft shoe, twirling a cane, and singing "Thanks for the Memories" with Bob Hope. He did have a fair singing voice, but the fact is that his act consisted of reciting speeches from *The Petrified Forest* and other films. And Mayo sang "More Than You Know," a song she was known for, and other tunes, accompanied on the accordion by Don Cummings.

By the time he got to North Africa, Bogie was known around the world, mostly from his gangster films. A measure of his growing international fame was that one day when he and Mayo were touring the ancient Casbah, an Arab man jumped out of a doorway at him. He lifted his arm as if he were holding a submachine gun and shouted a stream of foreign words at Dad, which turned out to be the Arabic equivalent of *"Rat-tat-tat-tat,* you're dead, you dirty rat!"

Though Bogie was a patriot who felt strongly about supporting the troops, he was his usual iconoclastic self when it came to the brass. At one point on the tour he and Mayo had a big fight. She locked him out of their bedroom. Bogie began pounding on the door to get in. A colonel showed up and, seeing Bogie in uniform (it was a USO uniform), told him to stop it. Then he asked for my father's name, rank, and serial number.

"I've got no name," Bogie told him. "I've got no rank. I've got no serial number. And you can go to hell."

Later, when Bogie was reprimanded for insulting the uniform of the United States Army, he apologized to the colonel, saying, "I didn't mean to insult the uniform. I meant to insult you."

In Naples, Italy, when Bogie threw a big party for a group of enlisted men, things got a bit rowdy. A general from across the hall complained about the noise, and Bogie shouted, "Go fuck yourself." Soon after that he was moved out of Italy.

Back home Bogie continued his military service by joining the coast guard reserve. He went on duty once a week. In fact, it was often on his coast guard weekends in Balboa that my father had secret romantic meetings with a striking young actress known as Lauren Bacall, also known as my mother.

I'm sure my father would have entertained the troops, no matter which party was in power during the war. But, as it happened, he was a liberal Democrat most of the time and he was an ardent supporter of Franklin Roosevelt. Bogie was not as politically active as Jane Fonda, or even Lauren Bacall, for that matter. But he did speak up for Democratic candidates, like Harry Truman, and he donated money to their campaigns.

The war, however, made Dwight Eisenhower very popular and both of my parents became early Ike supporters before anybody even knew if Ike would run for President. Bogie and Bacall hoped that Ike would run, and that he would run as a Democrat. But Ike went to the GOP. Though my folks still liked Ike, they began taking a second look at his Democratic rival, Adlai Stevenson. Especially my mother.

The more Mom heard about Stevenson, the more intrigued she became. She talked to friends about Adlai. She read a book about Adlai. She went to a party for Adlai in Hollywood. This was at a time when Hollywood was very touchy about politics, especially left-wing politics. In fact, at the party one well-known producer told Mother, "If you're smart you'll keep your mouth shut and take no sides."

Before long my mother had switched her allegiance from Eisenhower to Stevenson, and she was able to get my father to do the same thing. At one point Bogie was scheduled to fly to an Ike rally and, at the last minute, he changed his mind and went with Bacall to a rally for Stevenson. This was the early 1950s, of course, and by this time Bogie was one of the most famous movie stars in the world, so it was quite a coup for Adlai.

If my father was not quite as passionate for Stevenson as my mother, it might have been that she was much younger and more prone to political optimism. And also to the fact that she was a woman.

My mother is quite candid about the fact that she was smitten with Adlai Stevenson. After one trip to a Stevenson event, where she got to know him personally, she says, "On the trip home I was far away from Bogie, my thoughts on the man I had left behind. I tried to imagine his life. I had found out as much as I could from his friends, anyone who had known him in the last few years. In my usual way, I romanticized that he needed a wife—obviously his sister had taken the official place of one, but he needed someone to share his life with. I fantasized that I would be a long-distance partner, a pen pal, a good friend whom he could feel free to talk to about anything. A sympathetic, nonjudging ear. It took me a long time to dissect my feelings, but at that moment I felt a combination of hero worship and slight infatuation. This campaign had disrupted my life completely. I was flattered to have been included, flattered to have been singled out by Stevenson as someone a bit special. I was, after all, just twenty-eight years old. I'd just had a second baby and had been preoccupied with domesticity for the last couple of years. My career was at something of a standstill. I needed to dream. I needed to reach out, to stretch myself, to put my unused energies to use."

Not surprisingly, there were times when my father got sick of hearing "Adlai this," and "Adlai that," all the time, but his occasional fits of jealousy never got in the way of his political convictions. Bogie supported Stevenson, and Stevenson was grateful. (On the whole, my mother's relationship with Stevenson was a very positive force in her life, and I can remember playing on his farm not long after my father died because Stevenson was, for her, the kind of friend you turn to at such a time.)

Alistair Cooke, who also favored Stevenson, was sure that Eisenhower would win the election. He tells me that he made a ten-dollar bet with my father that Adlai would lose. When Ike won Bogie paid up, but not without a comment: "It's a hell of a guy who bets against his own principles," Bogie said. (Cooke, by the way, could vote in the election. He is an American citizen. A lot of people think he is a British subject because of all those *Masterpiece Theater*s he hosted.)

Because my father was a famous actor, he caught a lot of flack for taking public stands on political issues. In 1944, when he spoke up for Roosevelt in a radio speech, Bogie was assaulted with sacks of hate mail, mostly to the effect that actors should have no political opinions and if they do have them, they should keep them to themselves.

Dad didn't care for the mail. He shot back at his detractors in newspaper interviews and in a piece he wrote for the *Saturday Evening Post,* titled, "I Stuck My Neck Out." By this time his old friend Stuart Rose, now a *former* brother-in-law, was editor of the *Post.*

Bogie had little patience with the view that actors should keep their political opinions secret simply because their personal glamor might swing a few votes one way or the other. He said that idea was "idiotic."

"I dislike politics and politicians, but I love my country," he said. "Why should a man lose the freedom to express himself simply because he's an actor? Nobody ever suggests that a baseball star or a best-selling author should refrain from public discussion of political issues. I don't think anyone, and I mean anyone, should toss around a lot of political baloney, but I feel I know as much about politics and government as most guys on a soap box and if I disagree strongly with them I'm going to say so."

In 1950 when he was campaigning for Helen Douglas, the subject came up again. "Movie stars pay a tremendous income tax," Bogie said. "I don't even look at my paycheck. Just put my hand over it and sign it. It would buy an airplane, I'll tell you that. Anyone who pays $200,000 a year in income taxes darned well has a right to take an active role in politics. Of course, there are some Republicans who feel that a movie star should not have the right to engage in politics if he is a Democrat."

By this time my father was the highest-paid movie star at Warner, and had, in some years, been the highest paid in the world, though his paycheck was paltry by today's Hollywood standards. He had signed a fifteen-year contract with Warner Brothers in 1945 that, Benchley says, gave Bogie a million dollars a year.

Once when he was asked if he thought politicking would hurt his career, he said, "I think there are a few diehards in the backwoods of Pasadena or Santa Barbara who might not see my pictures because I'm a Democrat. But on the whole I don't think it makes much difference. People forget quickly, as soon as the election is over, whether you are a Republican or a Democrat. If you make a good picture and give a good performance people will go to see it anyway."

Perhaps. But there came a time when politics threatened to hurt a lot of careers and did, in fact, destroy some.

In October of 1947, three years before crazy Joe McCarthy got his witch hunt underway, a publicity-hungry congressman by the name of J. Parnell Thomas chaired something called The House Un-American Activities Committee (HUAC). Thomas decided that it was extremely urgent that the committee find Commies in the movie industry. Thomas, with the help of aides like Richard Nixon, came to Hollywood for "interviews," at which movie people were asked who they thought might be a Communist. People who gave names were considered "friendly." In reaction to this, nineteen Hollywood writers, directors, and producers formed a group that said it was none of Congress's business what their politics were or had been. Of those nineteen, eleven were asked to testify before Congress. One of the eleven, Bertolt Brecht (the guy who wrote *The Threepenny Opera*), skipped town. He went back to his home in Germany. The rest became known as the "Unfriendly Ten." A lot of people in the movie industry were outraged. They felt as if the ten were being accused of something, without being given a trial. They also thought that Congress should be making laws, not trying to enforce them. John Huston got a bunch of these movie people together and they formed The Committee for the First Amendment. Their purpose was never specifically to defend the Unfriendly Ten. It was to fight what they believed was an assault upon the Constitution and the Bill of Rights.

Huston, in fact, said some of these people really were Communists. "But they were well-meaning people who had no knowledge of the Gulag Archipelago or of Stalin's mass murders," he said. Huston went to a few Communist meetings and he found it all very childish. "I marveled at the innocence of these good but simple people who actually believed that this was a way of improving the social condition of mankind."

When an attorney for the Unfriendly Ten asked Huston for support, he got together a planeload of movie stars and, with Howard Hughes supplying the plane, they all went to Washington. Among them: Danny Kaye, Sterling Hayden, Richard Conte, Gene Kelly, Ira Gershwin. And my parents. "I remember going to a meeting that John organized at William Wyler's house," my mother recalls. "I told your father 'we have to go.' "

When it came time for testimony, the movie stars were there for moral support. The ten, led by writer Dalton Trumbo, told Thomas in so many words to shove his committee where the sun don't shine. They refused to answer questions, citing their First Amendment right to freedom of speech. But they did read statements. They wanted the Supreme Court to rule on whether or not the committee had the right to make a Communist identify himself as one.

Thomas banged his gavel and vowed to put them in jail for contempt of Congress.

The press, which until then had been friendly, now turned against the ten and against the Committee for the First Amendment. Soon the committee was being described as a Communist front organization, and one columnist wrote, "There is very good evidence that John Huston is the brains of the Communist party in the west."

After that Washington trip my father did some serious backtracking. He felt as if he had gone out on a limb, and had been assured that the Unfriendly Ten had been unjustly maligned. Now, as it became clear that some of them were Communists, Bogie was pissed because he felt as if he had been used.

"I am not a Communist," he said. "I detest communism as any other decent American does. I have never in my life been identified with any Communistic front organization. I went to Washington because I thought fellow Americans were being deprived of their Constitutional rights and for that reason alone.

"I see now that my trip was ill-advised, foolish, and impetuous, but at the time it seemed the thing to do. I acted impetuously and foolishly on the spur of the moment, like I am sure many other American citizens do at many times."

He told Ed Sullivan, "I'm about as much in favor of communism as J. Edgar Hoover. I despise communism and I believe in our American brand of democracy. Our planeload of movie people who flew to Washington came east to fight against censorship being clamped on the movies. The ten men cited for contempt by the House Un-American Activities Committee are certainly not typical of Hollywood. On every occasion at Washington we stressed our opposition to Lawson and his crew, so there could be no doubt as to where we stood. In fact, before we left Hollywood we carefully screened every performer so that no red or pink could infiltrate and sabotage our purpose."

My father's reaction had many interpretations. Some people felt that he was copping out, just trying to protect his career. Others say that he just didn't want to be part of something that he couldn't control. My mother, always looking for the best in Bogie, says that he realized that he was misled and he was angry about it.

I've given this some thought. I'm not sure that my mother's view makes sense. It seems to me that if Bogie and the others went to Washington to defend a principle, not the ten accused, then that principle didn't change just because some of the ten really were Communists. If he went to defend constitutional rights, then how was he misled or ill-advised? I happen to think that Bogie was wrong here, just as I have been wrong about hundreds of things. Maybe he was just trying to save his career. Maybe he was a human being and was expressing the simple human desire for self-preservation. Dad, apparently, came to feel the same way about his change of heart. Mother says, "He felt coerced into it, and he was never proud of it."

The ten were eventually convicted of contempt of Congress and sent to jail, some for as much as a year. One ironic twist, which I found satisfying: Some of them were sent to the federal prison in Danbury, Connecticut, and one of their fellow inmates was none other than J. Parnell Thomas, the great, self-righteous, Commie-hunter. Turns out he was a scummy little crook who was bagged for padding a payroll and taking kickbacks.

* * *

My father's role in the Unfriendly Ten, of getting involved politically and then dropping out, would not make for good cinema. Much more effective is the reverse, which is what Bogie often played in films: the man who does not want to get involved, wants to be left alone, but is eventually drawn in and compelled to take a side because a principle is at stake. Remember Charlie Allnut in *The African Queen?* When Hepburn's character suggests that they cruise on down the river and blow up a German ship he tells her she is nuts and he wants no part of it. Of course, he ends up designing his own torpedo and going after the Germans with Hepburn.

Casablanca is, of course, the classic example. Rick Blaine was this tough American who ran a café in Morocco. Even though he was flanked on every side by someone's political passion, he was the kind of guy who didn't take sides. He was cynical about all causes and he wanted to be left out of them. He was not into patriotism or nationalism or any other ism. But in the end he did the decent thing and he didn't expect to be praised for it. Rick was the guy that a lot of people want to be.

Was my father like Rick Blaine? Yes, in many ways. I don't think Dad was big on isms, either. He had ideals, but he was skeptical when other people talked about their ideals. He was big on compassion and loyalty, but his eyes tended to glaze over when other people went on too much about how compassionate and loyal they were. Maybe Rick Blaine would have handled the Unfriendly Ten controversy differently, but hell, nobody can be like Rick Blaine all the time, not even Humphrey Bogart.

Whether my father was a Rick Blaine or not, there is no question that *Casablanca* was the movie that gave the public its most memorable political image of Humphrey Bogart.

Alistair Cooke told me, "Your father is a legend, and a lot of it is tied up in that film, *Casablanca*. It was a stroke of colossal luck, that film appearing at a time when Hitler had demonstrated something we were loathe to admit: the success of violence. *Casablanca* first came to theaters just eighteen days after the Allied landing in Casablanca. This was one of the first great blows against Hitler. Then later, when they put the film in wider release, what was going on? Churchill, Roosevelt, and Stalin were holding a summit conference. And where were they holding it? Casablanca. Was it any wonder that the public got your father's character all mixed up with reality."

Cooke is right when he says there was a lot of luck involved. But Warner Brothers gave luck a little help. The movie was scheduled to be released later in 1943, but they rushed it to theaters after the Allied invasion of Casablanca in November of 1942.

Cooke, I found, was particularly interested not in Bogie's politics, so much as the effect that world politics had on my father's career. He says, "The gangster film fell out of favor when World War Two came along. How could you get excited about gangsters shooting a few people, when Hitler was doing things that Warner Brothers could never dream up? And out of the top gangster stars, like Robinson, and Cagney, and Raft, it was your father who seemed best suited to go up against Nazis in the movies."

Cooke once wrote of Bogie, "He probably had no notion, in his endless strolls across the stages and drawing rooms of the twenties, that he was being saved and soured by time to become the romantic democratic answer to Hitler's new order."

* * *

Like most people, my father was more likely to jump into a political issue that directly affected him. One of them was censorship.

In the late 1940s, with Hitler vanquished, gangsters were popular in films again and there was a lot of whining and hand wringing about the rising number of crime movies. For a short time crime movies were even banned by the Johnston office, which was the Hollywood censorship office at the time. The ban, like most censorship attempts, was effective only for a brief time. Soon more crime movies were reaching the screen and many people were upset.

Though my father had little patience with the complainers, he did concede a few points for their side. Discussing one recent prison movie he said, "It was a story of a bunch of bad eggs who broke out of stir and finally were put back where they belonged. I can see no reason for the picture." (This was a sentiment he had expressed before. Once, when his friend Mark Hellinger called to see what Bogie thought of the prison movie *Brute Force,* Bogie replied, "Why did you make it? A picture should have either entertainment or a moral. This one had neither.")

"But it's stupid to think that movies can foster crime," Bogie said. "When I was young we were reading about Billy the Kid. But that didn't make criminals out of us. If you want to find out what turns kids to crime look at their environment and particularly their family life. Parents who let ten-year-old kids stay out at night are the ones responsible for making criminals."

Dad deplored censorship and he said it would backfire. "The Johnston office made a ruling that a criminal can't use a sawed-off shotgun or a tommy gun in pictures," he said. "And movie cops have to be big and there has to be lots of them. So when you show a capture it appeals to a child's favor of the underdog. Like when I got caught in *High Sierra*. I was up on that mountain with the whole state against me."

Writing in the *New York Times* in November of 1948, Bogie came up with a "cure" for the gangster film.

Noting that he was a filmmaker and a man who was about to become a father, he said that he had a special interest in the problem. The "problem" which seemed to be emerging from all these antigangster film discussions was that the public was fascinated by the gangsters, not the police. "The reason for the gangster's popularity," Bogie said, "is that we don't hunt him singly or on equal terms. We call out a horde of squad cars, the National Guard, or the entire FBI and, after hunting him down like a rabbit, fill him so full of lead even his own mother wouldn't recognize him. Or, if we don't, for the average American the rest of the story stops moving until the gangster has by some good fortune or some charming device on the writer's part, got away and who in the audience at this point is going to say to himself, 'I like those policemen'?

"The young gangster, running out into the street, or up some alley, spraying the world he hates with bullets, may not be as morally acceptable as the young Crazy Horse outwitting an American army on the march, but as a dramatic device he will catch the same amount of sympathy, killer though he is.

"The cure for the gangster film, then, seems eminently simple to me. In *The Maltese Falcon* we sent a single individual out against a lot of gangsters, and the result was a whole series of pictures with the lone hero against gangsters instead of vice-versa. We called him Sam Spade, but you could call him Calvin Coolidge and still get the same effect if you held to the rule. Of course, I don't claim we're changing basic values. You have the cavalry for you winning money instead of the Indians, but you are going to get some killings in any event."

What I find admirable in my father on this censorship issue was not that he was against censorship, as I am, but that he was able to understand the other side, and not just paint one side of the question all black and the other all white. This, to me, is the mark of an intelligent person.

I suspect that, politically, I am much more like my father than my mother. I think of my mother as a kind of knee-jerk liberal, though it drives her crazy when I say that. I tend to be liberal on some issues, like abortion and civil rights. But I'm also conservative on others. For example, I believe in the death penalty, which horrifies my mother.

You might think that all this would make for lively arguments between myself and Bacall. Not exactly. It is true that, like my father, I love to argue. I'll be glad to take any side of an argument just for the fun of it. My mother enjoys a spirited discussion, also. But not with me.

My father, I think, was the more patient one of the two. I think that if he were around today he would listen to me. Politically, we are alike. It's not that he would agree with my views on each thing, but I think he would weigh each thing separately and not get caught up in the ism, whether it be liberalism or conservatism.

My father was also a "personal-religionist," which is a phrase I'd never heard until I read it in a press release about him. Basically, it means he didn't practice his religion. I'm not religious at all.

(Apparently, my own irreverence started early in life. When I was christened in the Episcopal church and the priest sprinkled water on my head, I said, "I don't like the drops," loud enough for everybody to hear. Then, near the end of the sermon, the priest said, "He shall enter the house of the Lord," and, again very loudly, I said, "If he wants to come in, then let him come in.")

"Bogie was not a religious man," my mother says. "But he was a great believer in the Ten Commandments and the Golden Rule."

Nat Benchley says, "His moral code was strict, and was based on, and almost indistinguishable from, the Ten Commandments. He didn't always obey them, but he believed in them."

I don't think learning about my father's politics changed my own politics in any way, though it does please me to know that he had strong convictions. My own convictions are a little closer to home than his. I'm more directed toward my personal world, my wife, my kids. It isn't that I don't care about the larger world; it's just that I don't care that much, and that I think I can do the most good at home. I find I don't tend to follow party lines, and, like my father, I am suspicious of people who do. Dad once said, "Politically, I am an anarchist. Just like John Huston." I'm not sure that he was kidding.

Bogie seems at every turn to be a man who is difficult to sum up. But when I went to see Alistair Cooke, I wanted to come away with some understanding of my father's politics, and I think I got it. Cooke often paused in our conversation about my father to read something he had once written about Bogie. And if the things he wrote don't tell the whole story, they at least tell a lot of it.

"Bogart," says Cooke, "was a touchy man who found the world more corrupt than he had hoped; a man with a tough shell hiding a fine core. He invented the Bogart character and imposed it on a world impatient of men more obviously good. And it fitted his deceptive purpose like a glove. From all he was determined to keep his secret: the rather shameful secret, in the realistic world we inhabit, of being a gallant man and an idealist."

When I return to the top of the stairway at the Mapleton Drive house, my mother is halfway down the stairs. Has she already gone into the bedroom without me? I wonder. Did she need to be alone there? I am relieved. I don't really want to go in there, though I haven't quite formed that thought in my mind. As I descend the stairs I hear the sound of a car going by on Mapleton. I think for a moment that it is like the sound of Daddy pulling into the driveway after a day at the studio. But this idea melts into a different memory.

We go off in the Thunderbird, my father and I. I'm aware that it's new and different. It's not the Jaguar. He boasts about the new car. He says two of his friends bought Thunderbirds, but his is better. We are driving to the studio where Dad works.

We pull into the lot. It's where they make the movies, he says. He says that going to the studio is like being allowed into the locker room of the Braves. He knows that the Braves are my favorite baseball team ever since Sammy Cahn took me to a Dodgers–Braves game.

At the studio everybody is friendly. We are on the set. Daddy says the movie is called The Desperate Hours. It seems very strange because my father is in a room, but it's not really a room and there are people all around with lights and cameras and microphones. I am sitting in the director's chair and people smile at me. They really say, "Quiet on the set," just the way they do in movies I have seen about movies. I'm feeling like a big shot because my *father is the star and I am his son. It's like being the son of the batting champ.*

6

Bogie was the most professional actor I have ever worked with. But his contract said he was off duty at six o'clock, and if it was six o'clock and we were in the middle of the scene, he was gone. He'd say, "It's six o'clock, we'll finish the scene tomorrow." Then he would go and have a drink.

—ROD STEIGER

When I began to write about my father I guess I believed that every major aspect of his life would cast light on my own, that I could easily find the ways in which I was, or was not, my father's son. His use of alcohol might say something about my use of drugs. His experience in private school might somehow preview my own trouble in private school. And I guess I thought that in looking at his career, in the way he conducted it, and the way he felt about his work, I might learn something about my feelings toward work.

Maybe. But the truth is there is little to be said about my work life. It's been like everybody else's, some highs, some lows. To go into my various jobs at length would be both boring and pretentious, sins which neither I nor my father would tolerate from someone else.

The most striking difference between my father and me on the matter of work is that he really cared about his craft. He was dedicated and, I think, he put work first. I, on the other hand, have enjoyed my jobs in television, and I think I have been good at them, but I have never really focused on work. I have always put family and friends above what I did for a living. Maybe if I had grown up with a father, and had not gone away to school, I would feel less strongly about the need for family life, and more strongly about career. Perhaps that is the way in which my father has really influenced me.

My father had no big career plan when he got out of the navy. He bounced around for a while. He worked at a biscuit company, then he had a job inspecting tugboats. He worked at other jobs, which didn't last long. The young Bogie had no idea of what he wanted to do with his life. He spent a lot of time horseback riding with friends in Central Park.

Though Bogie's parents were, supposedly, washing their hands of him, it is probably not a coincidence that he was hired as a runner for the Wall Street brokerage firm that managed their money. And it was while he was at that job that Bogie came under the wing of Bill Brady, Sr., the father of his long-time buddy Bill Brady. Brady senior was already an established producer of stage plays. Specifically, Dad said, "I got subway-sick one day in New York when I was running messages for the brokerage house and staggered off the subway near William Brady's theatrical offices—and, in a moment of desperation, asked for a job."

"How would you like to be an office boy?" Mr. Brady asked Bogie.

"Office boy?"

"It's not a big step up from being a runner," Brady told him, "but there are opportunities for advancement in a new business."

"What kind of business?" Dad asked.

"Movies, my boy, movies."

So my father became an office boy for Brady's company, which was called World Films.

Advancement came fast. Brady stopped Bogie in the office one day and said, "How would you like to be a director?"

"A director?"

"Yes," Brady said. He told Bogie that his picture, *Life*, was heading for the toilet, though he might have used a different phrase.

"I guess," Dad said.

Brady fired the director and handed the film over to young Humphrey. "Finish directing it," he said.

"How?"

"You figure it out," Brady said.

Unfortunately, Dad did not figure it out and the movie was a disaster.

The experience left my father with a belief, not that he could direct, but that he could write much better than some of the people who were getting paid for scripts. Soon he began hanging around the 21 Club, a speakeasy in those days, where he would sit at small tables and lean earnestly over his notebook, penning story ideas. He smoked a pipe, which he thought made him look more writerly. ("I like to smoke a pipe," he once said, "but it's too damn much work.")

When Bogie finally finished a story he sent it to Jesse

Lasky, who sent it to Walter Wanger, who announced that it was dreadful, and threw it in the wastebasket. (Years later Wanger's daughter, Shelly, would become one of my playmates, and Wanger would boast to people, "Bogie once wrote for me.")

When the writing thing went nowhere my father became a stage manager in New York, working for Mr. Brady. Bogie was responsible for baggage, props, and scenery. The stage manager actually runs the show backstage.

Even then Dad was flouting authority. One night when Brady brought the curtain up too soon after intermission, Dad brought it back down. Brady, so the story goes, kicked Dad in the stomach. My father got even by raising the curtain while Brady was on stage, making last-minute preparations for the next act. So Brady fired him. The next day Brady rehired my father. This, apparently, was a pattern which they repeated many times—an interesting precursor to Dad's battles with, and many suspensions by, Jack Warner.

My father's first acting job, if you want to call it that, occurred in rehearsals. The juvenile lead was sick, so Dad filled in, with only the cast for an audience. ("Juvenile" was the term for young, well-dressed men in minor parts.)

"It was awful," he said. "I knew all the lines of all the parts because I'd heard them from out front about a thousand times. But I took one look at the emptiness where the audience would be that night and I couldn't remember anything."

Fortunately, he never had to actually perform in the play because the show closed that night.

Awful or not, my father had the acting bug. He started alternating his stage-managing duties with acting stints when he could get them.

* * *

The acting bug is something that never bit me. Despite my pedigree, or perhaps because of it, I have never seriously considered being an actor. I did some acting in the eighth grade. I played Bianca in *The Taming of the Shrew.* Yes, I know, Bianca is a woman, but it was an all-boys school. I also acted a little bit at Milton. But, frankly, I'm a lousy actor. I'm comfortable being myself in front of people. But I'm not comfortable being someone else, and that's what acting is. If you're not comfortable being someone else, you'd better forget about acting. My mother keeps telling me I look great in front of the camera, but then, she *is* my mother.

Besides, early in life I decided that I wanted my work to have something to do with sports.

When Jady Robards and I used to go to Mets games we often sat in the bleachers, talking to each other as if one of us was the play-by-play man and the other was the color commentator.

"Yes, Jady, I think if the Mets can score more runs than the other team today they have a pretty good chance of stealing this ball game."

"Right, Steve, many of these players have fast speed and strong strength. And quickness, lots of very rapid quickness."

"Yes, and every one of them is one of the finest gentlemen in the game."

Even though we only had fun pretending to be sportscasters, I, at least, often dreamed of being one. And if I couldn't be a sportscaster, I still wanted some connection to sports.

"Well, go talk to Howard," my mother said. This was when I was in my early twenties. I'd been starting to think that maybe a person should have some focus in life, so I had talked to my mother about my sports dreams. The Howard of whom she spoke was Howard Cosell. She called him and I got an interview.

It's nice, I guess, to have a famous mother, because she, in turn, has a lot of celebrity friends. But, generally, I have a horror of taking advantage of that. Whenever I'm planning a trip to Disneyworld with my kids, for example, Mom says, "Call Michael, he'll help you out." She means Michael Eisner, chairman of Disney. But I never call Michael. Special treatment makes me uncomfortable; I don't want to feel as if I'm being pushed to the head of the line. So usually I don't take advantage of my mother's celebrity status. But hell, I was a sports nut, and this was Howard Cosell.

So I made an appointment, and one sunny morning I drove from Connecticut to ABC in New York. I sat in the receptionist's office waiting for Cosell to show up. After about ten minutes the elevator door opened and I heard someone doing this fairly good, but not great, Howard Cosell impression.

"Here he is, ladies and gentlemen, the great one has arrived. Yes, it's Howard Cosell, speaking to you from his palatial offices at the American Broadcasting Corporation Building."

I looked up and discovered it *was* Cosell, making a grand entrance, not as himself, but in a parody of his public persona. God, I thought, does he do this every day?

"And you must be the Bogart boy," he said. "I remember when I first met your mother, Betty. It was—" and he rattled off the exact time and place where he had met Mom, some fifteen years earlier. "Welcome to ABC," he said. He shook my hand and led me into his office. It was still another minute or two before he could break out of the impression he was doing of himself. After we talked for a while about Betty, and my father, we got down to business. I told him that I wanted to be in sports broadcasting. Cosell listened to me very intently, and earnestly, and finally he leaned across his desk and said, "You know, Steve, I could give you a job."

"Really?"

"Oh sure, I could make a few calls and you'd be working at nine o'clock tomorrow morning in some capacity or other."

"Anything would be great," I said. "Just a start."

"Steve," he said, "it would be the beginning of your sports broadcasting career."

"Yes," I said. Now my heart was pounding. This was it, my big break.

"But I have to tell you, Steve, it would also be the end of it."

"Huh?"

"The end, Stephen Bogart, the end. With no education, you wouldn't go anywhere in this business. Steve, I've been in this business a long time and I'll tell you one thing that I am absolutely sure of. You have got to go back to school and get your degree."

At the time I was crestfallen. It seemed as if my sports broadcasting dream was over and, after I shook hands with Cosell and thanked him for the advice, I left the building and I must have walked forty blocks along Sixth Avenue with my head down.

But at a deeper level I knew that Cosell was right and his words only tempered a resolve I was about to make: once and for all I would go to college and this time, for a novelty, I would graduate. So I will always be grateful for Howard Cosell's advice.

As it happened, there was a small trust fund that my father had left me. It had kicked in as soon as I got married and it came to about $600 a month, which was pretty good money at a time when my rent was only about $185 a month. But I had also from time to time petitioned for chunks of the fund, to get a car or whatever. By the time I spoke to Cosell I could see that this fund was only going to last about four more years. I did go back to school, the University of Hartford, where I majored in Mass Communications. And yes, I graduated.

So, like my father, I had turned to an older, established man. And each older man had done the right thing for the time. Brady gave a young man a job, Cosell did not. I lived in a time when you had to have a degree to get anywhere. My father lived in a time when success depended more on how high you were willing to pull yourself up by your own bootstraps.

My father was no sudden success. In his first appearance in front of an audience, Bogie played a Japanese houseboy. He had one line and he made the least of it. His friend Stuart Rose, who was in the audience that night, said, "He said his one line and he embarrassed me, it was so bad."

Dad's first significant role came as a juvenile in a play called *Swifty*. Almost all of Dad's early roles were juveniles. His performance in *Swifty* was not memorable for the audience, but Bogie would remember it for the rest of his life.

In fact, decades later he was sitting at 21 in New York with sportscaster Mel Allen, along with Hank Greenberg, the great Detroit Tigers slugger. Allen asked Greenberg about some of the home runs he had hit. Greenberg said that his greatest recollections were not about home runs that he had hit. They were about home runs he had wanted to hit, but had not. "I remember one home run I didn't hit with two men on in the 1934 World Series," he said. "And there was another home run I didn't hit when I wanted to in the 1940 World Series."

The failures had stayed in Greenberg's mind. When Allen reminded him about all the homers he *had* hit, Greenberg replied, "Some people only remember the unhappy things."

"That's a fact," my father said. "Newspaper people have been awfully nice to me and they've written some swell reviews. I couldn't quote you any of the good reviews. But I can quote you word for word the panning Alexander Woollcott administered to me twenty-six years ago when I was in *Swifty*. He said, 'The young man who embodied the aforesaid Sprigg was what might mercifully be described as inadequate.' That was back in 1921. A lot has happened since then, but I can still see those words."

Swifty, by the way, closed quickly, and my father carried Woollcott's review around with him for the rest of his life.

The first hit show Bogie appeared in was *Meet the Wife*. But even in a hit, he got into trouble. At one matinee he left the theater after act two, forgetting that he had to make a small appearance in act three. Later, when the stage manager asked him where the hell he had been, my father blew his stack.

His reviews during this time were mixed. The bad ones got to him, especially Woolcott's, and also one that said that Bogie and another actor "gave some rather trenchant exhibitions of bad acting."

"The needling I got about my acting in those days made

me mad," he said. "It made me want to keep on until I'd get to the point where I didn't stink anymore."

Over the years my father never raised much fuss about critics. He said, "I always thought they were fair, except for one, who wrote that so and so was bad in the part, but not as bad as Humphrey Bogart would have been if he had played it."

Dad appeared in dozens of plays during the 1920s, and in time his reviews got better, except perhaps from his mother, Maud, who made it clear that actors were not socially acceptable.

During this time my father drank lots of alcohol and dated lots of girls. Though it later became common for people to talk about my father as a man who had sex appeal without being handsome, the fact is that he was considered quite handsome then, and was even compared to Valentino in some reviews.

Though Bogie had not always had good reviews he had always tried hard. He was, and remained for all of his life, a student of acting.

One early story is that when Bogie was dating Mary Philips, who later became his second wife, he met an actor by the name of Holbrook Blinn, a stage star of the time.

"Hey, you're no taller than me," Bogie said to Blinn.

"So."

"But I've seen you on the stage. You always look taller."

"Watch," Blinn said. He turned around and took several steps away from Bogie. Then he paused for a few seconds and slowly turned back. Bogie was astonished. It seemed to him that Blinn had grown an inch or two right in front of him.

"How on earth?" Bogie said.

"Just think tall," Blinn said. "Just think tall."

From the beginning, it seems, he understood drama, and often during his life he would articulate on the subject.

Though his early parts were as juveniles, he sometimes called them "Tennis, anyone?" parts and that is why he is given credit for bringing that phrase into the language. He explained juveniles this way:

"The playwright gets five or six characters into a scene and doesn't know how to get them offstage. So what does he do? He drags in the juvenile, who has been waiting in the wings for just such a chance. He comes in, tennis racquet under his arm, and says, 'Tennis, anyone?' That, of course, solves the playwright's problem. The player whom the author wants to get rid of for the time being accepts the suggestion. The leading lady, who is due for a love scene with the leading man, declines. So the others exit and all is ready for the love scene between the leading lady and man. It doesn't always have to be tennis. Sometimes it's golf or riding, but tennis is better because it gives the young man a chance to look attractive in spotless white flannels."

My father had at least a couple of flirtations with the film industry before he made it in Hollywood. In 1930 the studios were looking for actors who could talk, so he went out to Hollywood. But so did a lot of others. Nate Benchley says, "Probably at no other time has so little talent been concentrated in one place."

He got into some pictures. They were boring and he was boring in them. So, fed up with Hollywood, he came back to the New York stage.

In 1934 he was in *Invitation to a Murder*, a play that was described by one critic as "high-voltage trash." But producer-director Arthur Hopkins saw it and wanted Bogie for the role in *The Petrified Forest*.

Whatever magical quality my father had seems to have shown up for the first time on January 7, 1935, in that play. He was thirty-five years old. What he had was that elusive something we call "star quality."

What is star quality? Nobody is quite sure, but Bogie, apparently, recognized it in himself. Sam Jaffe told me, "I was talking once to a director about this. He said there are some good actors, who you don't really notice when they come on the screen. But he said that when Bogie comes on the screen, no matter who else is there, your eye is drawn to Bogart. That's what makes a star. And this is something that Bogie knew about himself. He said to me, 'You know, Sam, I'm not the greatest actor in the world. Gary Cooper is not a great actor. But when he comes on the screen you watch him. And I have that quality. It's God given. That's what they call a star.' "

While Bogie might have slighted his own acting ability in that conversation, there were other times when Bogie told people that he was the second best actor in Hollywood, and Spencer Tracy was the first.

On this subject of star quality, John Huston said, "Bogie was a medium-sized man, not particularly impressive off-screen, but something happened when he was playing the right part. Those lights and shadows composed themselves into another, nobler personality; heroic, as in *High Sierra*. I swear the camera has a way of looking into a person and perceiving things that the naked eye doesn't register."

As Bogie developed his craft he became a teacher to others, just as Blinn had been to him.

In 1944, for example, when he was making *Passage to*

Marseilles, there was a scene where the cabin boy, played by Billy Roy, had to throw an orange. Every time Billy threw the piece of fruit he heard nothing but complaints.

"You're throwing it like a girl," the director said. "Throw it like a boy."

Billy kept trying, but he couldn't seem to throw the orange the way he was supposed to. Soon everybody in the crew was getting on him, and Billy was close to tears. It was my father who finally said, "Enough!"

He led Billy off to the side and took the time to teach him how to throw the orange. When Billy had it perfect they started shooting again.

Once when I was a kid my father brought six young actors over to the house to talk about acting. Frank Sinatra was there, too. All of the young actors were unknown at the time, but two of them made the cut, so to speak. One of them was Tom Laughlin, who later starred in the *Billy Jack* films. Another was Dennis Hopper.

Bogie sat on the floor, and the young actors, sitting cross-legged on the floor, gathered around him. "Keep working. Never be 'available,' " he told them. This was advice he had been given long ago, and he quoted it often. "Keep playing in theater or TV, anywhere, as often as you can. Eventually, if you're any good, somebody will see you. Of course the best way to get into the picture business is to go on the stage first."

"Why do you keep working, now that you're such a big star?" one of the young actresses asked.

"I don't know," Bogie said. "I have a charming wife, two beautiful kids, a gorgeous home, and a yacht. But I'll be damned if I know why I work so hard. Sinatra and I were talking about it the other day. Working is therapy, I guess. It keeps us on the wagon. This is a very bad town to be out of work in. After a week or so of not working you're so bored you don't know what the hell to do."

Bogart also told the young people, "If you want to be an actor be honest with yourself. Don't let them push you around. When you believe in something, you fight for it even though you may suffer for it. We actors are better judges than any studio as to what is good for us. As soon as your name gets known and you feel you can say, 'I won't do this,' if you think the part isn't right, go ahead, say it. In the long run it will pay off. Just remember to put some dough aside for the times you're suspended."

Dad asked Dennis Hopper why he wanted to be an actor.

"It's a lot of things," Hopper said. "To do something in life, to be somebody."

"But why acting?" my father asked. "Why not farming? Or something else?"

"I'm just best suited for acting," Hopper said. "I want, I don't know, I just have the urge to be better than—"

"Yes, all right, go on," my father said.

"To be better than the other guy," Hopper said.

"To get out of the millions?"

"Yes," Hopper said, "that's it."

My father smiled. "You're okay, kid," he said. He said "kid" a lot.

"Enjoy the applause," he told the actors. "It's wonderful. It has nothing to do with vanity. It's the satisfaction, like telling a joke and having everybody laugh."

And he told them, "Don't go to parties to meet people."

On the subject of publicity he said, "A star has to accept a certain invasion of privacy. If you get loaded in a bar, then you can't get mad if it's printed."

"What do you think a star is?" one of the women asked.

"Good stories make stars," Bogie said. "But if you want to be an actress, don't say, 'I want to be a star.' Just concentrate on acting, learn your trade. You've got to develop confidence if you're to play a scene right, and confidence comes from knowing the ropes. Personally, I think you're all in a hell of a mess, wanting to be actors, because they don't know what acting is in Hollywood. They think it's easy to act. They think actors are a necessary evil."

My father had some very definite ideas about acting and actors. He was skeptical about actors with a message. "If an actor has got a message he should call Western Union," Bogie said. "An actor's job is to act, nothing more. He owes the public nothing but a good performance."

Sam Jaffe told me, "Your father was not impressed with method actors. I remember being on the set with Bogart in one film and he was working with a young, so-called method actor. Bogie said to me, 'Sam, watch this guy. He thinks he's going to steal the scene from me.' So they started a new take and the other actor made a lot of noise and moved his body and his hands a lot. But when the rushes were shown it was Bogart who caught the eye. There was no way you could steal a scene from Bogie. He said he had two rules for playing with method actors. One was to let them improvise as much as they wanted, and the other was never to play an eating scene with them because they spit all over you."

My father once asked a young actor about the Stanislavski method.

"Well, Stanislavski claimed that the real interpretation comes from the subconscious," the young actor explained. "We can't touch it or control it, but if we release it, it will flow from the subconscious."

Bogie probably thought this was so much horse manure, but he replied politely. "If you'll pardon the expression," he said, "you've got me completely screwed up. But I know this, the audience is always a little ahead of you. If a guy points a gun at you the audience knows you're afraid. You don't have to make faces. You just have to believe you are the person."

Bogie said that the key to good acting was concentration. You might recall that first shot of Rick in *Casablanca* shows him playing chess alone. This was my father's idea, because playing chess alone was something he did often, and he associated it with his acting. He believed that his concentration at chess was what he needed in his acting.

While Bogie believed in talent and concentration, I suspect he would agree with Woody Allen, who once said that eighty percent of life is just showing up. Bogie was a guy who always showed up for work.

"Bogie was a man who was very disciplined," Sam Jaffe says. "People come to me and they often bring up the fact that he drank while he worked in a picture, and I say, you got the wrong man. Bogie came to work with a lunch pail. In it he had one bottle of cold beer. At lunch time he would go to his bungalow or his trailer and he would eat his lunch and have his beer. And he timed it. One half hour. Then he would lie down and go right to sleep for the other half hour. Bogie was anything but a drinker when he worked in pictures. He was completely sober because he was a man who came out of the theater and his acting and his art was something he revered and respected. He came to work like any disciplined worker and he knew his lines. He really liked what he was doing. But people used to say he was a drunkard. It's true he got in fights and drank when he was not working, but not on the set."

This is something that everybody says about my father. He was never late, always knew his lines, and would rehearse for as long as necessary for the other actors so that they didn't have to talk to a wall. In fact, one beef my father had with Sinatra, even though they were close friends, was that he felt Frank was not a professional as an actor, though he certainly was as a singer. Bogie felt that Sinatra treated acting too lightly. During the later years of his life, Bogie would be in bed by ten o'clock when he had to work the next day, and he often chided Sinatra for being such a carouser during the making of a film.

Actually, there is one recorded time of my father letting booze interfere with his work at Warner Brothers. He got drunk one night and the next morning refused to work. Instead, he zoomed around the Warner Brothers lot on his bicycle, shouting, "Look, no hands, no hands," like a ten-year-old who had learned a new trick.

Finally, Jack Warner came out to talk to him.

"Bogie, what the hell are you doing?"

"Riding my bicycle," Bogie said.

"It's time to go to work," Warner said.

"I don't feel like working."

"You don't, huh?"

"That's right, I don't."

"Well," Warner said, "there's a lot of people in there who do feel like working and they get paychecks that are less than what you spend on scotch."

"So," Bogie said. "What's your point?"

"My point is that these people are depending on you. If you don't work, they don't work."

That pretty much ended that conversation. Bogie put

his bike away and went to work, and never showed up drunk again.

Though Bogie was disciplined about acting, he claimed not to be sentimental about it.

"I take my work seriously," he said, "but none of this art for art's sake. Any art or any job of work that's any good at all sells. If it's worth selling, it's worth buying. I have no sentimentality about such matters. If someone offers me five dollars a year more than I'm getting I take it."

Sounds nice, but it simply is not true. Bogie also said, "The only reason to make a million dollars is so you can tell some fat producer to go to hell." And the fact is that Bogie, who was the highest-paid actor in Hollywood in the late 1940s, often gave up a great deal of money in order to play the roles he really wanted.

"Your father was an intellectual, for an actor," Phil Gersh says. "Generally, actors aren't very smart. But he was very well read. One time he came to my office and he said, 'Phillip, have you read this book, *The Caine Mutiny*?'

"I said yes.

" 'And do you know Stanley Kramer?' he said. Stanley was going to direct *The Caine Mutiny*.

"I said, 'Yes, I know Stanley very well.'

"And your father said, 'Well, I'd like to play Captain Queeg.'

"So I called Stanley and he said he thought Bogie would be great as Queeg, and I called Harry Cohn, who was head of Columbia. Now, at that time the top salary for a big star was about $200,000 per picture. So I told Cohn that's what we're looking for and Cohn says, 'No, no, he wants to play this part, we'll pay him $75,000.' And Bogie ended up doing the movie for a lot less money than he could have gotten for another film. Every studio in town knew they could get Bogart for cheap if he really wanted a part."

Bogie must have had good instincts about Queeg, because the role earned him his fourth Oscar nomination. Marlon Brando beat him out that year, for *On the Waterfront*.

But Bogie's instincts were not always so good about films. He made some bad ones, and he knew it. When he was in Italy with Huston making *Beat the Devil*, for example, he sensed that the film was in trouble. He thought the first script was a dog and that maybe he and Huston should drop the whole thing. Instead, Huston brought Truman Capote over to rewrite. Capote turned what had been a complicated adventure into a parody, but not all of the actors knew that. The result was a dopey, oddball movie that was supposed to be a spoof of caper movies, but just did not meet with everybody's taste. When the movie came out it was a financial failure. In fact, one theater placed an ad apologizing for showing the film, but, noting that they were obliged to run it a few more days, offered to give the admission price back to anybody who thought it was as lousy as they, apparently, did.

Critically, the film was given good marks and bad. One reviewer said that no matter where you came in during the movie you felt as if you had missed half of it. Dad, it seems, agreed that *Beat the Devil* was a disaster, and he said that the people who thought it was funny were phony intellectuals.

Beat the Devil would later have a cult following, but that doesn't make it a good film. Many Bogie films have cult followings and many of them are bad. *The Big Sleep*, for example, has many devoted fans, and the movie is great fun, but is also a confused mess. Bosley Crowther says, "So many cryptic things occur amid so much involved and devious plotting that the mind becomes utterly confused." And when my father was asked what happened to the chauffeur in the movie, he replied, "I'm damned if I know."

Though my father made a lot of money as an actor, and did not spend it foolishly, he was not a man who accumulated great wealth from investments. At one time he owned a few Safeway supermarkets, but they went to Mayo Methot when he divorced her, as did a large chunk of cash. His only other significant investments were in movies, and he tended to make these investments more with his heart than his head. He had put some of his own money into *Beat the Devil*, probably as an act of faith in his friend John Huston.

But that was not his last movie investment. Throughout his career, my father was often concerned about the quality of movies he appeared in. In 1947, he decided to put his money where his mouth was, and he formed his own production company, Santana Pictures Corporation, with the help of Sam Jaffe and Sam's partner, Mary Baker. Bogie said that some day all big stars would have their own production companies, so they could acquire properties and control what films they appeared in. This was a bizarre idea at the time. Jack Warner, of course, was pissed off. He called Sam Jaffe.

"Sam," he said, "you are the most destructive force in the movie industry today."

"Why is that, Jack?" Sam asked.

"You have made an actor into an independent company," Warner said. "That sets a terrible, terrible precedent."

Sam asked, "How does that hurt the industry? Bogie is a name above the title and he wants his own company."

"It will destroy the industry," Warner said. "These actors will want everything. Maybe you can talk Bogie out of this terrible thing he is about to do."

"I don't think so," Sam said. "Seeing as how, it was my idea that he could have his own company."

Sam Jaffe told me that Warner never forgave him. In fact, because Jack Warner saw Santana as a great danger to the business, he refused to use Jaffe & Baker clients in films. As a result the agents lost many stars. But they held their ground.

Santana, unfortunately, never made a *great* film. There were four Santana films made between 1949 and 1951: *Knock On Any Door, Tokyo Joe, In a Lonely Place,* and *Sirocco.* None were very popular, which was embarrassing to Bogie, because he had quit Warner Brothers in order to make better films. But my father had struck a blow for artistic freedom, and he was proved right. Today many, if not most, big stars have their own production companies, and choose their own movie projects. So there, my daddy was right!

Whether he was working for others or for himself, Bogie, I have learned, was usually not difficult to work with. But he expected other people to be as professional at their jobs as he was at his, and from time to time this would put him in conflict with a director.

Sam Jaffe says, "One day I was on the set of *The Desperate Hours* with your father and Fredric March. Willie Wyler was directing. Wyler was the type of man who could not articulate what he wanted. He was like a lot of directors who can put together a fine picture in the cutting room but really don't know how to tell an actor what they want. All they can do is say, 'Do it again.' So he kept doing this to Bogie and Bogie said, 'Look, what is the point of me doing it again if you can't tell me what it is you want different, or what it is you want me to do.' That was characteristic of Bogie. He was analytical. But, he had embarrassed Wyler and the two men got together and talked quietly and made peace with each other, then they shot the scene again, and I guess Wyler communicated what he wanted from your father."

Oddly, Phil Gersh also told me a story about Bogie and Wyler failing to communicate on this same film.

Bogie had it written into his contracts that he was done for the day at six o'clock, and one day during the filming of *The Desperate Hours* he called Gersh up from the set at ten minutes to six.

"Phil," Bogie said, "Wyler's driving me nuts."

"What's the problem?" Phil asked.

"I've got to walk upstairs to the second floor in this scene."

"So?"

"So, I do it, and Willy says I'm too slow. Then I do it again and Willy says I'm going too fast. No matter what I do, it's not right. I've run up and down those stairs about twelve times now and it's almost six o'clock."

"Make him show you," Phil said.

"Huh?"

"Just tell him, 'Willy, you go up the stairs. Show me how you want it done.' "

So Bogie went over to Wyler. "Look," he said, "why don't you just go up the stairs the way you want me to."

Wyler looked at him for a moment, then looked at the stairs. "It's a wrap," he said, and Bogie was out by six o'clock.

Most directors found Bogie easy to work with. As did most actors. Rod Steiger says, "Bogie was the ultimate professional. Even when he was not in a scene with me he would stand off camera and feed me the lines, so I had someone to talk to. And Bogie was very generous. We'd be shooting a scene and he'd say, 'Jesus, this kid is blowing me off the screen,' and I'd say, 'Well, Mr. Bogart, we can switch parts,' and he would just smile. He could have gotten me out of the picture if he wanted to, or he could have had my close-ups cut out, the way a lot of stars did in those days, but he never did any of those things."

There were, however, a few actors who found working with Bogie not quite so joyous. One was William Holden.

Holden did not care for Dad. He called Bogie "an actor of consummate skill, with an ego to match."

When Holden was twenty-one and appearing in *Invisible Stripes*, in 1939, he was to be in a scene where he drove a motorcycle, with my father in the sidecar. He overheard Dad say, "Get my double to do it. I won't ride with that son of a bitch. He'll crack it up." Years later Holden allowed for the fact that "son of a bitch" could be an endearment coming from Bogie, but at the time he was steamed, and he was so anxious to prove Bogart wrong that he cracked up the motorcycle with Bogie's double in it.

Fourteen years later my father and Bill Holden were making *Sabrina* for Paramount. The making of *Sabrina* was by all accounts a lousy experience for my father. And, by all accounts, Bogie was at least partially to blame for that.

"It didn't even start off good," Phil Gersh says. "I called Billy Wilder. I said, 'Billy, you've already got Audrey Hepburn and Bill Holden. I think Bogie would be marvelous as Linus Larrabee.' Billy said, 'Meet me at the tennis club on Saturday, we'll talk.' So we talked. Then two weeks went by and he called and said, 'I've been thinking it over, can I meet with Bogie?' So we met at five o'clock and we all schmoozed and it got to be seven o'clock and we still hadn't even discussed the movie. Everybody had appointments. Finally, Bogie said to Billy, 'Look, let's just shake hands on it, and you take care of me.' They shook hands and that was it, there was nothing to worry about. They hadn't even talked about the script. Bogie was just trusting Billy to treat him right.

"So the picture starts shooting thirty days later and Bogie calls me all upset. He says, 'Look, this guy is shooting the back of my head, I don't even have to put my hairpiece on; I'm not in this picture.' So I went to Billy Wilder and told him, 'Look, Bogie is very unhappy, he's going to walk.' There was a lot of yelling and screaming, he's not being taken care of. So Bogie put his hairpiece on and came off great in the movie."

Bogie might have come off great, but the movie, I learned, was troubled from day one. Wilder started shooting without a complete script, reminiscent of Bogie's *Casablanca* experience. Pages were being delivered every day. One day they were delivered to Holden and Hepburn, but not to my father, who already felt like an outsider among these "Paramount bastards," as he called them. He walked out, forcing a shutdown in the production.

One reason that Dad felt like an outsider was that William Holden, Audrey Hepburn, and Billy Wilder, who was directing, would get together for drinks every evening after shooting, but they never invited Bogie to join them, and it hurt his feelings. More than once he was heard to say, "Those Paramount bastards didn't invite me. Well, fuck them," which is the way I talk when my feelings are hurt.

Billy Wilder says the reason Bogie was not invited to join everybody for drinks at the end of the day was, "We just didn't think he was fun to be with. Since he was excluded he reacted with anger and became worse than ever. This caused extreme tension on the picture."

More than one movie journalist has said that Bogie was not at his best during the filming of *Sabrina*. Some say he was still identifying with the character of Captain Queeg from his previous movie, *The Caine Mutiny*—paranoid and unhappy. He was, some say, irritable, on edge, apathetic about the film. He is said to have complained about his costumes, told reporters the movie was "a crock of you know what," and often referred to Billy Wilder as a "Kraut bastard Nazi son of a bitch," even though Wilder is, in fact, Jewish.

Dad also did not care for Audrey Hepburn. Though he said gracious things about her in interviews, he privately thought that she was unprofessional.

Even on this movie, which he was unhappy about, Dad knew his lines cold and he often got impatient with Holden and Hepburn, both of whom had a tendency to blow lines. Supposedly, Bogie had a whole laundry list of complaints besides this. Hepburn couldn't do a scene in less than twelve takes, he said, and she had rings under her eyes because she was up late seeing Holden. Holden, who was married at the time, also blew cigarette smoke in my father's face. In one scene Dad was on camera and Bill Holden, because he was out of the shot, read his lines from the script. Holden was smoking and when my father got frustrated because he was blowing his lines—something he had never done—he told Billy Wilder, "It's that fucking Holden with his script and his cigarettes in the air."

Holden and my father exchanged words, but apparently they made up later while drinking alcohol, a love they shared.

Another actress who was less than enamored of my father was Bette Davis. Conrad Nagel, the actor who helped to start the

Academy of Motion Pictures, says that Bette Davis did not like my father, and it was because of something that happened when she was making her first movie, *Bad Sister*, with him.

According to Nagel, there was a scene in the movie where Bette Davis had to diaper a baby. Davis, Nagel says, was sexually inexperienced and easily embarrassed, and she had assumed the baby would be a girl. She was twenty-three and supposedly had never seen male genitals, but when she unwrapped the baby, there they were. Davis got terribly embarrassed and blushed. Nagel doesn't say that my father arranged for a male baby, just that Bette Davis always believed that Bogie had gathered the cast and crew to watch her reaction. As she saw it, he got a big laugh at her expense. Bogie, she has said, was "uncouth."

Though Davis and Bogie were never close, they did have a drink together now and then to bitch about Jack Warner, and she says they came to have a "grudging admiration for each other."

I suppose a grudging admiration is what I came to have for my father's work as I learned more about it. I learned that he took his work seriously, that he stood up for other actors, that he studied his craft. All these things are admirable. But his job, like his boat, had deprived me of time with him, so I suppose I have always resented it. I've come to see it differently—to do another take, as it were. He did, after all, have to make a living. And, perhaps more to the point, Bogie didn't know that he was going to die when I was only eight years old. Maybe if he did know, he would have slowed down and not made so many pictures. I've learned, too, that passion for work can be an acquired trait, particularly as your kids grow older and less in need of your time. And maybe a lot depends on what the work is. I never cared enough about my jobs to put them first, but that doesn't make me right and him wrong. The fact is that lately I've been writing a series of mystery novels, and I find that I think about them even when I don't have to, just as I imagine Bogie must have thought about his roles, even when he was sailing off the coast of California. So maybe one of these days I will take my notebooks and pens and find a Greenwich Village drinking establishment, where I can sit at a small table, penning story ideas. And maybe I'll smoke a pipe while I work. Or maybe I won't. Maybe, like my father, I'll think it's too damn much work.

Mother and I enter the kitchen just long enough to say how different it is. But in that fragment of time I remember my first taste of alcohol.

I am eight years old. My father has been sick for a long time now and he comes down from his bedroom only in the afternoons to be with his friends in the butternut room. The grown-ups still laugh, which makes me think things will be all right. And they still drink liquor, which is the word I know for everything that they pour into glasses. It is late afternoon, unusually cool outside and not a day to play. I have been trying to do my homework, but I am bored. I come downstairs to the kitchen, and there is nobody there. I can hear them all talking in the butternut room. On the sink there is a tray of empty glasses. But May is not there. No one is there. A few of the glasses still have liquor in them, and I am suddenly excited, thinking this is my chance to taste liquor. For some time I have thought about these drinks that grown-ups have. Which glass is Dad's? I wonder. Is his one of the ones that still has something in it? My heart is pounding, as if I am about to do something wicked. I hear the voices in the butternut room. I move close to the sink, where the tray of glasses is. I count the glasses. There are four of them. Which one is my father's? I wonder again. I move closer, thinking I want to taste liquor and tell the kids about it. I sniff the glasses, thinking I can tell which one is my father's. Two are the same, one is different. The smell is not really pleasant. It feels warm to my nostrils, like breathing hot air. But I am sure the taste will be good. Even if it's not, I think, I will have tasted liquor. Finally, thinking I know which glass is my father's I pick it up. There is only a small amount of liquor in the bottom of the glass. I wait for the sound of laughter, so I will know they are all still in the butternut room. I lift the glass to my mouth and let the liquor pour over my tongue. It feels hot and disgusting. I quickly put the glass back on the tray and I start spitting into the sink, trying to get the taste off my tongue. I turn on the faucet and pour water into my cupped hands and drink it. These people must be nuts to like this stuff, I think.

7

Bogie had an alcoholic thermostat. He just set his thermostat at noon, pumped in some scotch, and stayed at a nice even glow all day, automatically redosing as necessary.

—NUNNALLY JOHNSON

One time, a few years before I was born, my father was out all night drinking. When dawn came he was staggering around on unfamiliar Hollywood streets. He was hungover, unshaven, and disheveled, looking more like a gutter rat than a movie star. As he walked along one side street in the early morning, he noticed a light glowing in the window of a small house. He slipped between two hedges, crept across the lawn, and peered in the window. There he saw a woman in her kitchen, cooking breakfast for her family. By this time Bogie was getting hungry, apparently, and he stood by the window for a long time, sniffing the smell of bacon. Finally, the woman turned toward the window and she saw him peering in at her. At first she was startled at the sight of this scruffy-looking guy. But as she stared longer at him she realized that she was looking at one of the most famous men in the world.

"My God!" she called to her husband, "it's Humphrey Bogart."

"What about him?" the husband asked.

"He's in our front yard," she said.

"Well, let's invite him in."

So the husband invited Bogie in. The kids came down for breakfast, and everybody gathered around the kitchen table. There, the not-quite-sober movie star wolfed down bacon and eggs, and regaled these ordinary folk with tales of Hollywood moviemaking and what it was like to kiss Bette Davis and get shot dead by James Cagney and Edward G. Robinson. After he said good-bye that morning, Bogie never saw the people again, but for the rest of their lives they had a story to tell.

There are any number of anecdotes concerning my father and alcohol. Dad lived, after all, in a time when there were no Mothers Against Drunk Driving, when getting loaded was still amusing. So he made no efforts to hide his drinking, and many of his drinking stories found their way into print.

My father, in fact, was somewhat chauvinistic about booze, often hinting that people who drank were of a higher order than those who abstained.

"The whole world is three drinks behind," he said in 1950. "If everybody in the world would take three drinks, we would have no trouble. Of course, it should be handled in moderation. You should be able to handle it. I don't think it should handle you. But that's what the world needs, three more drinks. If Stalin, Truman, and everybody else in the world had three drinks right now, we'd all loosen up, and we wouldn't need the UN."

Bogie once announced, "I'm starting, maybe I should say uncorking, a campaign for more civilized, more decorous drinking." He named his favorite "gentlemen guzzlers." On his list were Winston Churchill, Ernest Hemingway, Errol Flynn, John Steinbeck, Don Ameche, Ed Gardner, Toots Shor, Pat O'Brien, Paul Douglas, and John Nance Garner. And on his all-star drinking team he put Mark Hellinger, Robert Benchley, and W. C. Fields.

He wouldn't allow women on the team. He said that you could not have peaceful drinking when there were women around. "You don't have fights in men's bars," he said. "The fights are in night clubs, when women come flirting around. Women should be allowed one cocktail as an appetizer, and they should be made to drink that at a table. Women don't drink attractively. They look a little crooked when they drink. They fix their hats till they get them tilted and crooked."

Whenever Bogie talked at length, which was often, some reference to drink was almost inevitable, and he has become highly quotable on the subject. "I think there should be some space between drinks," he said. "But not much." When he came back from Italy he said, "I didn't like the pasta so I lived on Scotch and soup." When asked if he had ever been on the wagon, he replied, "Just once. It was the most miserable afternoon of my life."

Bogie also said, "Something happens to people who drink. They live longer." But he knew better. When his sister Catherine, whom he called Kay, died of peritonitis after a ruptured appendix, the doctors said she had been weakened by too much alcohol. "She was," said Bogie, "a victim of the speakeasy era."

Kay, who had been a Bergdorf-Goodman model, died in her thirties. She had been as prodigious a drinker as my father. George Oppenheimer, cofounder of Viking Press, was once her steady date, but he couldn't keep up with her drinking. Bogie once said, "The trouble with George is that he gives out just as Kay is ready to give in."

So yes, there are some cute stories about Bogie's drinking and there are lots of funny lines. But the simple truth is that my father had a drinking problem, and that can never be a good thing.

"My father was a functional alcoholic," I said to a woman one time. I have said that a lot.

"Watch what you say," she said. She was very upset with me.

"Huh?"

"There's no such term as 'functional alcoholic,' " she said. "It doesn't mean anything. Alcoholism is a disease and we should be very careful about how we use our terms."

Well, maybe.

I do know that Bogie functioned. He was never drunk on the job (except, of course, for the time that Jack Warner had to coax him off his bicycle), never hauled into jail or hospitalized for drinking, and never ravaged by booze, though certainly it was a factor in his cancer. Bogie did not usually get drunk, at least so that you could tell. He was what he called a good drinker. "A good drinker," he said, "doesn't let drinking interfere with his job. He can get absolutely stiff and the fellow next to him doesn't know it."

Patrick O'Moore, one of my father's actor friends, said

that when he drank with Bogart, he realized there was something wrong with his own drinking.

"I thought we drank the same," he says, "but I noticed that Bogart was still cold sober at the end of the evening and I wasn't."

One day on the *Santana,* O'Moore said to Bogie, "There's something wrong with my drinking, Bogie. I don't know what it is, but you can be all right when you want to and I can't."

Bogie replied, "Well, kid, you don't handle it right. You've crossed the line."

My father rarely crossed the line. He took great pride in that.

Yet, this is a guy who, when he wasn't working, started drinking by noon. He drank when he went to Romanoff's. He stopped for drinks on the way home. He drank when he got home. He drank on his boat. He hung out with people who drank. Drinking was one thing my father did a lot of. The fact is that my father liked to drink and smoke, and that's what eventually killed him. It seems to me at least that this is a description of a drinking problem.

John Huston said, "Bogie loved to drink and play the roughneck. Actually I don't think I ever saw Bogie drunk. It was always half acting, but he loved the whole scene."

Maybe Huston never saw Bogie drunk, but a lot of other people, including my mother, did. The results were not always attractive. Just like Jason Robards, Bogie could be charming when he was sober, but often unpleasant when he was drunk. Bogie was not always drinking for fun.

Mom says that when Bogie drank too much with her, he felt remorseful. And when he drank too much he often had a temper. She tells me there were times when Bogart was so loaded he didn't even know where he was or who she was.

One night—I think it was her first night on the boat, and they were still dating secretly—he got frighteningly drunk and she watched as his personality turned from adorable to ugly. It was Jekyll-and-Hyde time. There had been no arguments, no cutting remarks, nothing to predict an outburst. But, suddenly Bogie began pounding on the table.

"Actresses!" he shouted.

"Bogie, what's the matter?" Mother asked. She was only nineteen at the time and this was the first time she was seeing Bogie's temper.

"All you damn actresses are what's the matter," Bogie shouted. "You're all alike."

"Well you ought to know," Mother said, trying to make light of things. "You married three of them."

"I said that ninety-five percent of them were morons," Bogie shouted. "And the papers got all over me for that. Well, I'm revising the figures, goddamn it! I'm saying that ninety-eight percent of them are morons."

Though these same comments had been amusing when the sober Bogart said them to reporters, he now sounded furious.

"Actresses! Who needs them, damn it," he shouted. Again, he pounded the table.

My mother felt a mixture of emotions. She didn't understand what had set him off like this. "Actresses," she figured was code for women like her, and his three wives, and perhaps even his mother. Mom had never seen him so upset. She was afraid that people would hear him shouting. She was afraid she would lose him. And she was terrified that if she managed to hold on to this volatile personality, she would never learn how to deal with all the drinking that he and his friends did. My mother had never been around so much drinking before.

Finally staggering, and railing against the world in general and actresses in particular, Dad stormed off the boat and disappeared into the night. Mother cried for hours. In the morning Bogie was back, filled with remorse for his behavior. It was only much later that Mother came to the conclusion that Bogie had been fighting and drinking for so long with Mayo Methot, to whom he was still married at the time, that he had established a terrible pattern, and in his drunkenness he must have thought Bacall was Mayo.

The fact is that a lot of Dad's fears came to the surface when he drank, and one of them, certainly at this time, was that he would lose Bacall. From her viewpoint this was ridiculous. She was in love with him and if anyone was in danger of heartbreak it was her. After all, he was a highly desirable, witty, wealthy, intelligent, and famous man whom many women found very sexy. In fact, she often saw, or thought she saw, other women coming on to him. But from my father's point of view, he was a nearly fifty-year-old guy whose looks were gone, and she was a beautiful young and talented actress who could get any man she wanted. The result was the friction of two insecure people. My mother, fortunately, was not a big drinker. But Bogie, of course, was, and when he drank he would worry and often he would lash out at my mother.

I'm relieved to say that I did not inherit my father's addiction to alcohol. I'm not a drinker. I don't like the taste of alcohol or the smell of it. In one year I might have only six or seven drinks, and even those will be something innocuous, in which the taste of the alcohol is well disguised.

I am, however, interested in my father's drinking habits because I had a substance addiction of my own. Drugs. I think my father's experience and mine were similar in some ways. And they were different in some ways, the most obvious being that his drug was legal and mine was not, and that I gave up drugs, but he never really stopped drinking.

Certainly Bogie and I, both of us shy, used our drugs as a social lubricant. There doesn't seem to be a time in Bogie's adulthood when booze was not at the center of his social life.

In the twenties he was part of the jazz age. He ran around with brazen women who smoked cigarettes, and he drank bootleg whiskey distilled by the same machinegun-toting gangsters that he would later portray in the movies. After his first early successes on the stage, when he had some money in his pockets, Dad used to spend a lot of time in Times Square watering holes and Greenwich Village bars, speakeasies, and places like the Harlem Cotton Club. Often he stayed up drinking all night.

Later, when he got into movies, at six o'clock he would go to his dressing room and shout "Scotch!" That's when his hairdresser would get drinks ready for Bogie and any guest who happened to drop by. On his way home from work he would stop for drinks with pals—writers mostly, like Mark Hellinger, John O'Hara, Nathaniel Benchley, Nunnally Johnson, and Quentin Reynolds. When he got home he would drink again, and often go out later, looking for guys to go drinking with.

His first three marriages, particularly his marriage to Mayo Methot, were largely a drinking orgy. But when my father married my mother, it seemed he had found the missing piece in his life, and his drinking habits improved. He stopped drinking mixed drinks and he stopped mixing his drinks.

"Mark Hellinger told me I was drinking like a boy and he was right," Bogie said. Hellinger had told him that he was drinking like a kid because he mixed his drinks. Before Hellinger, Bogie would have martinis before dinner, beer with dinner, and Drambuie after dinner. But during the Bacall part of his life he was strictly a scotch man. "Scotch," he said, "is a very valuable part of my life."

Though my mother has often been given the credit for reducing Bogie's alcohol consumption, she doesn't see it quite that way.

"I didn't persuade him to cut back," she says. "That would have been foolhardy. You couldn't nag Bogie. That would be counterproductive. I didn't try to keep up with him, and I didn't bawl him out when he was hungover. I simply ignored him. He would try to get me to pay attention when he was drinking but I did not. The fact is that Bogie drank because he was insecure. Once he realized that he had emotional security, and professional security, too, he cut back on his drinking."

After he married Bacall, Bogie didn't go out to drink as often, but he still drank every day, usually with friends in the butternut room. During this later part of his life Bogie said, "This is my recreation. I like to sit around and gab, enjoy my drinks and my family. That's what a man wants when he's over fifty. Drink never caused me any harm."

Quite simply, Bogie's social life, throughout his life, could fairly be described as "drinking with friends." And I know how that goes. A lot of my young adulthood could fairly be described as "smoking dope with friends."

My mother, of course, never knew about all this drug-taking until much later. But drugs—or, at least, the drug culture—still got me in trouble with her during this period, when I was living in her apartment.

One day in 1968, while my mother was in Europe making a movie, my friend Peter, from New Jersey, came up to the Dakota.

"Bogart, let's have a party," he said.

"Great idea," I said. "Who shall we invite?"

"Everybody."

So we invited all our friends, and we told them they could bring friends.

Before the party, Peter and I headed down to Greenwich Village to buy a pound of grass. By the time we got back to the Dakota, people were already showing up for the party. All of them had one thing in common: Neither Pete nor I had the vaguest idea of who they were.

I guess when we put out the word about the party, we thought we'd end up with a few dozen people. But by ten o'clock that night there were three hundred to four hundred people tromping in and out of Mother's beautiful apartment, including a few people that Pete and I actually knew. In those days word of a party would spread like a virus. One person would tell another where there was a party and soon strangers would show up, completely untroubled by the fact that they didn't know who was running the party or any of the people there. So they came—long-haired guys and longer-haired girls. Some brought cake, or a brick of cheese. Or a bowl of cauliflower. All of them brought drugs. Joints were passed from hand to hand, Mary Jane brownies were munched, platters of acid made the rounds. Even some old-fashioned types brought alcohol. Every five minutes the doorman would buzz the apartment and tell me somebody wanted to come up.

"What's their name?" I'd ask and I'd hear him asking them, "What's your name?"

"John and Cherry," they'd say, or "Windsong and Harmony." And I'd say, "Send them up." I didn't know who the hell they were. It didn't matter to me. I was stoned and I was surrounded by peace and love and good-looking females. They could have said their names were Huey, Dewey, and Louie and I would have invited them up.

We all had a great time, and kind of a miracle occurred that night. It wasn't a miracle then, but it would be today. Here were four hundred drug-addled hippie strangers roaming around the luxury apartment of a movie star, and not one thing was stolen or broken in that apartment. Times were definitely different. Today everything would be stolen or wrecked or used as evidence in a negligence suit.

So, since nothing was stolen or broken, my mother was happy for me that I had four hundred friends drop by at her place, right? Well, not exactly. After all, Pete had said there was no possibility that she would find out, because she was in Europe.

However, the doorman at the Dakota thought Bacall might be interested in the fact that half the unwashed people in New York were dancing on her carpets. So he called her in Europe and told her.

She, not surprisingly, called me. We discussed it.

"Stephen," she said, speaking in the coldest tones I have ever heard. "I have just received a very disturbing telephone call from the doorman there."

"Mom, it's not so bad, there's nothing broken—"

"Stephen," she said, stopping me in midsentence, "what

you have done is so monumentally bad, so unforgivable, that I am beyond even screaming."

"Look, Mom, everybody's gone. Nothing got stolen, nothing got—"

"Stephen! My hands are trembling on the phone. Trembling. I don't know if I will ever again be able to trust you."

She might as well have shoved an ice pick in my heart.

"Mom, I'm sorry. I didn't know so many people would show up."

"How many?" she said.

"I don't know. Forty, maybe fifty."

"I see," she said, which either meant that fifty was a horrendous number, or that she knew the truth. "Now I will only say this once, Stephen, I want that apartment spotless. Do you understand?"

"I got you, Mom."

"I don't want to see a stain. Do you understand me? I want to walk into my apartment and believe that this was all a nightmare, that what I have heard tonight never really happened."

I spent the next three days cleaning things that didn't need to be cleaned.

Despite one bad acid trip and the incident with my mother, over which I still feel guilty and embarrassed, I don't think smoking grass and tripping, on the whole, did me much harm. That, however, cannot be said for cocaine, a much more seductive drug and, I know now, a much more dangerous one.

I first started snorting cocaine in my late twenties, when I went to the University of Hartford. It was not a problem at first. For the first couple of years I would do it maybe once a month. It was around 1980, when I was working as an assistant producer at ESPN in Bristol, Connecticut, that my cocaine use started to escalate. My marriage to my first wife, Dale, had been lousy for a long time, but the impact of a bad marriage had only just started to get to me. I was lonely, and I guess cocaine took the edge off my loneliness.

At ESPN I'd be assistant-producing games and doing lines of coke at the same time. We had a telex machine, where you went to get the scores. Guys would put coke on the plastic top and slice it up with a razor blade. Of course, all this sounds reckless as hell today. But then cocaine was the "good drug." It was party time, Studio 54 and all that. Cocaine was not the social evil that it is now. It wasn't even all that expensive.

At ESPN I still felt that I had my coke habit under control. I'd buy some and I'd use it, and that would be it. I didn't go screaming through the streets for more. Sometimes I'd go to people's houses and do cocaine until four in the morning. But the next day I would stay away from it. So I was cool, I thought.

But cocaine is seductive. You don't realize that you are getting addicted. I started using it more and more. Soon I was doing it on my day off, and twice a week I would make a two-hundred-dollar coke buy. That's four hundred bucks a week to get drugged. Ten thousand bucks a year, and even that was small change compared to the habits of some guys. Trouble is, I was on track to become one of those guys.

I would do cocaine on a Friday night and I wouldn't sleep until Saturday night. I would space out. I would get selfish and refuse to share my coke with anybody. Then the paranoia started. The fear, the sweats, the jitters—all came with the crash that followed the high. I stopped eating. I lost weight. My strength was sapped and I couldn't work out.

Still, I went to work in New York every day, which meant I had to commute eighty-five miles each way from Connecticut, and I would do coke. I didn't miss much time at work, but still I was getting worse.

With cocaine, as with alcohol, you reach a bottom. That is, if you don't kill yourself first. Everybody has a different bottom. I think I know when I reached mine.

It was in 1984 when I was working for NBC as a writer for the affiliate news. I had been doing cocaine all night. I needed to get ready for work. By this time I was divorced from Dale and I was living in New York again, at my mother's place at the Dakota.

This particular morning, after the all-night coke session, I was a wreck. I knew I couldn't go to work, but with the insane optimism of the coke fiend, I figured maybe later in the day I'd feel just great and I could go in to work. So I called NBC and told them that I was in Connecticut.

"My car stalled out," I said. "I don't know how long it will take to have it towed and fixed."

I said I was calling from a pay phone. I felt guilty as hell, lying to them, but I figured I'd get in to the studio later and everything would be fine.

Of course, the way to take the edge off a cocaine high is to drink alcohol when you're coming down. That was no pleasure for me, because I don't like alcohol. But I drank it, anyhow. I'd done it before. I drank half a fifth of vodka. I'd pass out for a while, wake up and think I was getting a grip on things, then pass out again and wake up later. I figured if I could last for an hour then I knew I'd be okay. Around midday I began to believe that I was pretty straight, so I got dressed and started walking to NBC. When I got close to Rockefeller Center I started to think, "Shit, they'll smell the vodka I've been drinking." So I called NBC from a pay phone right outside of the building. I told my supervisor that I was still in Connecticut having the car fixed. "I know you are," he said, meaning, of course, that he knew I was what we affectionately called a lying sack of shit.

Before I hung up, he said, "Watch out or you're going in the shitter," or something like that.

I guess that's when it hit me. I already was in the shitter, whatever a shitter was. I was spending all kinds of money on cocaine, I was allowing it to interfere with my life, and now I was in danger of losing my job because I had turned into a lying, scheming cocaine addict. I sensed suddenly that I was not cool, that I was one of these guys who had a problem and that everybody in the world could see it.

Shortly after that I went into therapy. I went to therapy alone. And I went to therapy with my mother. And I went to couples therapy with Barbara, who was then my new girlfriend.

I give most of the credit for my sobriety to Barbara. It was she, more than anybody else, who helped me to give up drugs. Barbara had been two years sober after a serious substance abuse problem of her own. Alcohol and drugs. She had gone through a long and difficult time, and as I fell more deeply in love with her I came to admire her greatly for overcoming her addiction. She took me to her AA meetings. She loved me and supported me and told me I could kick the habit.

"Steve," she said, "it's easier to stay straight than to keep up the addiction. And you have more fun."

Being with Barbara was important because she was a winner, a person who had become sober. If you are going to get rid of a substance abuse problem you must associate with winners. You can't hang out with drug addicts.

In therapy I came to see what need cocaine was filling in my life. I could see that I had become a very lonely person. I had gotten into cocaine at a time when I was lonely in my marriage because Dale and I had become practically strangers. After my divorce from Dale I had gotten even lonelier because I no longer had a daily relationship with my son, Jamie. And I was lonely because, even though I had some friends, I didn't feel truly intimate with them. Cocaine had somehow taken the edge off that loneliness. Did I take cocaine because I am Humphrey Bogart's son? No. But I think the loneliness that led to cocaine began when my father died and I began to build a wall around me.

Not surprisingly, my father's name came up from time to time during therapy. In those dark, introspective days, I felt a real bond with Dad. We both had a substance abuse problem. I talked a lot about him, or about his absence, I guess. I learned that I was full of regret for the fact that I never had a father in my life to teach me male things, to show me exactly what it meant to be a man. I began to think that he and I were similar. It seemed to me that he had been lonely, too.

Now, having talked to many people about my father, I am more sure than ever that Humphrey Bogart was tightly wrapped around an inner core of loneliness.

"There was something very sad about Mr. Bogart," Rod Steiger told me. "You could see it in his eyes."

"He seemed to be a sad man," Jess Morgan said.

I heard similar comments from others.

My father, I have learned, was a very guarded man. Though he was famous for speaking his mind, I don't think he let his true feelings out to anybody, at least not often. Maybe this had something to do with the fact that his mother didn't really give him the attention that he needed. Sometimes I think of him as a kid pulling pranks at Andover, and the image of him melts into the image of myself doing the same things at Milton. For me, all that mischief was a kind of mask. I bet it was for him, too.

And at the other end of his life, when Bogie supposedly had close friends, maybe he didn't feel truly intimate with them. We know that he did not feel close enough to any of them, including Mother, to really talk about the fact that he was dying. There was no last conversation with his wife or his kids. You would think he would want to talk about death. But he didn't. He just wanted people to ignore his illness until he died, and then he wouldn't have to deal with it. Maybe, despite the surprise birthday party and all the many get-togethers with pals, Bogie still never really believed that he was loved. After all, there were things to dislike about Bogie, and maybe in the privacy of his thoughts, those are the things that he focused on. Maybe there was a reason why he drank.

I don't know. But there are two things I am sure of. One is that my father was neither a saint nor a devil. He was human. And the other, learned from my own experience with drugs, is that nobody just happens to drink constantly, day in and day out. It is too goddamned punishing. There is always a reason.

The reason can only be guessed at. But certainly my father was troubled and insecure, and the drinking was not unrelated to those things. Pat O'Moore said, "There came a time when the pressure built up inside him and he had to drink. I used to see him so frustrated with anger that he would sit and quiver all over."

And Phil Gersh says, "The insecurity of Humphrey Bogart was amazing. He was terribly insecure."

Gersh remembers one particular lunch at Romanoff's. Usually, at lunch, Gersh would tell Bogie about possible jobs, or at least bring him a couple of scripts. This time the two men talked about other things.

After Bogie had put away two scotches, he looked at Gersh and said, "No scripts, huh?"

Gersh said, "No, I don't have any today, Bogie, but I will have some."

Bogie looked depressed. "Well," he said, "nobody wants me."

"Bogie, what are you talking about?"

"I guess I'll go down to the boat," he said. "I'll call Betty and tell her to bring the kids down."

"Listen," Gersh said, "I'm getting a script from Hal Wallis tomorrow. It will probably be great for you."

"No," Bogie said, "I'll go down to the boat."

Gersh says, "He really thought, then, that nobody wanted him, that maybe his last movie was his last movie. Bogie had a great ego, but he had great insecurity, too. One time we walked out of Romanoff's and the people were there. A bunch of kids ran over for autographs, and I said, 'Doesn't that bother you?' and he said, 'No, it would bother me if they didn't come.' "

If I got a better understanding of Bogie in therapy, I also got a better understanding of my mother during this time. But the moment of insight didn't come from a therapist. It came from my sister, Leslie, who lives in California, where she and her husband both teach Yoga.

I was talking to Leslie on the phone one night, griping about Mom.

"Why does she always have to be in control all the time?" I said. "Why can't she ever be just pure emotion?" (Two weeks in therapy and I was starting to sound like Leo Buscaglia!)

"Well," Leslie said, "Mother never got the chance to express her emotions, and maybe she came to believe that expressing your emotions was not a necessary thing. Because of this silly game she and Dad played, never talking about the fact that he was dying, she never got to say to Father, 'I can't believe you're dying. How could you do this to me? I gave up my career. You gave me two kids. And now you're leaving, damn you!' Instead she had to say, 'I adore you,' and so forth. I don't know if this is something she would have said if she could have, but when you are allowed to have your grief you go through all these stages and one of them is anger. And I know that that's what I would have said. But she never got a chance to say it. He didn't leave her with that much."

God, I thought, Leslie's right. And I knew that what was true for Mom was also true for Leslie and for me. If my father had died when I was an adult I might, like so many others, regret that I hadn't told him I loved him. But he died when I was a kid. I had hugged him, I had told him I loved him. I was, as they say, okay with that. But I had never gotten a chance to say, "Damn you, Daddy, for dying on me when I need you." And maybe all those years of denying him were my way of saying it.

So here I was, having insights left and right and I breezed through therapy and never touched cocaine again, right? No, of course not. Life is never quite that simple.

After Barbara and I were married there came a day when I slipped. She was away and I did some cocaine, even though

I had been sober for a period of time. When I told Barbara about it, she didn't scream and yell at me. She didn't even preach. She made things very simple for me. She told me she would not be married to a cocaine addict. I could do cocaine or I could be married to her. Not both. No contest. I have been sober since.

Like my mother with Bogie, Barbara does not take credit for getting me sober. And in a way she is right. Nobody can really get you off drugs. You have to get off them yourself. But in Barbara I think I found what my father found in Bacall, that one great love which, even if you have nothing else, is enough. Whatever hole I'd been trying to fill with drugs has now been filled.

As we move through the house on Mapleton I am aware of my mother's voice. I hear it now not as the famous voice of an actress, but as the voice of my mom, echoing through the house so many years ago. It mixes musically with a variety of voices, all female. There is the voice of my sister, little Leslie, giggling at times, whining at other times. I hear the laughter that rose out of her when Dad would pick her up and swing her in the air, and the shriek of delight when he would trap her in the up position on the seesaw. There is the voice of May, the cook, deep and full of authority. It always seemed she knew things that the rest of us did not. And I hear the voice of Grandma Natalie, thick and maternal, sometimes lyrically reading stories to Leslie and me, sometimes stern and exasperated at our misbehavior. I notice that the voices are all female, that in this moment I am not hearing the voice of my father, the voice of any male, and I feel that something is missing and it makes me lonely.

I think, when he married me, Bogie thought I would be, like his other wives, a companion for his semibachelor existence.

—LAUREN BACALL

For decades it has been whispered that my father had the biggest schlong in Hollywood. I like to think the rumor is true, but I don't know who to ask. Who keeps track of these things? I do know that it's not the sort of thing I can discuss over tea with Mother.

Whether it's true or not, the fact is that my father was not a major-league cocksman.

People who knew Dad say he almost never looked at other women. Film critics have said that Bogart was at his least convincing on the screen when he was supposed to be leering at dames. And Bacall says, "Not once in our years of marriage did Bogie ever suffer from the roving eye."

The party line on my father and women is that he was not a skirt chaser, not a ladies' man, and only occasionally a flirt. In fact, much of his movie appeal to women seems to come from the fact that he doesn't need them. Bette Davis said, "What women liked about Bogie, I think, was that when he did love scenes, he held back, like many men do, and they understood that."

On the other hand, my father was married four times, and in at least two cases, he was wriggling under the sheets with the future wife before the present wife became a past wife. Which kind of knocks the shit out of my Peter Lorre quote: "Bogie is no ladies' man. Maybe it is deep-down decency. He has very set ideas about behavior and morals in that respect."

Still, it is clear that my father would rather have sailed to Catalina with an all-male crew than dance until dawn at the El Morocco with a beautiful blonde. He liked a good horse race and a round of golf more than a great set of gams. Bogie did not squire hundreds of girls around town, and when he did get attached to a female he tended to marry her.

I am very different from my father in that respect. I have always found the female form a hell of a lot more compelling than a birdie on the fifteenth hole, even though I am a golfer. This can be a problem. Like any man, including Bogie, I have from time to time been controlled by anatomical parts much lower than the brain. After I got kicked out of Boston University, for example, and was staying at Dale's parents' home in Torrington, I got the boot when Dale's mother came home from the hardware store one day and caught us screwing in the living room. I did manage to get back in after I wrote a long, apologetic letter.

Howard Stern once asked me on the radio if I had ever

used my role as Bogie's son to get laid, and I told him I hadn't, at least not consciously. In fact, I said, sometimes when women asked me if I was related to Humphrey Bogart I told them I wasn't, because I didn't want to be Bogie's son, always being compared to him. And I especially did not want a girl to be interested in me because of who my father was. Sometimes I even lied about my name. But, now that I think about it, I suppose there were those other times when I was with a woman who was keenly aware of my bloodline, perhaps impressed by it, and I did what I could to make the most of it.

Anyhow, having made sex and romance—not necessarily in that order—priorities in my life, I took a special interest in finding out about my dad and women.

I learned that his first known girlfriend was named Pickles, though my guess is that that was not her given name. Bogie was a teenager when he fell in love with Pickles at Fire Island, where his family was staying one summer, a change of pace for them since they usually spent their summer vacations upstate at Camp Canandaigua, the place where Bogie learned to sail. Pickles was, he once said, "a girl with laughing eyes and freckles on her nose." At summer's end Pickles returned to her home in Flatbush and, as much as he was in love with her, it apparently was not enough to make worthwhile the long train ride to Brooklyn. So, after one postsummer visit, young Humphrey scratched Pickles off his dance card and took up with a girl from New Jersey.

Bogie did a fair amount of oat-sowing with a succession of young women, and when he finally did get serious, it was with an actress by the name of Helen Menken. He met Helen when he was working as a stage manager for a touring company of a play called *Drifting*. One day some of Bogie's sets fell on poor Helen's head and the two of them got into a peppery battle over it. Later he said, "I guess I shouldn't have done it, but I booted her. She, in turn, belted me and ran to her dressing room to cry."

We'll never know whether these two literally smacked each other, or if Dad was just trying to be colorful when he talked about this, but the fight between man and woman led, as it often does in the movies, to romance. It was only a matter of weeks before Humphrey and Helen had a license to get married. And a matter of hours after that before Bogie had second thoughts.

Menken was a well-known and well-connected actress who could help Bogie in his acting career. But he was concerned about marrying a woman who was more successful than himself. He had grown up in a home where the wife was dominant and he didn't care for it. So Bogie backed out.

He told his friend Bill Brady, "God, I don't want to marry that girl."

Brady replied, "If you don't, Humphrey, you'll never get another part on Broadway."

Maybe Dad was worried about what Helen could do to his career. Or maybe it was just that Helen was persistent. Either way, the result was that Bogie reconsidered, and he and Helen did get married in the spring of 1926.

The wedding was a horror. Helen's parents were deaf mutes and the minister, also deaf, performed the ceremony in sign language. That would have been fine, but the deaf minister tried to speak the words, too, and the sound that came from him was unlike any known language of the time, dragging the whole affair down to the level of tragicomedy. By the end of the ceremony Helen was crying hysterically, and she ran from the reporters who were covering the wedding.

Helen recovered, but the marriage, clearly, was doomed, and indeed it went straight to hell. Bogart and Menken fought over everything, including the fact that Helen wanted to feed the dog caviar, and my father, despite being a dog lover, thought hamburger was good enough for a pooch. "This would lead to that," my father said, and "one or the other of us would walk out in a fine rage."

The unhappy lovers separated once or twice and their reunions were short-lived. Eighteen months after the wedding they were permanently split. Dad worried about the gossip but he told one friend, "When the whole thing is over Helen and I will be good friends. She's a wonderful girl."

Though Helen blamed Bogie for the failed marriage at the time, years later she told my mother that it was her own fault, that she had put too much emphasis on her career and not enough on her marriage.

Bogie, who was twenty-seven when things went sour with Helen Menken, later said, "I'd had enough women by the time I was twenty-seven to know what I was looking for in a wife. I wanted a girl I could come home to."

Perhaps, but after Helen he dated other actresses.

One of them was Mary Philips. She would become wife number two, and his romance with her also began with a fight scene.

Bogie had a small part in a play, and during his one good scene, this actress, Mary Philips, was supposed to be walking away from him, drifting out of sight and mind as he went into his speech. One night during his big moment Dad observed that Philips was putting too much of what he called "that" into her walk. It was a bit of feminine swaying that was sufficient to draw the audience's attention away from his speech and on to her derrière. Later he confronted her.

"You can't do that," he said.

"Do what?"

"That thing you do. That walk."

"Really?" she said.

"Yes, really," he said.

"And why, pray tell, not?"

"That's my scene," Bogie said. "You can't just steal a scene from me like that."

Mary was amused. "Well," she said, "suppose you try to stop me."

If Bogie were telling the story today he might say something like, "Well Stevie, I smacked her a good one and she smartened up." But the truth is he did nothing. He explained once, "I didn't try to stop her, because while I was talking I suddenly became aware that here was a girl with whom I could very easily fall in love."

Bogie did fall in love with Mary Philips. But not just then. A few years after the derrière incident he ran into her after a showing of *The Jazz Singer,* the first talking movie. They started dating, going mostly to plays when they were not performing in them. Mary, like Helen, was more successful than Bogie and, like Helen, she encouraged Bogie to pursue his craft.

After he proposed and Mary accepted, Bogie told a reporter, "Marrying her is probably the most wonderful thing that could happen to me."

As it turned out, something more wonderful happened to Bogie. He was invited to Hollywood. He tested for a role in *The Man Who Came Back* and was offered a contract at $750 a week. Dad had it in his head that he would take his bride out to California, that he would make it big in Hollywood, and they could live in great style. But Mary, it turns out, was not interested in being "a girl you can come home to," and something large came between them: the United States. Mary had her own career and it was firmly rooted in the stages of the east coast, not in front of Hollywood cameras.

The result of all the bickering over careers and coasts was that my father and Mary agreed that while he was out in California becoming a movie star, he could see other women and she would be back in New York with the freedom to date other guys.

When this was told to me I found it interesting because in my first marriage I did somewhat the same thing, though by that time it had a name: open marriage. I was very young when I married Dale and became a father. It wasn't long before our marriage became little more than a device for keeping both of Jamie's parents under the same roof. It seemed to me that I was changing and my wife wasn't, though of course, Dale saw it differently. Anyhow, with a toddler to care for, Dale and I didn't want to break up, so we went the open marriage route, popular in those days. It's not as though I would come home and say, "Oh, by the way, I screwed Lulu last night," but we had an understanding that if either of us wanted to see someone, we could. Truth is, it didn't work all that well. For the last seven years of my first marriage, Dale never got to know the people I hung out with, and I didn't really know the people she was close to. We were emotionally separated. We didn't fight much, but that was probably because she worked days then, and I worked nights.

Dad's open marriage experiment didn't fare much better. Mary Philips, apparently, was a woman of her word. She said she would see other men, and that's what she did. She fell in love with the actor Roland Young, while Bogie was in Hollywood. But when Bogie got back to New York, he and Mary hashed things out. They brought the marriage in for repairs and vowed never to be separated again, which was fine with Bogie since he was now disillusioned with Hollywood for the second time. For his $750 a week he had not been hired to star in *The Man Who Came Back*. He had been hired to work as a voice coach for the star, Charles Farrell, who you might remember as Gale Storm's father on *My Little Margie*.

Bogie's marriage to Mary Philips lasted for a decade, though not without its occasional plot twists. These were the depression years and the young acting couple struggled financially. Mary had some luck, performing in summer stock in New England, but through much of the thirties many lights were dim on Broadway. What money the couple did have was mainly brought in by Mary. Bogie couldn't even borrow money from his parents, because by this time Belmont had made a number of bad business deals and the Bogarts were not as affluent as they had been. (Eventually, Belmont would give up his practice and run away to become a ship's doctor aboard freighters. He returned to New York a morphine addict, and died ten thousand dollars in debt. My father would eventually pay off the debt.)

So Bogie and Mary pooled money with friends and wore a lot of sweaters.

Though Mary would prove to be a little lamb compared to wife number three, the Bogart–Philips marriage was in some ways a preliminary bout for the Bogart–Methot marriage that would come next. Mary, for example, almost bit off a cop's finger one night when he arrested her for being drunk, along with Bogie and their friend Broderick Crawford, who had a career as a movie actor before my generation got to know him as Captain Dan Matthews on *Highway Patrol*.

On Bogie's next visit to Hollywood Mary went with him. They lived in the Garden of Allah, a legendary cluster of bungalows on Sunset Boulevard, where celebrities and wannabes drank, laughed, and occasionally bedded down together.

But Mary was homesick for the smell of greasepaint. Broadway was where she belonged, she felt, and when she got a chance to perform there in *The Postman Always Rings Twice*, she told Bogie she wanted to return to Manhattan. Bogie was deeply hurt that she wanted to leave.

"The postman always rings twice?" he said. "What the hell does that mean, anyhow?"

"I don't know."

"It doesn't mean anything," Bogie said. "I read the book. There's no postman in it and nobody rings anything once, never mind twice. Guy just made up the title. You want to be in a play where the guy just made up the title?"

"Yes."

"It's all wrong for you," Bogie said.

"I want to go," Mary cried.

"For God's sake, Mary," Bogie said. "This is my first chance to really prove that I can support a wife, maybe have kids, and here you are getting ready to hop on the first train back to New York."

"I have to go," Mary said.

"Then go, goddamn it, but I'm telling you the play is not right for you," Bogie said.

Mary left, and it was during her absence that Bogie met Mayo Methot.

* * *

Some say Bogie met Mayo at the home of his friend Eric Hatch. Others say he met her at a Screen Actors' Guild dinner. He spotted her eyeing him from a balcony and found her so fetching that he broke off a decoration of a nude woman from a column of some sort and presented it to her.

"Your Academy Award, madame," he said. "For being the most exciting actress present."

Mayo, a native of Portland, Oregon, had been a child actress. She was still an actress, and in many ways she was still a child. Like Bogie, she had been married twice. A year earlier she had divorced her second husband for mental cruelty, claiming that he wouldn't allow her to rearrange the furniture.

Bogie took Mayo on his powerboat at Newport Beach. This was before the *Santana*. Mayo, whose father was a ship's captain, loved the sea and that was a big point in her favor. Mayo loved to drink, another point. Bogie had fun with Mayo. Unfortunately, Mayo Methot was a raging alcoholic, and her fits of temper and violence made Bogie's occasional outbursts look kittenish by comparison. With Mayo, who has been described as a combination of Mae West and Edward G. Robinson, Bogie began a relationship that was as famous for its fury as his later relationship with my mother was for its romance.

When Mary came back from New York and found Bogie and Mayo staying at the Garden of Allah, she felt that a divorce was in order. After the divorce, Bogie was not really in a marrying mood, but, once again, he had gotten himself into a position where he felt he had an obligation. Sam Jaffe's partner, Mary Baker, said, "Bogie was trapped in a situation and didn't know how to get out of it."

It is interesting that my father, who is famous for doing

exactly what he wanted and compromising on nothing, seems to have entered with some reluctance into each of his first three marriages. With Helen he had tried to back out at first. With Mary he had had major doubts, but had been financially dependent on her. And now, with Mayo, again, he told people he wasn't at all sure that he wanted to marry her. In some ways all three of these women were the dominant person in the relationship, and even in his fourth marriage— well, it is no secret that my mother is a strong, controlling sort of woman. So Bogie, the very symbol of male independence, married women who could, at least in part, control him. A Freudian might say that he was trying to replace his domineering mother. Others would say he married women who could help his career. Nat Benchley, who gave this matter a good deal of thought, came to the conclusion that none of the handy theories fit. Not all of Bogie's wives were financially helpful. Not all of them were older than him. (My mother was twenty-five years younger.) And not all of them could help his career. (He was already a big star by the time he married Mayo and my mom.) Benchley concludes that the answer is much simpler than that. My father, Benchley says, "was a gentleman, like his father, and he felt that once he had gone a certain distance with a woman, he was obliged to marry her."

I know that that self-imposed feeling of obligation weighed heavily on my father, because I have gone through the experience, though in a slightly different way. A generation ago, Dale and I had planned to go to the great Woodstock lovefest. We couldn't make it, so we stayed home and had a lovefest of our own. The sex was, shall we say, impetuous. A few months later Dale had some interesting news to tell me.

"I'm pregnant," she said.

I was still a kid, really, and getting married was not on my list of things to do. But I knew I had an obligation, and it was one I had created long ago when I swore that no kid of mine would ever go through life without a father.

Though abortion was out of the question, Dale did not insist on wedding bells. She was not interested in acquiring a husband who didn't want to be acquired.

"I'm keeping the baby," she said. "You do whatever you really want to do."

Of course, there was never any doubt about what I wanted to do. I wanted to be a father to my kid. I asked Dale to marry me.

And in 1938, Bogie did the same thing. He asked Mayo Methot to marry him.

Shortly before their wedding Bogie said of Mayo, "One reason why we get on so well together is that we don't have illusions about each other. We know just what we're getting, so there can't be any complaints on that score after we're married. Illusions are no good in marriage. And I love a good fight. So does Mayo."

It's a good thing that Dad loved a good fight because Mayo gave him a lot more action than he ever saw when he was in the navy. He was thirty-eight when he married her and there were some who wondered if he would make it to thirty-nine.

They got married on August 21, 1938, at the home of Mary and Mel Baker in Bel Air. Bogie cried at the wedding.

"He cried at every one of his weddings," my mother says, "and with good reason."

On their wedding night Bogie and Mayo had a fight, so he went off to spend the night with Mel Baker while she spent the night with Mary. There is even a report that Bogie went off to Mexico for some male bonding.

Soon he and Mayo moved into a house on Horn Avenue near the Sunset Strip. They filled it with pets, and they fought constantly. Bogie nicknamed Mayo "Sluggy." In front of their house they had a sign that said SLUGGY HOLLOW. They also had a dog named Sluggy. And Bogie named the thirty-eight-foot cruiser that he kept in Newport *Sluggy*.

Mayo was a devoted and adoring wife when she was sober, but, like her husband, she was a prodigious drinker of scotch, and when she was drunk she could be hell on wheels. The neighbors remember the nightly shouting and the sounds of breaking glassware. The battles were strangely, or perhaps fittingly, theatrical. For example, one night the couple came out of the house drunk and Mayo had tied a rope around Bogie's neck. But it was Bogie who was shouting, "Sluggy, you miserable shrew, I'm going to hang you."

"The Bogart–Methot marriage was the sequel to the Civil War," Julius Epstein says.

An interesting turn of events for the man who once complained that he had to hide under the blankets and cover his ears to block out the sound of his parents fighting.

"The marriage was very stormy," says Gloria Stuart. "Their relationship was mutual; they hit each other. But it was really Mayo who did most of the hitting. I remember once when Mel Baker and my husband and I were at their house and Mayo threatened to shoot all of us. When she was drunk she was very combative. Sober she was fine. But I think the fighting excited them, it got them all worked up."

While friends agree that Bogart liked to needle Mayo, all agree that she was the violent one. And Mayo was also every inch the needler that Bogie was. She often referred to him as

"Mr. Bogart, the great big Warner Brothers star," and after he made the smallest remark she would say, "Quick, call the newspapers. Mr. Bogart, the great big Warner Brothers star, has spoken."

"Mayo resented Bogart's growing popularity," one friend says, "and the fact that she gave up her career to be just Mrs. Bogart. The resentment always showed."

Mayo was insanely jealous, too. Maybe drink made her jealous, or maybe jealousy made her drink. Either way, Mayo often had her claws out for Bogie's leading ladies. Being married to a top male actor would be difficult for any woman, but for Mayo it was war. So when Bogie had to take a beautiful actress in his arms you could hear Mayo's roar all the way to Fresno. Mayo was especially jealous of Ingrid Bergman when Bogie made *Casablanca*. After the film came out a reporter asked Bogie what he thought of it. "I don't know," he said. "I wasn't allowed to see it."

Dad's early movie career, of course, was not as a romantic lead or a sex symbol. A condemned murderer or gun-toting racketeer was not the kind of guy most women were looking to fall in love with. But in 1940, during this marriage to Mayo, Bogie was making a personal appearance at a New York movie house when something happened to change all that.

The show that evening opened with dozens of Bogie's movie death scenes flashing across the screen. Then, when the lights were turned up, there was Bogie lying on the stage, face down as if he had been rubbed out by gangsters. He got up slowly, grinned at his audience and said, "Boy, this is a hell of a way to make a living."

It was a magical moment. Suddenly, movie fans who had known Bogie only as a thug, saw a guy with a sense of humor, a guy who could laugh at himself, which it seems to me is a definite aphrodisiac for women. After the show there was a mob of women outside of Bogie's dressing room. Mary Baker called Warner Brothers to tell them about all the female adoration. Jack Warner was skeptical, but in time Bogie did become a rather unlikely heartthrob.

Bogie actually claimed to enjoy Mayo's jealousy.

"I like a jealous wife," he said. "I can be a jealous husband, too. Mayo's a grand girl. She knows how to handle me. When I go to a party and the party spirit gets at me I'm apt to flirt with any amusing girl I see. But I don't mean it. My wife's job, and Mayo has promised to take it on, is to yank me out of the fire before I get burned."

If Bogie looked at another woman, Mayo would hit him, punch him, or throw something at him. Once she threw him into a harbor because she thought she caught him eyeing a girl getting off a boat. One night at Peter Lorre's house she hit him over the head with a large wooden spoon for the same offense. Not all of Mayo's rages, however, were about other women.

Mayo didn't always need a reason to fight. Like so many alcoholics, she simply turned into a violent, insecure, and dangerous person when the booze kicked in. One night, for example, she actually set the house on fire. Naturally, the incident was handled discreetly by the local fire department.

And then there was the time that Bogie was sitting at home with a friend when Mayo went into a rage about something. She picked up a bottle and threw it at him. Bogie just sat still and let the bottle pass by.

He turned to his friend. "Mayo's a lousy shot," he said. "Besides, she's crazy about me. She knows I'm braver than George Raft or Edward G. Robinson."

I found out about another time when they were having Thanksgiving dinner with Raymond Massey and his wife. Bogie made some remark and Mayo hurled the turkey platter at his head. As the story is told, Bogie smiled, picked up the food, put it all back on the platter, and they all enjoyed their meal. Bogie, it seems, had a tremendous ability to remain calm during tense moments.

Mayo often became paranoid when drunk. One night she came into the living room where Bogie and some guests were talking.

"You bastards are talking about me," she said.

"No, we're not," Bogie said.

"Of course you are," she said. "Do you think I'm stupid, that I don't know when I'm being talked about?"

"Sluggy, will you sit down," Bogie said. "Nobody is talking about you."

"You *are* talking about me," she cried. "I know it."

Then she ran out of the room and dashed up the stairs to their bedroom.

A few minutes later, when the group was about to sit down to dinner, they heard a gunshot from upstairs.

"Forget it," Bogie said to his friends. "It's just Mayo shooting her gun."

Then there was another shot.

"I guess we'd better go upstairs," Bogie said. He went up. Mayo was locked in the bedroom.

"Open up, Sluggy," Bogie said.

"No," Mayo screamed.

Bogie started pounding on the door. "Sluggy, open the door or I'm going to break it down."

"Get away or I'll plug you," Mayo said.

Finally, Bogie managed to break the door and get in. He found Mayo lying on the bed, crying.

In the press they became known as "The Battling Bogarts." They were notorious for breaking crockery and glassware at a number of fine business establishments.

One typical fight occurred when they were in New York and they got an early morning phone call. Mayo answered the phone then turned to my father. "It's for you," she said, then she dropped the phone on his face.

Bogie, annoyed, smacked her.

Then both of them leaped out of bed naked and started throwing things at each other. This went on for a while, then Mayo picked up a potted plant to hurl at Bogie, but she lost her balance with it and fell on the floor. The two of them had a good laugh and went on with their lives.

Sam Jaffe says, "I remember one time they were in New York, at the Algonquin. I went to see them. Right then and there they got into an argument over Roosevelt. She threw a lamp at your father. Bogie rushed out. Later Mayo kept calling me and saying Bogie had probably been killed in traffic. When your father called me the following morning he told me he had spent the night with one of his previous wives, Helen Menken."

The battling Bogarts got into battles in nightclubs with each other, and sometimes, with the two of them on the same side, against some heckler. At one point Bogie and Mayo were barred from 21 as a couple. They could come in separately, but not together. 21, by the way, was not the only place to bar them as a couple. When they went overseas to entertain the troops they were so rowdy and fought so often that the USO made a rule, forbidding husband and wife teams to tour the army camps.

Dad told the Mayo stories with great relish. But one incident Bogie did not boast about was the night Mayo stabbed him.

Bogie came home that night from the Finlandia Baths on Sunset Boulevard. He had gone there to get away from Mayo, but she was convinced he had gone to a whorehouse. When he came into the house Mayo was humming "Embraceable You," which was always the signal that she had crossed the line from a sober Jekyll to a drunken Hyde. He could see that she had been drinking and that she had been crying. He said nothing.

But a few minutes later they had gotten themselves into a violent argument, when suddenly Mayo lunged at Bogie with a kitchen knife. Bogie ducked. He ran for the door. Mayo came after him.

"The great movie star, Humphrey Bogart, thinks Roosevelt's a grand guy, does he? Tell it to your whores," Mayo shouted.

"Cut the crap, Sluggy," he shouted back.

But when Mayo caught him she jabbed the knife into his back. Bogie, feeling faint, went to the phone. Instead of calling a doctor, he called Sam Jaffe.

"Sam, we have a problem," he said.

"What's the matter?" Sam said.

"I think you'd better come over here," he said.

"Why?"

"Mayo stabbed me."

"Jesus!"

Sam sent Mary Baker to Bogie's house. When Baker got there Mayo was hysterical.

"I didn't do anything, I didn't do anything," she was shrieking. But Bogie was on the floor, just regaining consciousness after passing out for a few minutes, and his jacket was red with blood. He explained to Baker that he and Mayo had gotten into an argument over Roosevelt, and that Mayo had stabbed him. Baker told Mayo not to pull the knife out of Bogie. Baker called the doctor. The doctor was bribed not to tell the story. Bogie was patched up and Mayo, as always, was stricken with guilt and was full of affection and kisses for her husband.

One morning after the stabbing, Dad invited Sam Jaffe over to the house.

They sat in the living room, Dad still slightly shaken by the incident. "Sam," he said, "look at the seltzer bottle there." He pointed to a glass bottle in the corner.

"What about it?" Sam asked.

"Well, she threw it at my head the other day. She missed."

"So?"

"So someday she might not miss."

"And?"

"And it might not be a bottle," Bogie said. "I think you ought to have insurance."

"Not necessary," Sam said.

"Look," Bogie said. "You've invested a lot of time and money in my career. If Mayo's aim ever improves you could lose it all. Get some insurance."

So Jaffe & Baker took out a hundred-thousand-dollar life insurance policy on my father. Fortunately, Mayo's aim never did improve.

Long before this, Mayo had been diagnosed by a psychiatrist as a paranoid schizophrenic. She had even made at least one legitimate suicide attempt, slashing her wrists. After the knife incident the psychiatrist recommended that Mayo be institutionalized. Bogie refused. He said at the time, "My wife is an actress. It just so happens that she is not working right now. But even when an actress isn't working she's got to have scenes to play. And in this case I've got to give her the cues."

There was also a night when Mayo pulled a gun on Bogie. He casually mentioned that he wanted to go off on a trip alone, and Mayo freaked out. She came after him with a gun. Dad retreated to the bathroom where he called a studio publicist for help. While the publicist drove over to the house, others in the studio gathered around the phone and listened to the drama. They heard Bogie shouting through the door, trying to calm Mayo down, but all she did was get more hysterical. At one point Mayo got so frustrated that she started shooting Dad's suitcase. This was so absurd that Bogie started laughing, and so did the studio people who listened on the other end. Though I'm sure at first my father must have been afraid that this time Mayo really would kill him, he apparently came to the conclusion that she couldn't really do it. When the publicist arrived at the house, he found Bogie relaxing in the bathtub. This incident, like many others, was covered up by the studio and never made the papers.

Growing up, I heard many of the Bogie and Mayo stories. I've heard a lot more since I began asking about my father. But something has always bothered me about all these stories. They seem almost unbelievable. There is a show business quality to them. They sound like something out of a screwball romance of the thirties—two people throwing things at each other, then laughing about it minutes later.

I can't deny that the fights actually occurred. Certainly, some of the stories have been embellished over the years, but basically they are true. Many reliable people remember these physical battles between my father and Mayo Methot. The skirmishes represent one of the more bizarre episodes in Hollywood lore. To me, what is most bizarre about the battles is not that they happened, but the spirit in which they occurred, with so much good humor. Why would two people who fought like cats and dogs stay together?

"These fights," one friend says, "were a kind of mating dance. They liked to fight because it made sex better. Their marriage was kept together because of the fighting, their fantastic physical attraction for each other, and their love of sailing."

In fact, quite a few people state with remarkable certainty that the fights made their sex hotter, though I assume this is secondhand knowledge, at best.

For me the key to understanding my father's relationship with Mayo, and, indeed, much of my father's life, is in something he said in an interview before he married her.

"We have some first-rate battles," he said. "Both of us are actors, so fights are easy to start. Actors always see the dramatic quality of a situation more easily than other people and can't resist dramatizing it for them. We both understand that one of the important things to master in marriage is the technique of a quarrel."

Later, when he was married to Mother, Dad wrote, "Each of my wives has been an actress. Betty's a good one as well as a good-looking one. I guess it would be plain hell to marry a bad actress. I never could have stood that. Of course, when an actor marries an actress, their differences usually develop into something more intense than they started out to be. You find you are playing a dramatic scene. And some of the arguments I've had in my time in married life have gone on long after either of us remembered what the tiff was about. I guess we were each thoroughly enjoying a leading role."

Certainly Mayo's jealousy and paranoia were real. Certainly the alcohol problem was real; she eventually died of alcoholism. But I think in some way the fights were also staged; Bogie and Mayo were, in part, acting out their anger and frustration. Bogie loved a good joke and he loved to dramatize. You can imagine what would happen if he married a woman who felt the same way, and when he married Mayo he did marry a woman who felt the same way. She once said of Bogie, "I married a man who conducts himself like a man. A man who doesn't only offer me security, but a certain excitement." To some extent Bogie and Mayo were putting on an elaborate show for the public. And, I think, to some extent, Bogie did that with his whole life.

One thing that always troubled me about these stories was the hitting. Did my father actually hit his wife? Did he hit women?

"No," Gloria Stuart told me, "your father did not hit people. He did not hit women. But he did hit Mayo and she hit him. She always hit him first. It was part of the relationship. In fact, I only saw your father hit her back one time."

So Bogie did not hit women. But still, it is difficult to talk today about my father and women without it seeming that he was as politically incorrect as you can get. He lived in a different world from the one I live in. He called women "girls," and it was perfectly acceptable. He said, "I have an aversion to any group of women with a purpose or a mission." He made jokes about a woman's role and that was fine.

"This was a different time with men and women," Gloria Stuart says. "This was a time when people still joked about rape. Men and women just talked differently then and nobody thought anything about it."

For example, when Dad came back from filming *The African Queen* he took a ribbing in the newspapers because a photo had been taken of my mother hanging laundry supposedly while he was snoozing on his hammock. DID BOGIE BRING BACALL TO AFRICA TO DO HIS LAUNDRY? the newspaper headline asked. Bogie denied that he had. "You think Baby would do this for me back home?" he said. "Not on your life. I take her half way around the world and suddenly she becomes the perfect housewife. In Hollywood she never once washed a handkerchief. No kidding!"

The story now seems quaint, but today it would take on an entirely different spin, and Bogie would be made out to be some sort of sexist monster.

His public interviews are peppered with comments about women that would be regarded as outrageous today, but were kind of endearing in their time. He once said, "Women have got us. We should never have set them free. They should still be in chains, and fettered to the home where they belong." And after he made his statement about not being a Communist, and being "ill-advised" about his trip to Washington, one reporter asked him if the statement also represented his wife.

"I am making the statement," he said, "but it includes her. I still believe the man wears the pants in the family and what I say goes for the whole family."

Much of how Bogie thought about women can be inferred from what he said about actresses. In 1953 he did an interview for the *London Daily Mirror* and he talked about "four real hot babes that stand way out in my twenty-five years of movie making." If he talked about hot babes today he would have to duck fast. The four were Katharine Hepburn, Bette Davis, Barbara Stanwyck, and, of course, Lauren Bacall.

"I'm not saying anything against the sweet and shapely glamor girls in the business," Bogie says. "They're okay. But for me, you act with them, then forget them. Whatever they've got is laid right out on a platter for you. Now that doesn't appeal to Bogart. For me an actress has to have unassailability. This, in plain language says, here it is, now come and fight for it. Which I reckon is a good thing for all women to have.

"Hepburn has unassailability. She is a dyed in the wool eccentric. There is nothing phony about her. She is not beautiful, more like a nylon-covered skeleton. She's no chicken any more either, but she's really fascinating with a tremendous off-beat kind of sex appeal which throws out a challenge that not any hunk of man can take up. She's shy, though. At interviews she shakes like a leaf, although she has the guts not to show it. She's got maybe half a dozen friends in Hollywood and she just circulates among them. You never see her at the nightclubs. When you spend six weeks on a boat in the jungle with a woman and all around you are down with malaria you kind of get to know her. I got to know Katie like a favorite book.

"Bette Davis is different. She's not as well-organized as Katie, mentally. She's got very definite opinions and it's sure hard to shake them. I made *Dark Victory* with Bette and although I haven't any scars from it, I'm not forgetting it either.

"I've never had any trouble with her, but it may be true some guys find her hard to get on with. The fact is she's a talented, tough, temperamental filly with a strong mind of her own. Unless you're very big she can knock you down. She's

Dad and me looking at his model of the Santana.
The Oscar sits on top of the case.
(1952) (PHOTO COPYRIGHT © 1978 SID AVERY/MPTV)

ABOVE: *Dad in his element, on the* Santana.
(1952) (PHOTO COPYRIGHT © 1978 SID AVERY/MPTV)

BELOW: *Sinatra — yachting cap and all,*
on the Santana. *(1952)* (COURTESY STEPHEN BOGART)

ABOVE: *The Mapleton Drive house.* (COURTESY STEPHEN BOGART)

BELOW: *Dad in the pool with Leslie at Mapleton Drive.* *(1954)* (COURTESY STEPHEN BOGART)

ABOVE: A stroll on Waikiki Beach.   BELOW, LEFT: We went to Hawaii during a break in the shooting of The Caine Mutiny. *(1954)   BELOW, RIGHT: "What did you say, Mom?" in Hawaii.   OPPOSITE: One more pose, then let's go in the water.*
(COURTESY DAVID FAHEY)

ABOVE: A wink and a smile—Dad on board the Santana. *(COURTESY STEPHEN BOGART)*

OPPOSITE: Dad teaching me how to ride a bike. (1955) (COURTESY STEPHEN BOGART)

BELOW: A contented man—on the Santana. *(COURTESY STEPHEN BOGART)*

*ABOVE: The mob outside the funeral at All Saints Church.
(1957) (COURTESY STEPHEN BOGART)*

*BELOW: The whole clan after Mom's marriage to Jason Robards
at Disneyland. From left: Mom, Leslie, Jason III, Dopey, Snow
White, Happy, Sarah, Jason, me. (COURTESY STEPHEN BOGART)*

RIGHT: My first wife, Dale, holding my first son, Jamie. (1971) (COURTESY ARTHUR RUBENS)

BELOW: Jamie and me in Florida. (1989) (COURTESY STEPHEN BOGART)

ABOVE: Mom and me at my wedding to Barbara. (1985) (PHOTO BY JEFF ALAN)

BELOW: My old family with my new family and some friends. From left: Mom, Sam, me, Jamie, Barbara, Jean (Barbara's mom), Donna (Barbara's sister), Melissa (another sister), and Melissa's daughter Katie. (PHOTO BY JEFF ALAN)

ABOVE: *Barbara and me.* (PHOTO BY JEFF ALAN)

*ABOVE: In Florida—Mom holding my daughter Brooke. Son
Richard seated in the background.
(1989) (COURTESY STEPHEN BOGART)*

*BELOW: Back in the northeast with Brooke and Richard.
(1993) (COURTESY STEPHEN BOGART)*

ABOVE, FROM LEFT: Me, Mom, Sam, and Leslie. (1993) (COURTESY STEPHEN BOGART)

ABOVE: Sam, Leslie and me in New York. *(1994)* *(PHOTO BY MIKKI ANSIN)*

ABOVE: Me on the Santana *with its current owner, Ted Eden, San Francisco. (1994)*

ABOVE: *Richard, Barbara, and Brooke in New Jersey.*
(1995) *(PHOTO BY KATHRYN OXBURG YEW)*

getting along a bit, so if people treat her rough she can get kind of crotchety. But she's a hell of a gal.

"When she was younger she used to be a real dish—not my type, though. I like a good figure and Bette's a wee bit too well-stacked and a shade heavy in the legs. But I'm sure fond of her. She's got a highly developed intellect and she can act the pants off most of the other ladies in the business. When you take Bette Davis you've got to take everything else that goes with it. And I guess I like all the things that go with Bette Davis.

"Barbara Stanwyck has unassailability by the truckload. She's got a wonderful figure and talent that bursts out in every scene.

"I can't stand bad actresses. When I act with them they throw me so hard I can't speak a line. But Stanwyck, that girl acts like she really means it. We made a louse of a film together called *Conflict*. It bored the pants off both of us. But Stanwyck was good. If she had an emotional scene to play, we'd all have to wait while she'd go for a little walk to work up steam. Then she'd come back all ready to emote. God help the technician who interrupted at the wrong moment. She's a fine type is Stanwyck, solid material. Her hair is going gray. She's putting on the years, but she still makes movies with a kick in them.

"As for Lauren Bacall, well sure, she's Mrs. Bogart. But she doesn't figure in my favorite foursome just because of that. She's a big beautiful baby who's going to make a big name for herself in the business. She's bright, brainy and popular with women as well as men. Look at that face of hers. There you've got the map of Middle Europe slung across those high cheekbones and wide green eyes. As an actress she hasn't got a lot of experience. It's going to take a long time to get it. But Baby is going to get there. She's not the type that hangs around being stalled by the boss's secretary. As a woman she holds all the cards. She's beautiful, a good mother, a good wife, and knows how to run a home.

"She's a honey blonde and in her high heels she comes up to the top wrinkle in my forehead. She's got a model's figure, square shoulders, and a kid's waist. Met her in the film *To Have and Have Not* then afterward we made *The Big Sleep*. After that film I said, 'That's my baby,' and I've called her Baby ever since."

I focus more and more on my mother's voice now. She is talking about him. "Your father loved the dogs," she says. Then something else. "He always wore that terry robe when he was out by the lanai." She is talking to me, but not checking to see if I am listening. She knows that when she has talked about Dad in the past I have not always listened. She moves about, reciting her memories like lines from a movie. And the words she speaks resonate with a headful of images that have been passed to me over the years from things she has said and things I have heard from friends. Mother has told me many times about her love affair with Humphrey Bogart. I vow that from now on I will listen carefully.

9

When the picture's over Bogart will forget all about you. That's the last you'll ever see of him.

—HOWARD HAWKS TO LAUREN BACALL

During the last week of 1943, director Howard Hawks took my mother, then nineteen, to the sound stage where Humphrey Bogart was shooting *Passage to Marseilles*.

At the time my mother was under personal contract to Hawks, and while he was certainly interested in finding a role for her, he made no mention of it that day. He did tell her, however, that he owned the film rights to *To Have and Have Not* written by his friend Ernest Hemingway, and that he was hoping to get Bogie for the lead.

During a break in shooting, Hawks brought Bogie over to meet Mom. "There was," she says, "no fireworks, no thunder, just a pleasant hello and how do you do." Mostly, Mom remembers being struck by the fact that Bogart was much smaller than she had expected him to be.

A few weeks later there was some Bogart excitement in my mother's life, but it was not of the romantic variety. It was career excitement. Hawks told her that she would get a screen test for a role in *To Have and Have Not*.

"And by the way," he said, "I've got Bogart."

The scene was the famous "You know how to whistle" scene, and Mother rehearsed it over and over with a well-established actor, though she was always embarrassed by the requirement that she kiss him every time she did the scene. Bogie, meanwhile, had gone off to Casablanca to entertain the troops. In any case, it would have been unusual for an actor of his stature to play in a screen test for an unknown actress like my mother, who at that time was still Betty, not yet Lauren. A few days after the screen test was shot, Bogie was back and Mom ran into him at the studio.

"I saw your test," he told her. "We'll have a lot of fun together."

Mom had the role. She was ecstatic. She was also a nervous wreck and would remain that way for the next several weeks.

"On the first day of shooting I was ready for a strait-jacket," she says. She remembers doing the "Anybody got a match?" line again and again, being all knotted up inside, trembling, perspiring. "Your father tried to joke me out of my nervousness," she said. "He was wonderful about that, trying to put other actors at ease."

Though Bogie was kind to Bacall right from the beginning, and sensitive to her youth and inexperience, he did not flirt with her. Mom was a flirt, but Bogie had a reputation as a man who never flirted with actresses in his films. So the relationship that began during the filming of *To Have and Have Not* began as a friendship, which perhaps is why it lasted. From the beginning they called each other Slim and Steve, which is what the characters in the film called each other, even though the characters' names were really Marie and Harry.

Bogie and Bacall talked nonstop, and probably it was obvious to others before it was obvious to them that something was happening between them. Mom talked about her childhood and her dreams of success in Hollywood. She adored Bette Davis, she said, and Leslie Howard, and she was thrilled to learn that Bogie actually knew them both. It must have been pretty heady stuff. Bogie gave her acting tips and he talked about his early days on the stage. He told her the twenties were "the good old days." And he talked about his marriage to Mayo. He joked about the fighting with "madame," as he called her, but Mom could see that he was lonely.

The relationship progressed in this platonic fashion until one day about three weeks into the shooting of the picture, Bogie came by Mom's dressing room to say goodnight.

"He was standing behind me," she says. "We were joking, the way we always did. Then suddenly he leaned over and he placed his hand under my chin. He lifted my face toward his and he kissed me. It was very romantic, very sweet really, and your father was quite shy about the whole thing. Then he took an old matchbook out of his pocket and asked me to write my phone number on it."

That night Bogie called Mom. He just wanted to see how she was doing, he said. They talked for hours.

After that, Mother says, things were different. They lit up when they saw each other. During breaks they gravitated toward each other, as if there were no other place to be. When Bogie played chess on the set, Mom would stand behind him and watch. Where they used to eat lunch separately—Mom from a brown bag at the studio and Dad at the Lakeside Golf Club—now they both went to Lakeside. One day gossip columnist Hedda Hopper called Mom and said, "You'd better be careful or you might have a lamp dropped on your head," a reference to Mayo's well-known penchant for throwing things. Another columnist wrote, "You can get your B&B lunch any day at Lakeside," an item which must have been of special interest to Mayo Methot.

Bogie and Bacall were suddenly giddy with romance. They acted like kids, exchanging cornball jokes like, "What did the ceiling say to the wall? Hold me up, I'm plastered."

The attraction was real. In fact, the sexual tension between my parents was so palpable that changes had to be made in the script of the movie. Originally, Bogie was supposed to have a relationship with a different woman, but no amount of acting could disguise the fact that Steve wanted Slim and Slim wanted Steve.

Years later Bette Davis commented on this chemistry: "Up until Betty Bacall I think Bogie really was embarrassed doing love scenes, and that came over as a certain reticence. With her he let go and it was great. She matched his insolence. Betty came along at exactly the right time for Bogie. He was mature and she was a kid, and I think he had a ball showing her what life was all about."

After a day's shooting they used to drive off in separate cars and then they would pull onto a small residential side street where there was no traffic. Bogie would get out of his car and climb into Mom's, where they would squeeze an extra twenty minutes out of the day, holding hands and talking love talk. Then Bogie would go back into his car and head for home and Mayo. Mom would follow in her car, and when Bogie turned off for Horn Avenue, he would wave to her, and she would wave back and continue home to Beverly Hills, where she would spend another sleepless night.

Hawks, who had a financial interest in my mother, and probably a romantic one as well, saw the romance developing. He stewed in silence over it for several weeks and then one day he blew up at Mother.

"You damn fool! Bogart's forty-five years old," Hawks said. "He's a boozer. He's married. This relationship is going nowhere. It means nothing to him. This sort of thing happens all the time, he's not serious about you. You are throwing away a chance anyone would give their right arm for. And I am not going to put up with it, I tell you." Hawks threatened to send Mom to Monogram Pictures, which in the context of the time was like telling a young *New York Times* reporter that he was being sent to the *National Enquirer.*

Mother was nearly hysterical with tears by the time Hawks finished. It's not true, she thought, it's not true. Bogie is not like that. But, still, there was a little part of her that was not so sure. Maybe she was just a Hollywood fling for him. Later, after she cried in Bogie's arms, she felt better. He assured her that he cared for her, that he would protect her, and that she was too promising a talent for Hawks to let her go.

As the days of shooting passed and Mother looked painfully forward to the day when they would no longer have this movie to throw them together every day, she couldn't eat, she couldn't sleep. All she could do was think about Bogie. At night she often spent time commiserating with her friend Carolyn Morris, who also was in love with a married man.

When the dreaded last day of filming came, Bogie and Bacall were parted. He went back to his wife, and she to a pillow to cry on. A week later my father sent his first love letter to my mother.

"I wish with all my heart that things were different," he wrote. "Someday soon they will be. And now I know what was meant by 'to say good-bye is to die a little' because when I walked away from you that last time and saw you standing there so darling, I did die a little in my heart." He signed the letter, "Steve."

It was around this time that Mom started driving down to Balboa with Carolyn Morris, to secretly visit Bogie on his coast guard weekends. Carolyn would go off somewhere, and Bogie and Bacall would sit in the car and talk and smooch. Whenever they met this way they each brought a letter, to be read after they were separated.

He wrote, "Baby, I do love you so dearly and I never, never want to hurt you or bring any unhappiness to you. I want you to have the loveliest life any mortal ever had. It's been so long, darling, since I've cared so deeply for anyone, that I just don't know what to do or say. I can only say that I've searched my heart thoroughly these past two weeks and I know that I deeply adore you and I know that I've got to have you. We just must wait because at present nothing can be done that would not bring disaster to you.

"It seems so strange that after forty-four years of knocking around I should meet you now and fall in love with you when I thought that could never again happen to me. And it's tragic that everything couldn't be all clean and just right for us instead of the way it is because we'd have so much fun together. Out of my love for you I want nothing but happiness to come to you and no hurt ever."

* * *

Howard Hawks was not the only one who was unhappy about the budding romance. My mother's mother also warned her that she was hurtling toward heartache because Bogart was an actor, thrice-married, in his forties, and, perhaps worst of all, he wasn't Jewish.

I'm sure that my mother thought her mother was being unreasonable at the time, objecting to the love of Betty's life. But the generations have an eerie way of repeating themselves and Bacall eventually became the mother who disapproved of her son's mate. Flash forward to the time when Dale was pregnant and we decided to get married. Bacall was not happy.

"Stephen, you're too young, it's too soon, you're making a terrible mistake."

"How can it be a mistake for a kid to have a father?"

"But this girl, she's not right for you."

"What's wrong with her?"

"Well, Stephen, let's be serious. Torrington, Connecticut! Is this where you see your future?"

And so forth. Mother probably said to me the same things her mother had said to her. But I was adamant. My kid would have a father.

After I married Dale, she and Mom still did not get along. I'm sure Mom resented Dale for getting pregnant and hauling her young son into a less than perfect marriage. But there was another issue. It was that my mother didn't think I was doing enough to keep the memory of my father alive. At the time Mother viewed all of what I was doing—the failing grades, the blue-collar jobs, the move to Connecticut, the marriage—as denying the existence of my father.

"Stephen, I want you to be proud of being Humphrey

Bogart's son," she would say, which I thought was code for, "Move to a real city, get a career underway, and do something with your life."

My mother has never fully understood that I was neither proud of, nor ashamed of, my father; I just didn't want to be smothered by him. All of my behavior, which she saw as destructive, was simply my trying to outrun his shadow, trying to get away so I could be myself. Mother thought my wife was holding me back in the small Connecticut town, that Dale was responsible for my not expanding, not growing. But that's how I wanted it.

Though nobody thought my marriage to Dale would last very long, including me, it endured for thirteen years. Of course, much of that was the open marriage phase, but still the marriage lasted longer than any of my father's.

I don't know if marriage was on my mother's mind when she met Bogie, but certainly she was in love. Ever since her father had left her when she was a kid, she had keenly felt the need to love a man, and in Bogart she had found that man.

Mother hated the sneaking around. Not only was she consumed with guilt, but she had to worry about Mayo's temper. One time Mother went to visit Bogie on a friend's boat, and she had to hide in the head when Mayo showed up.

While Hawks, my grandmother, and others were against a Bogart–Bacall wedding, the public was all for it. Though word of the romance got into the papers, Bacall never had to take flack as "the other woman" or "home wrecker." The public loved her and they knew what a looney tunes Mayo was.

On May 10, 1945, Bogie and Mayo divorced. Though Dad was anxious to marry Mom, he had put off the final break with Mayo several times out of fear that she would shoot him, Bacall, herself, or possibly all three. But there was more to it than that. As anyone who has ever been divorced knows, the years of shared experience exert a powerful influence, and leaving is rarely easy. Bogie and Mayo had once been deeply in love. They'd had many great times together and, when she was not drinking, Mayo could be a sweet and dear woman. Despite her jealousy, she was on the whole very supportive of Bogie's career. It was Mayo who got Morgan Maree to be Bogie's business manager. And when Bogie's mother, Maud, became ill with cancer, Mayo welcomed her and treated her kindly until the end came. And when Maud died, at seventy-five, Mayo made all the funeral arrangements. My father was grateful for these things, despite all the savagery in the relationship.

There is, perhaps, one other reason why my father found it so difficult to leave his mentally ill wife. There was another woman in his life who was mentally ill. His sister, Frances, known as Pat, had been in and out of treatment for years. In 1930, Pat had gone through twenty-seven hours of torturous labor before delivering a baby girl, Patricia. The ordeal left her permanently unbalanced. She became manic depressive and had to be hospitalized off and on. In 1935, Maud insisted Pat divorce Stuart Rose, to free him from the burden of being married to her. Then she was transferred to a west coast hospital and my father took over her care. Because of her condition, she was rarely able to see her daughter, but they did correspond. And from time to time, Pat was able to visit her brother, the movie star.

"She was a tall, strongly built woman, easy to visualize on a horse," my mother recalls. "She looked a lot like your father. She was shy and sweet and totally normal when I saw her. Your father was very gentle with her and she adored him."

If the problem of Mayo and Pat accounted for some of

the sadness my mother detected in Bogie's eyes, it explained, too, why he was so overjoyed to have a beautiful young woman, sane and sober, who loved him so. Eleven days after the divorce from Mayo, Bogie and Bacall were married on Louis Bromfield's Malabar Farm in Ohio. Bromfield, who went back a few decades with my dad, was a well-respected novelist who had fallen in love with the soil and become a farmer. His politics were very different from Dad's. He was a Republican, but the two men had great respect for each other's intellect.

The wedding had the potential to become the media circus of its time, with reporters and photographers from all over the world surrounding the house. Despite police guards a few managed to sneak into the house. Mother was a wreck throughout, and she kept running to the bathroom.

Mom writes, "My knees shook so, I was sure I'd fall down the stairs. Bogie standing there looking so vulnerable and so handsome—like a juvenile. Mother as nervous as I, trying to keep her eyes from spilling over, a smile on that sweet face. My knees were knocking together, my cheek was twitching—would any sound come out when I had to say 'I do'? We turned the corner. When I reached Bogie he took my hand—the enormous beautiful white orchids I was holding were shaking themselves to pieces; as I stood there, there wasn't a particle of me that wasn't moving visibly. The judge was speaking—addressing me—and I heard a voice I'd never heard before say those two simple words of total commitment. Bogie slipped the ring on my finger—it jammed before it reached the knuckle, the trembling didn't help, and then it finally reached its destination. As I glanced at Bogie, I saw tears streaming down his face—his 'I do' was strong and clear, though. As Judge Shettler said, 'I now pronounce you man and wife,' Bogie and I turned toward each other—he leaned to kiss me—I shyly turned my cheek—all those eyes watching made me very self-conscious. He said, 'Hello, Baby.' I hugged him and was reported to have said, 'Oh, goody.' Hard to believe, but maybe I did."

The days that followed were no less romantic than the days that preceded. Mother, who was no cook, vowed to learn all the requisite skills of a housewife in those days, even though Bogie, set in his ways, planned to keep his cook, May, and his gardener, Aurelio.

They lived first at the Garden of Allah, the friendly cluster of bungalows where Bogie had many friends and drinking companions. "It was a great place to be a bachelor," my mother says. But Bogie was not a bachelor, and already Mother was looking forward to the day when they would live in a house suitable for raising children. Still, the social life at the Garden of Allah was exciting. Bogie's friends there were fascinating people with keen minds and sharp tongues, most of them writers, all of them drinkers.

Bogie wasted no time getting Mom into the sailing fraternity, or tried to. He introduced her to his Newport Beach boat friends, all of whom were in businesses other than show business, and most of whom thought actors were strange, save for their friend Bogie.

"Your father took me to Catalina on his boat when we were first married," Mother says. "This was before he bought *Santana* from Dick Powell. He was so excited. It was important to him that I love the sea as much as he did. He showed me how to steer the boat and I made lunch in the galley. When the boat started to sway I thought, Oh my God, I'm going to be sick. I felt nauseous. I wanted to hide this from your father more than anything because I knew what sailing meant to him. After a while I felt better and we ate lunch, which was a mistake. Again I felt nauseous. Finally, your father caught on and he told me to stare at the horizon, that would settle me down. It seemed to work. We went to Catalina many times after that and I loved the island, but I never really cared for the getting to it."

The relationship that developed during the early days of my parents' marriage has often been compared to that of Nick and Nora Charles in the *Thin Man* movies. It was lively, it was romantic, it was witty and loving. It was a verbal tennis match in which Bogie usually won the point but Bacall somehow ended up winning the set.

He said things like: "I should have remained a bachelor. I never learn. You think it's going to be all right, that you've learned all the tricks. You've learned that you must put away that bath towel and not leave bristles in the basin after you've shaved. And then the next time it's something different. You have a cupboard for drinks and you want the glasses arranged so you can get at them, and you find your wife likes them fixed in neat pyramids, and you're wrong again."

She said things like: "Bogie does nothing around the house, but nothing. He is not a house man. He wants everything to be just so, but he doesn't build barbecues or stone walls and he has no recipes for spaghetti." During the four years of their marriage before I was born, Mom was certainly free to pursue her career. Dad had decided that he would not interfere, but he also would make no heroic efforts to help. That is, he would not insist that Bacall be used in any of his films. To Mother, however, it seemed that people forgot she was an actress. They saw her now as Mrs. Humphrey Bogart.

Critically, she went through the wringer. After *To Have*

and Have Not came out, my mother was the hottest thing going. The critics compared her favorably to every big name actress of the day. They predicted great things for her. Next she appeared in *Confidential Agent* ridiculously miscast in the role of an Englishwoman, and the critics savaged her. They had been wrong, they said. Bacall, they said, had no future. But when *The Big Sleep* came out they announced that they had been right all along, that Bacall was a great emerging talent with a huge future. She must have had her own big sleep through *Confidential Agent* they said, cleverly, when in fact Mom had actually made *The Big Sleep* with Dad first.

It was after Bogie and Bacall made their third movie together, *Dark Passage*, that Mother talked Dad into buying the house in Benedict Canyon, where I would be conceived. Benedict Canyon was not developed yet, and this was a real farmhouse which was owned by the actress Hedy Lamarr. It had eight rooms all on one floor, a pool, and a yard for ducks and chickens.

Along with the feathered pets at Benedict Canyon, my parents had a few four-legged ones. Louis Bromfield had given them a boxer as a wedding present. Bogie named the dog Harvey, after the invisible rabbit in the James Stewart movie of the same name because, Bogie said, "Harvey's the invisible hound. He's never around when you want him." Later my parents got a mate for Harvey and called her Baby. (In fact, Harvey had been one of Dad's pet names for my mother when they first started seeing each other and she was supposed to be "invisible.") When Harvey and Baby had pups, they kept one and named him George.

Oscar Levant said that whenever he visited my parents at the Benedict Canyon house the biggest hazard, aside from my father, was the two large boxer dogs. He says the dogs would snooze all through the evening in the middle of the living room and everybody had to talk loud because the dogs would snore. However, the dogs apparently had another habit more troubling than snoring, because Levant recalls everyone lighting wooden matches to get rid of the smell.

My father was devoted to the dogs. Benedict Canyon was still very rural then, and one night he found that Baby had been bitten by a rattlesnake. He stomped the snake to death, then took Baby to the hospital. When he came back he found that Harvey was being harassed by a wildcat, which Bogie chased off with a rifle. The paper heard about the incidents and portrayed Dad as a hero, standing up for his pets.

I was just a baby at Benedict Canyon, so my memories of the dogs don't show up until after we moved to Mapleton Drive. One incident gives you an idea of what a dog lover Bogie was.

The dogs often barked late at night and after a while a few neighbors, including Art Linkletter, signed a petition to have the dogs muzzled.

When my father was told about one of the men who complained about the dogs barking, he said, "The son of a bitch doesn't like dogs? What kind of monster is he? He ought to be glad he can hear the wonderful sound of dogs barking."

Some time later, after this dog thing had blown over, the same man was circulating a harmless petition concerning changes he wanted to make on his property. Dad was talking on the phone with Sammy Cahn, who just happened to mention that he had signed the man's petition.

"What?" Bogie said. "You signed it?"

"Sure," Sammy said. "What do I care?"

"How could you sign anything for that goddamned dog-hater?" Bogie asked.

After Bogie hung up he mulled it over for a long time. He couldn't stand the thought of his friends helping a man who had criticized his dogs. Finally, he called back.

"Sammy," he said. "That petition for the dog-hater. Did anybody actually see you sign it?"

"Well, no," Cahn told him.

"Then it's not legal," Dad said, and he hung up.

The same year that Bogie bought the house in Benedict Canyon for his true love, he also bought his other true love, the *Santana*.

"The boat was owned by Dick Powell and June Allyson," Mom says, "but Dick was having sinus trouble and he had to stay in dry climates. So he had to sell the boat, which was agony for him, because he was in love with the sea as much as your father was. So we went sailing with Dick and June. Bogie, of course, fell madly in love with the *Santana*. After he bought that boat Bogie had everything he had ever wanted."

So it seems that from the moment he met Bacall my father's life was just one headlong rush to pure happiness, with no bumps along the way, save for splitting from Mayo. And maybe that's how it was.

But, as with so much of my father's life, there is another version of the story.

Vera Thompson, a hairdresser and toupee expert, says that she had an affair with my father that began when he was still married to Mayo Methot, and continued long after he married my mother.

Vera says she met Bogie at a wrap party and later that night they went out dancing and drinking. Bogie, she says, called her the next day for lunch.

"Then," she says, "he surprised me. He said, 'I'll go back over to the set and see if they're going to need me. I'll play sick or something and meet you at your place in about an hour. Is that okay with you?' "

Vera was surprised, not just because Bogie was married to Mayo at the time, but because Vera, herself, also was married. She said yes.

She says that the affair ended when Bogie got involved with my mother, but that three months after his marriage to Bacall, they resumed their affair. She signed on as his hairstylist she says, and they began meeting secretly at her house, on his boat, and at the Beverly Hills Hotel. She says that she thought my parents would get divorced, at least up until the time I was born, and then she gave up hope of that. In 1982 she put all of this stuff in a book called *Bogie and Me*.

Is any of this true? Is all of it true? I don't know, and I really don't spend much time worrying about it. However, it seems to me that my father was probably a lot hornier than he is generally given credit for. I don't think that my father fooled with other women after he married my mother. It's not, of course, that Dad was a saint. But it seems to me that he liked too many other things for him to take the time and energy to be sneaking around with another woman. He was, as I've said, a man's man—a drinker and sailor and poker player—not a lover. Also, he was one of the greatest stars of his day and I don't think Thompson would be his first choice out of all the ladies who would have been available to him if he had been interested in a dalliance. But, unfortunately, we live in a time when a lot of people are "remembering" that they had an affair with some celebrity who is dead and can't deny it.

On the other hand, I can't say for certain that it never happened.

I have learned that there was an impenetrable part of my father, that he did not reveal every part of himself to anybody, including Bacall. We tend to paint legends in absolutes: "Bogie always told the truth." "Bogie had an unshakeable moral code." And so forth. But legends start out as human beings, and human beings are never consistent. *Nobody* always tells the truth.

Bogie, for example, put out a lot of phony stories when he first got to Hollywood. One was that he owned a train station in France. Another was that he went to jail to prepare for his role in *The Petrified Forest*. And nobody, as far as I can see, has an unshakeable moral code. So did Bogie screw around on Bacall? I doubt it. But if he did, it is not the smoking pistol that proves he was imperfect. He was, like the rest of us, imperfect to begin with.

Horny or not, unfaithful or not, I do believe that my father was a romantic and a man deeply committed to the idea of love.

"I believe in the institution of marriage," he said. "The institution is right, it's the human beings who are wrong. I believe in love, but not the 'one love of a lifetime' as pretty a tale as that always makes. There couldn't be just one love. Among fifty million people that would be pretty hard to find."

"Love is very warming, heartening, enjoyable," he said, "a necessary exercise for the heart and soul and intelligence. If you're not in love, you dry up. After all, the best proof a man can give of his belief in love and marriage is to marry more than once. If you're not married or in love you're on the loose and that's not comfortable. Love is comforting, too.

It is the one emotion which can relieve, as much as is ever possible, the awful, essential loneliness of us all."

These are feelings I share with my father. He spoke these words before he met Bacall, so maybe he did find that one love of a lifetime. Everybody seems to agree that they adored each other. I know that I have my own love of a lifetime in Barbara. And I know that, perhaps because of my childhood, I have always put that first. And that is something I have never regretted.

"Perhaps we should look at the bedroom," my mother says. I am alarmed. I thought I would avoid it.

"I thought you did," I said. "When we were upstairs."

"No," Mother says. She stares off into space. "I didn't go in there."

We move across the dining room. Toward the stairs. I am aware of an airplane somewhere off in the distance. I'll be flying home to Barbara and the kids soon, I think.

The sound of the airplane brings another memory. It is not really a memory of an event. It is the memory of how I saw the event in my mind when I was old enough to know about it.

It is March 12, 1951. I am two years old. My father has been signed to star with Katharine Hepburn in The African Queen *under the direction of his friend John Huston. My father is anxious to work with Huston again, because, he says, "John is my friend and he makes good movies."*

Both Bogie and my mother are going to Africa. They will be gone for four months, one sixth of my entire life at the time.

While my parents are on the dark continent I am to remain in the care of my nurse, Mrs. Hartley, a florid, full-bodied woman who holds me tightly in her arms on the tarmac as I watch my mother and father climb into some mysterious huge metal machine. It is, she says, a big silver bird. Coaxed by Mrs. Hartley, I wave my small hand at Mommy and Daddy one last time. The airplane rolls down

*the runway. God knows what anxiety I am feeling as I
watch the big silver bird fly into the sky with my parents
and zoom off away from me. I cling to Mrs. Hartley. I
don't understand why Mommy and Daddy are gone, but
at least I have my nurse. And in that moment, while she
is holding me, while my parents are disappearing beyond
the horizon of the nighttime California sky, Mrs. Hartley is
seized with a cerebral hemorrhage and falls dead.*

10

You suddenly say to yourself, "Where the hell am I going—what am I doing?" Then, of course, you know what you're doing—you're going with your husband who believes in no separations in marriage, who is working. Your life with him cannot stop for your son.

—LAUREN BACALL

Of course, I don't consciously remember the airport death of Mrs. Hartley. I was two years old. But I have the story from no less a source than Hollywood columnist Louella Parsons, published in the next day's *Los Angeles Examiner.*

Little Stephen Bogart, two-year-old son of Lauren Bacall and Humphrey Bogart, barely escaped injury when his nurse, Mrs. Alyce Louise Hartley, who was

holding him in her arms, suffered a cerebral hemorrhage and died almost instantly.

Fortunately, Carolyn Morris's mother, who was
also at the airport, rushed to take the boy from the
stricken nurse's arms, thus preventing Stephen from
being dropped.

That's what happened, and while I don't remember it, I
think it's fair to say that I was terrified by the event. However,
Mrs. Hartley's death is not the worst of it. What happened
next is something that I've thought about all of my life.

My mother did not come back.

My father, of course, *had* to go to Africa. He was an actor.
This was how he made his living. This was a chance to work
with Hepburn and Huston. But my mother was not in the
movie. She didn't *have* to go.

In her book, *By Myself,* Mother writes with some candor
(though a noticeable retreat into the second person) about
leaving me. She writes, "I have a pain in my solar plexus
when I remember how it felt to leave Steve behind. . . . Your
life with [your husband] cannot stop for your son. And—
admit it—you want to see these unseen places. So the brain
whirs—the heart tugs—the gut aches. I must have turned
around a hundred times to look at Steve and wave and throw
kisses and get teary-eyed."

My parents were on a stopover in Chicago when they got
the news about Mrs. Hartley.

"I agonized about coming back," Mother says, "I knew
you were being taken care of by my mother, but I wondered
if maybe I should have come back. I talked to your doctor,
Dr. Spivak, many times on the phone. He told me not to
worry, that he would interview nurses and find one who was

acceptable. In the meantime my mother was there with you. By the time the plane landed in New York, Dr. Spivak had found a nurse. I interviewed her for a long time from a phone booth in 21. I talked to the servants and they promised to report to me. I tried to talk to you, Stephen, but you refused to speak to me. I talked to the doctor again. He told me you would be fine. There was never any issue of your physical needs being taken care of."

This is true. But it's the emotional needs that I have always wondered about. There are people who would say that a two-year-old boy needs his mother when his father has gone away and his nurse has just dropped dead while holding him.

On the other hand, a defense could be made of my mother's decision. I have made it many times. I did, after all, have a safe and beautiful house. I had servants to feed me. I had the new nurse to dress me and take my temperature if I got sick. I had my grandmother to look after me. I wasn't exactly being left in a basket in the woods.

And frankly, my mother was under great pressure to stay with Bogie. She was incredibly devoted to him, and wanted to be with him. And Bogie was a man who believed that a woman's place was with her husband. Because he was twenty-five years older than Bacall, I can imagine that he must have felt that each moment with her was particularly precious. Even if they both lived to the same age, there would still be twenty-five years that he would never share with her. He certainly didn't want to be robbed of four months every time he had to shoot on location. I can understand that; I hate to be separated from my wife even for four days.

So I know that I would have handled it differently if it were me and my kids. I would have come back. But each of us does what he or she feels is right, and that's what my mother did in 1951.

What I did in 1951 and for most of my life was to feel angry and resentful about it. It has always been an issue between Mother and me. I'm sure a good therapist would tell me it's not so simple:

"Steve, you've got to understand that your feelings of being abandoned are not just about your parents going to Africa. They are about your father dying, and your sense of identity being stolen by people who think of you only as 'Bogart's son,' " and so on and so on and blah blah blah.

Probably true. But I do my own therapy. Half the time I say, "Steve, your feelings are justified," and the other half I say, "Get past it Steve, it was forty-three years ago." I believe that I am now past it.

But, because this episode has loomed so large in my life, I knew when I began asking about my father that I wanted to learn what those four months were like for my father and my mother. To find out, I talked to my mother and her friends and people who knew my father. But, mostly I talked to Katharine Hepburn.

I've known Kate Hepburn all of my life, because she has been a good friend to my mother ever since those *African Queen* days. I remember being a boy of six and going to her house for the first time. It was high on a hill in Beverly Hills, California. In my mind, that house is like a castle, kind of spooky and mysterious. Spencer Tracy was there, too, and I've always regretted that I never really got to know him.

It was during the filming of *The African Queen* that Kate and my father developed their enormous affection and respect for one another.

"I loved him and he loved me," Kate says. "He was a real

man, your father, there was nothing about him that wasn't manly. He was an aristocrat, and he was a gentleman. He was very proud to be an actor and that is rare. Your father was an angel, a true angel."

My father admired Kate, too, but typical of him, he expressed his affection in less direct ways. When he and Huston first went to see her, Kate made some comment about plain women knowing more about men than beautiful women. Dad later remarked to Huston, "She's a crow, so she should know." But after filming *The African Queen,* he told the press, "I found no one is sexier than Kate, especially before a movie camera, and she has legs like Dietrich. You learn to brand as rank slander the crack that you can throw a hat at Katie and it'll hang wherever it hits."

The African Queen, a book by C. S. Forester, is the story of Charlie Allnut, a gin-swilling Cockney ne'er-do-well riverboat captain, and Rosie Sayer, a skinny, hymn-singing missionary. An odd couple if ever there was one. There had once been a plan to star Charles Laughton and Elsa Lanchester in a film version of the story. Still later, it was to be John Mills and Bette Davis. By 1951, producer Sam Spiegel wanted Bogart and Hepburn.

It was a movie, my father says, "about a woman who starts out to become a missionary but after spending some time in a small boat with me winds up being a woman."

Though my father had known Spencer Tracy well for years, he had known Hepburn only casually. By the time he and John Huston drove to that California house, to lobby Kate for the part of Rosie, Bogie had heard terrible things about her and he went, he said, "entertaining righteous skepticism." Bogie had heard that Kate drove hard Yankee bargains with producers, that Hollywood was only a necessary evil to her, that she didn't sign autographs and, most shocking, that she didn't drink.

"Your father was a bit nervous about me," Kate says. "He thought I was an ogre."

Hepburn, likewise, was fearful of Bogie and Huston because she had heard that they were reprobates. After she lectured them on the evils of drink, Bogie said to her, "You're absolutely right, Kate. Now pull up a chair and have a drink with us."

Kate, who was forty-two at the time and still quite glamorous, was being asked by Huston to do something daring: play a woman of fifty-five.

"Rosie was haggard," Kate says. "She was worn out. She was being dragged through the muck of Africa. This was not a glamorous role. I loved it."

My father loved Forester's story, too, and he saw it as a change. "We all believed in the honesty and charm of the story," he said. "And I wanted to get out of the trench coat I wear in the movies whether I'm devil or a saint." Bogie, who usually avoided sentiment, was sentimental about *The African Queen.* "We loved those two silly people on that boat," he says.

Actually, according to John Huston, my father was not crazy about Charlie Allnut to begin with.

"Bogie did not like the role at first," Huston said. "But all at once he got under the skin of that wretched, sleazy, absurd, brave little man and would say to me, 'John, don't let me lose it. Watch me. Don't let me lose it.' "

After they all met, it was agreed that Kate would play Rosie and that my father would play Charlie Allnut, except that Allnut was changed to a Canadian to accommodate Bogie's accent. So all the adults were off to Africa.

Well, not exactly. After my parents left me and the late Mrs. Hartley at the airport they did not go straight to Africa. In New York they boarded the cruise ship *Liberté* and sailed to England. When they got to London they learned that some of Spiegel's backers had jumped overboard and the money to make *The African Queen* wasn't there. Financial decisions were made hurriedly. One was that my father would put up some of his own money to make the film. Another was that Bogie, Hepburn, and Huston would defer their salaries until there was money coming in.

"I did insist on having my hotel room in London paid for," Kate says. "I didn't mind doing the film for nothing, but I certainly wasn't going to pay for the privilege."

In Europe they drove through the French countryside, having a fine time while I was sulking in Holmby Hills. They stopped at roadside cafés. In Paris they visited the Eiffel Tower, the Arc de Triomphe, and they ate dinner on the Seine with Art Buchwald and Frank Capra. They stayed at the Ritz, and they ate, my mother says, "incredible French breads." My mother fell in love with Paris for life. But it was Italy that my father loved most, and he would later make two movies there.

My father liked to pick up a pen from time to time, and of his European adventure, he later wrote, "Like most Americans I have my greatest linguistic difficulties in France. My theory is that Parisians understand my Phillips Andover French and pretend not to. On the other hand, Italians pretend, out of natural politeness, to understand my experiments with their language when actually they don't. Either way I am in trouble."

Perhaps it was best that my parents had these idyllic days on the Continent. Because typical of Huston, whom my father referred to as "The Monster," *The African Queen* was to be shot in the most remote jungles of the Belgian Congo (now Zaire) and Uganda. Generally, my father didn't care for location shooting. He preferred the comfort of a studio. But he knew that when you made a film with Huston you had to be prepared to relocate in jungles and on mountains.

Bogie had already gone on tough locations with Huston. They had gone to a remote village in Mexico to make *The Treasure of the Sierra Madre.* "John wanted everything perfect," Bogie said of that excursion. "If he saw a nearby mountain that could serve for photographic purposes, that mountain was no good. Too easy to reach. If we could get to a location site without fording a couple of streams and walking through snake-infested areas in the scorching sun, then it wasn't quite right."

The filming in Africa was, by all accounts, a nightmare.

"We lived in bamboo bungalows," Kate says. "Half the time we didn't know what we were eating, and we didn't want to know. I found a snake in my toilet."

Personality conflicts among the major players were relatively minor. My mother and Kate got along nicely. However, early in the adventure Kate did seem a bit too haughty for Dad. "There we are a million miles from nowhere sleeping in bamboo huts and she wants a dressing room with ankle deep rugs and a star on the door," he said later, with affection. But at the time what he said to Kate was, "Kate, you ugly, skinny old bag of bones, why don't you come down to Earth?"

Kate's reply was, "Down where you're crawling? All right!" Perhaps that was the beginning of their beautiful friendship.

Bogie and Huston, of course, were already friends. And

Kate got along well enough with Huston, even though she did see in him a sadistic streak, an unfortunate Huston quality that others have also noted. I remember John Huston best for his kindness to me when I was a child. He was a fascinating and complex man and you can get one very compelling view of him in the novel *White Hunter, Dark Heart,* written by Peter Viertel. Viertel was the screenwriter on *The African Queen* and his novel, about Huston in Africa, was later turned into a movie with Clint Eastwood in the Huston role.

Though I had always imagined that my parents were off in some exotic world enjoying a glamorous vacation, I have since learned that the cast and the English crew of *The African Queen* were visited by plagues of biblical proportions. The first of these was bad drinking water. Everyone except Bogie and Bacall got dysentery. My mother, apparently, was just lucky. My father was saved because he drank no water, only scotch.

"His strength was scotch," Huston says. "I think all of us were ill in some way or another, but not Bogie."

"I was sick with dysentery," Kate says, "because I drank water all the time, hoping to shame Huston and your father out of drinking liquor. Well, the water was full of germs. I got the trots so bad I thought I would die."

Dysentery, however, was mild compared to some of the other diseases that threatened the crew. For example, much of the filming was to be done on or near the Lualaba River in Pontheirville in the Belgian Congo. Huston loved the river because it appeared to be black, due to the tannic acid from the surrounding vegetation. However, human waste had infested the Lualaba with parasitic bacteria that could cause incurable blood disease. There was one affliction, apparently common in the area, that caused worms to grow under the skin. When my father learned about this, and the fact that the river was well populated with crocodiles, he thought it might be best if the scenes of him and Kate submerged in the Lualaba were shot not on location, but later at the studio in England.

Also, it rained often, shutting down the shooting. When that happened, Huston, who fancied himself a great white hunter, went off to stalk elephants. My father, who did not like the idea of killing animals, stayed at the camp. There he drank scotch, told stories, slept in a hammock on a river raft, and read the many books he had brought with him.

The rain, unfortunately, did bring on some of those minor personality conflicts. Kate, for example, thought Huston was a murderer for going hunting, though she took comfort in her belief that Huston "could not hit an elephant with a bean shooter."

My father also was annoyed when Huston went hunting. Dad thought the director ought to pay more attention to the movie even if rain had shut down the actual filming. It wasn't just that Bogart wanted to get back to his comfortable air-conditioned house in California. It was also that in the movie industry, more than most, time is money and in this case a lot of the money being lost was his. Huston, on the other hand, was never anxious to leave exotic locations. He seemed to thrive in swamps and deserts.

In addition to rain and disease, there were bugs. "Bugs were everywhere, especially on the personnel," Bogie said. After the first two-day rainstorm, which occurred almost as soon as they arrived, mosquitoes hatched by the millions and they seemed to have no trouble working their way through the netting around the beds. Kate says everyone was soon itching and scratching and covered with red welts.

Except for my father, of course. He claimed that when the mosquitoes bit him they either died or got drunk. "I built a solid wall of scotch between me and the bugs," he said. Later, an army of man-eating red ants invaded, driving the filmmakers out of their campsite, to another site outside of Entebbe in Uganda. There it rained more and several members of the crew got malaria. Oh yes, they were having a grand time.

There's more. There were also problems with the Ugandans. When it came time to burn an entire village, which the crew had built for the scene, Huston worked a deal with a local chief to populate the film village with natives. On the day of the scheduled shooting, the hired natives didn't show up. It turned out that cannibalism was still common in the area, and the natives were afraid that Huston was setting a trap to capture them and eat them. (If this sounds crazy to us, you can imagine how crazy they thought Huston and these other white people were, building an entire village and then burning it to the ground.) There were natives working with the film crew, too, and at one point they went on strike for higher wages.

The centerpiece of the filming was a bizarre caravan of four rafts, all tied together. The first was a replica of *The African Queen,* Charlie Allnut's boat. Most of the shooting was done there. The second raft carried the lights and props. The third raft carried the generator to power it all. And the fourth raft carried Kate's dressing room, including a privy and full-length mirror. After a few days Kate's raft had to be cut loose; the boat was towing too much. At one point *The African Queen* sprung a leak and sank. It took five days to raise it by hand. "The natives were supposed to be watching it," Bogie said. "They did. They watched it sink."

Even though my father didn't get sick in Africa, he nevertheless griped constantly about the heat, the dampness, the stink, and all the crawling things. So, while I was at home alone, he and Bacall were not having such a great time. Kate, however, didn't gripe, and Bogie marveled at how Kate, who was ill and exhausted almost all of the time, handled herself through the ordeal. Often he was heard to shout, "Damn Hepburn, damn her, she is so goddamned cheerful."

"Huston and I drank," he said. "But what is good for me and John Huston has got to be bad for the rest of society. Katharine Hepburn didn't drink, and breezed through her stay as if it were a weekend in Connecticut. She pounces on flora and fauna with a home movie camera like a kid going to his first Christmas party. About every other minute she wrings her hands in ecstasy and says, 'What divine natives, what divine morning glories.' Brother, your brow goes up."

A few years after the filming of *The African Queen*, my father wrote slightly more seriously in *The American Weekly* about one incident with Hepburn. He described going into the jungle with John Huston to find the caravan of trucks that was carrying cameras, lights, and sound equipment. When they found the trucks, which were being driven by local natives, some of the vehicles were stalled on the road. Others were overturned, and the drivers had taken the calamity as an opportunity to chat with people in a nearby village.

"The block and tackle is as mysterious to a native as the workings of the atom bomb is to me," Bogie said.

Seeing there was no way to hurry the natives, Huston and Bogie decided to scout for locations in the jungle.

"Katie could have remained behind," he wrote, "but she

preferred to march through the jungle with us, as John and I knew she would."

Bogie was sitting in a small jungle clearing with Kate and John Huston, when a huge wild boar showed up with his family. "It was a gruesome creature," Bogie said, "big as a large sheep dog with vicious tusks springing from both sides of its mouth.

"Fortunately, we had a downwind, or the creature would have smelled us and charged. I froze. So did Huston. But not Katie. Before we could stop her she had stepped into the clearing, with her sixteen-millimeter camera to her eyes. Huston and I dared not yell to Katie to come back for fear the boar would charge, nor could we move for fear of panicking him and we could not shoot since Katie was between us and the boar.

"As she walked slowly toward the thing, with the camera finder to her eye, it stared straight at her. I was frozen but fascinated, and in those horrendous moments of waiting that seemed like hours I learned something rare and wonderful about Katie.

"I thought, there's a fearless woman. I also sensed that Katie, who is a remarkable woman, could not believe that an animal would hurt her. She is not stupid but I suddenly knew that she felt if she wanted the boar's photograph, he could not possibly object. Approaching him fearlessly, as she did, she communicated no fear to him. Huston and I were the ones who were afraid, but in a desperate situation, I'll take Katie before Huston—or myself—any time."

Maybe. But in one desperate situation it was Bogie who had a moment of bravery. My parents and Peter Viertel were going for a ride down the river in a small gasoline-driven boat. Their boatman, however, had trouble getting the engine started, and he flooded it. When he went down to look at it with a lighted match, the whole damn thing blew up. When the boatman came running up to the deck he was on fire and he quickly put himself in the water. Meanwhile, the boat was in danger of burning. It was Bogie who threw a line to another boat that was tied up and somehow he got buckets of sand, then went below deck and put out the fire. It could have been a real disaster.

The filming in Africa came to an appropriately dramatic close. When the schedule called for two more days of shooting, Huston announced that he needed three days, which raised havoc with airline schedules and inland transportation. Bogie was mad as hell and he thought Huston and Hepburn were in cahoots to keep him in Africa forever. Huston, however, got his way. Equipment was moved out gradually so that on the last day nothing was left but Bogie, Hepburn, Huston, and the camera. My mother and my father went to London together, where they were to meet me at the airport.

"Your plane arrived around noon and I was a nervous wreck," my mother says. "The door opened and there you were. Immediately you made this face that you always made and you came running down the gangway, smiling, and I was so happy to hold you again. I missed you terribly in Africa. Your father was very emotional, too, at seeing you again. You just kept talking and talking, chattering a mile a minute. We had never heard you talk so much before. I was really happy that the Africa adventure was over and we were all back together as a family."

The Africa adventure, of course, was not over for me. For decades I would carry around the belief that I had been abandoned by my mother. Sometimes when I watch my home movies of Mom and Dad and Kate working and playing in Africa, I can't help thinking that most parents of a two-year-old, especially their first, don't want to miss a day with the child because he is learning to talk better each day and he is constantly making new discoveries. I know that's how I felt about my kids. It makes it harder to understand.

The months that my parents were in Africa were, undoubtedly, a formative time for me. It was also a time of passages for others. It was in Africa that Kate found out that her good friend Fanny Brice had died. It was there that my father learned that Mayo Methot had died. And it was in Africa that John Huston learned that his wife had given birth to a baby girl. They named her Anjelica and today, of course, she is one of our top screen actresses. (I finally met Anjelica Huston a few years ago. Her first words to me were, "It's about time we met.")

Some wonderful things came out of that African adventure. One was my parents' friendship with Kate Hepburn. Another was that the work those people did in the jungle produced a great film. And a third was that later that year my father was nominated for an Academy Award as Best Actor.

My father certainly did not expect to win the Oscar. He thought it would go to Marlon Brando, who was up for *A Streetcar Named Desire*. Bogie admired Brando immensely, even if Brando was a method actor. He considered him to be the best of the new actors. Bogie also thought that Montgomery Clift had a decent shot for *A Place In the Sun.*

Also, my father was embarrassed by the whole thing. He had, after all, derided the Oscars, saying that the only way a Best Actor award would make sense would be if each actor donned black tights and recited Hamlet. Years earlier he had ridiculed the Oscars by concocting the idea of giving Academy Awards to animals. The first year he gave the award to Skippy, the dog in *The Awful Truth*. The following year he gave the Oscar to a water buffalo in *The Good Earth*. Though he intended all this as a joke, the animal award later became real in the form of the Patsy, awarded annually by the ASPCA.

But the big night came and Bogie was there. My mother sat beside him, tensely holding his hand. The award for Best Supporting Actress went to Kim Hunter for *A Streetcar Named Desire*. Then the award for Best Supporting Actor went to Karl Malden, from the same movie. Then Bogie and Bacall sat through the disappointment of having Kate lose out on the Best Actress award. The award went to Vivien Leigh. Three straight acting awards to *A Streetcar Named Desire*. Brando, for Best Actor, would make it a sweep. And then came the announcement for Best Actor. Greer Garson announced, "The award goes to Humphrey Bogart for *The African Queen*." The cheers were deafening.

My father, always so quick with a quip, stumbled over his planned ad-lib. Clearly, he was touched by the award.

"It's a long way from the Belgian Congo to the stage of this theater," he finally said. "It's nice to be here. Thank you very much." He thanked Kate, and Huston and Spiegel and the crew. "No one does it alone," he said. "As in tennis, you need a good opponent or partner to bring out the best in you. John and Katie helped me to be where I am now."

What stunned my father, though, more than the award itself was the fact that his was such a popular victory. He never believed that people in Hollywood liked him as much as they did, and he was very moved by it all. Long before there was a Sally Field crying, "You like me, you really like me," my father felt the same way.

Back in the press tent after the awards, Bogie reverted to form and wheeled out his old jokes about actors donning tights and reciting Hamlet. But he didn't fool anybody. They knew he was pleased and touched to have been chosen.

Later, among his friends at Romanoff's he admitted as much. Now my father was at the height of his career. He had an Oscar, a beautiful young wife, an adorable son, and a daughter on the way.

I don't know if a three-year-old boy has the sophistication to turn a small metal statue into a symbol of his anger and resentment. But I seem to recall that when my father brought home the Oscar, visible symbol of all that he had accomplished in Africa, I wanted to pick it up and hurl it at him.

That Oscar, by the way, is now on a shelf in my home.

When we get to the room that was my parents' bedroom I feel pain. I have been expecting it. Now the room holds the possessions of another Hollywood family, but I look through them and I see the room as it was. I remember the position of the bed, the table with the chess set, those nights watching TV with my father, the good-night kisses, the smell of medicine.

"God," I say to my mother, "this is so strange. I remember coming in as a kid. The bed was against the wall. I remember standing by the bed, seeing him a lot, lying down in that bed."

"Well, he was only lying down toward the end," she says.

"I have a picture of him in my mind," I say, "and Leslie and me coming up. I can really see him," I say. I am talking more to myself than to Mom.

"He would be sitting up," my mother says. "He would be sitting up when you saw him."

Despite my pain and the memories, I smile. It suddenly seems funny that Mom would be uncomfortable simply agreeing with something I say.

"Yes, Stephen, you are absolutely right," I say out loud, but she doesn't get it.

A sensation of sadness sweeps through me.

"God, thirty-six years ago," I say. I can still feel the pain, but I don't think my mother is aware of it.

I know what I am feeling. The pain is not about memories of being in the bedroom. It is about the times *when I was not allowed into the bedroom. I try to push the pain from my mind.*

11

When a man is sick you get to know him. You find out whether he is made of soft or hard wood. I began to get fonder of Bogie with each visit. He was made of very hard wood, indeed.

—DR. MAYNARD BRANDSMA

I remember the wheelchair that my father needed during the final weeks of his illness. It was a fascinating metallic contraption with hinges and shiny spokes, and a leather seat that made a snapping sound when it was opened. Dad would roll across the floor in it, grabbing at the wheels with his withering, bony hands. The wheelchair was visual, it was exotic, it was something that I understood because it was something that I could have built with an Erector set. So it is the wheelchair that is the most vivid image I retain from those mostly faded memories of my father's illness.

Our gardener then was Aurelio Salazar. Now he is old,

brown as a coffee bean from decades in the sun, and always bent slightly toward the earth he has tended so long. But back then, Aurelio was young and sturdy, and I can remember that every day at around five o'clock Aurelio would go up to my father's bedroom. He and my mother would help Bogie get dressed in his trousers, casual shirt, and smoking jacket. Bogie would make jokes about having to gain weight and he would fret about his boat, asking if they had finished the work on the hull. And then Aurelio would slip his strong arms under my father's shoulders, lifting Bogie from the bed and into the wheelchair. My father, fussing and mumbling and still insisting on doing whatever he could for himself, would roll the chair himself across the bedroom to the dumbwaiter shaft which was built into the corner of the bedroom.

Then Aurelio would lift Bogie again, and carefully place him in the dumbwaiter, which had been altered to serve as an elevator for my father. My father would sit on a small stool. The top of the dumbwaiter had been removed to accommodate him, but, sadly, nothing else had to be done. My father's weight loss had been gradual, and as a kid I didn't realize what I know now, that my father, thin to begin with, had become skeletal. Toward the end he weighed as little as eighty pounds.

Aurelio would go down to the kitchen and pull the ropes that would slowly lower my father through the dumbwaiter shaft. The shaft was dark, and though the entire ride took only about twenty seconds, it must have been a painful, even humiliating, ride for my father, alone in that dark shaft, reduced to the size of a child, and face-to-face with his own helplessness.

But once Aurelio had pulled my father out of the shaft and put him back in the wheelchair, my father would begin what, for him, was the best part of the day: cocktails with friends. He would roll into the study, swing into a more comfortable chair, smooth down his trousers, and light a cigarette. Mother would hand him a glass of scotch.

"Haven't you people got anything better to do than come over here and bother me," he would say to whoever had come to visit on that particular day. Then the banter with pals would begin and for an hour or so, despite the pain, despite the moments of despair, my dad would again be Bogie.

This is one of the precious few memories I have of the period from February 1956 to January 1957, the time of my father's illness.

I was seven years old then, and I would certainly not have understood talk about malignant cells, biopsies, radiation treatments, drugs for pain. But those were the realities of my father's cancer. So to a large extent, my father's illness was a mystery to me, a nameless thing that invaded our home one day and forever changed our lives. Certainly, I understood that Daddy was sick. But I had gotten sick, too, and I'd always gotten better.

I do remember sitting with Leslie and my mother in my father's bedroom some nights, the four of us watching television. And I remember going up to his room every night with Leslie to kiss him good night. I remember being in my pajamas, and the feel of my terry cloth bathrobe, and the smell of medicine in the room. I remember a couple of trips on the *Santana,* when he was no longer able to scramble around the deck and sing and be as cheerful as he usually was on the boat.

But, sadly, it is not the moments with my father during his illness that I remember most strongly. It is the moments without him. I remember a feeling of not being allowed to see him when I needed to. I remember that I was not supposed to jump on him, that I was not to let the dogs get too lively with him. I remember that he no longer picked me up and swung me around.

Until recently I was not especially troubled about my lack of memories. I took it on faith that my father's illness and death must have been traumatic and that I had simply blocked much of it out.

When I talked to my sister about it, she, of course, remembered less. She was only three years old when he got sick, four when he died.

"I remember Daddy in a bathrobe and sitting in a chair," she said. "I do remember that from the time he became ill, Mother felt you were old enough to understand and I was not, so all she could deal with was you, and her, and Father, not me, and I guess I felt angry and jealous about that. I don't remember a lot of family stuff from that time, either. I don't remember him being around. But whether he was around or not and whether we remember it or not, he was our father and he must have had a huge effect on us. He was a big presence whether we realized it or not."

Leslie was right. My father's dying must have had a great effect on me, whether I remember it or not. So as I began my search for my father I knew that I wanted to ask his friends about the last months of his life, months that may very well have shaped me in ways I don't even understand. I wanted to know about the spaces between my memories, the world that Humphrey Bogart lived in during those painful months. And

I hoped that in the asking, and in the telling, I would remember much of what I had forgotten.

One of the first people I talked to was Julius Epstein, the cowriter of *Casablanca*. Epstein is a small bald man, now eighty-five years old. I went to see Julius in Boston where he was visiting his son, the fine novelist Leslie Epstein.

Julius Epstein was not one of my father's intimates. They knew each other mostly in connection with *Casablanca*. But all of Hollywood was in the grip of my father's illness and Epstein remembered those final months, not so much as a man who saw my father, but as a man who was part of the world my father lived in.

"As I recall, it was right around Christmastime," he said. "That would be 1955. This was after your father had filmed *The Harder They Fall*. Bogie was drinking orange juice at Romanoff's. That, of course, was his hangout. And he found that it hurt his throat to drink the orange juice. And there was a lot of coughing. So he went to see the doctor."

In fact, it was Greer Garson, the actress who had announced Dad's Oscar, who dragged Bogie to her doctor one afternoon because she didn't like the sound of his cough.

Garson's doctor, Maynard Brandsma, told my father that his throat was inflamed. My father took it casually, even though he'd been having lengthy coughing spells long before the orange juice incident. The doctor put him on a better diet and told him to cut back on the scotch and cigarettes.

"Sure, Doc," Bogie said.

"And come back in three weeks."

"Sure, Doc."

When Bogie got home and told my mother he'd been to the doctor, she was not alarmed. However, the mere fact that Bogie had even gone to a doctor was disconcerting. He had been coughing for years, but her suggestions that he see a doctor had always been met with stony silence or a scornful reply.

Three weeks later Bogart was back in Brandsma's office. It still hurt to swallow.

"Did you do what I told you?" the doctor asked.

"No."

"Well, I can't help you if you won't help yourself."

"Yeah, yeah, well it will clear up," Bogie assured the doctor.

Somewhat nonchalant about his coughing and the fact that it hurt him to swallow, Bogie continued to prepare for his next film. He and my mother, who had already starred together in *To Have and Have Not, The Big Sleep, Dark Passage,* and *Key Largo,* were planning to make their first film together since *Key Largo,* eight years earlier. This one was to be called *Melville Goodwin, USA,* with my father as a military officer, and my mother as a character based on Claire Booth Luce.

But the coughing got worse and, finally, Bogie began to worry. He called the doctor.

"Bring in a mucus sample," he was told.

The mucus sample that my father brought in made Brandsma suspicious. He asked Bogie to come back in for a bronchoscopy, a procedure for scraping a tissue sample from the esophagus. Though Bogie was still having trouble eating and had lost weight, he and Mother still thought they were dealing with nothing worse than a viral infection of some sort. So, after the bronchoscopy they went off to Frank Sinatra's house in Palm Springs, so that Bogie could rest for a week.

By the time my parents came back from Sinatra's, the doctor was sure. Bogie had cancer. "The malignancy is small and we're finding it early," Brandsma told him. "I think we can get it out of you."

"Great," Bogie said. "Let's do what has to be done. As soon as I finish this movie we'll get to it."

"They tell me you're not a man to be lied to," Brandsma said.

"That's right," Bogie said.

"Well, I'm telling you, you'd better get to it now. If you delay surgery to make a movie, it will be your last movie."

"I can't put off this film," Bogie said. "It will cost the studio too much money."

"Do the movie," Brandsma said, "and all the cast and crew can come to your funeral."

So surgery was scheduled and the film was put on hold. The press was told nothing about the cancer, just that Bogie was going into the hospital with a swollen esophagus.

I remember the day that my father left for the Good Samaritan Hospital, February 29, 1956. My mother brought me and Leslie into the living room. She sat us down somewhat formally, then crouched to speak to us at eye level.

"Daddy is going away for a while," she said. "He has to have something taken out of his throat by a doctor. It's nothing to worry about, but he will be gone for a few weeks." We didn't really understand, but I guess we nodded our heads and figured everything would be all right. A few minutes later a big white limousine pulled up in front of the house. Dad kissed Leslie and me good-bye, and off he went in the limo. Perhaps if I had been the son of an auto mechanic who came home every night, this would have been upsetting. But during my short life my father had often gone away for weeks, even months at a time. Leslie and I were not alarmed.

The next morning when my father went into surgery,

the doctors found that things were not all right. Dr. John Jones, the surgeon, saw that the cancer had spread to Bogie's lymph glands. Jones took out the lymph glands, along with the esophagus. There was more. The surgical team had to move my father's stomach around so they could hook it up to the tab that was left. To do that they had to open his chest as well as his abdomen, so they could take out a rib to get at a few things. When they explained the procedure to my mother they also told her that from now on Bogie would feel food go directly to his stomach and that it would probably nauseate him until he got used to it. For my mother it must have been a nightmare to hear all this. Neither of my parents had had much experience with doctors and hospitals.

Dad went through nine and a half hours of surgery. Mother, of course, stayed at the hospital, calling home every few hours to tell us that everything was fine, not to worry.

When Bogie first came out of surgery my mother was horrified to see that his left hand and arm had swollen to four times their normal size, a consequence of being in one position during the hours of surgery.

For the next three weeks Leslie and I saw little of our mother. She called often, but came home usually just long enough to change clothes and rush back to the hospital. Though I was often petulant at the time, I know now that those weeks were an incredible ordeal for my mother. She had to watch helplessly as the man she loved was injected with needles, surrounded by tubes and bottles, and hooked up to cold, robotic medical machines. She had to listen while kind but often incomprehensible doctors explained the carpentry they had done inside her husband's body. She had to obey when competent but sometimes officious nurses told her when she could and could not see her husband.

"He hated the suction machine most of all," she tells me. "They needed it to clear his lungs so that he wouldn't get pneumonia. But it was awful. Once when they were getting ready to put him on it, I heard him cry, 'Please, no more.' Your father had to be in great, great pain, for him to say something like that. Through the entire ordeal of his illness, that was the only time he complained."

As my father improved he saw more and more visitors. Not only his close Hollywood friends came to see him in the hospital, but other Hollywood luminaries whom he knew less well, people like John Wayne and Fred Astaire. At some point my mother decided that he was well enough for a prank. John Huston flew in from England, and hid outside my father's hospital room. When Bogie went to the bathroom, Huston climbed into his bed and hid under the covers. Bogie came out and eyed the mysterious lump under his sheets. Then Huston leaped up, surprising Bogie, and the two men had a fine laugh.

They talked about the movies they had made together, and the ones they would make in the future. Huston, of course, had already directed my father in five great movies. Now he was looking forward to Bogie's recovery, he said, because he wanted to pair him up with Clark Gable in Rudyard Kipling's tale, *The Man Who Would Be King*. (The movie, of course, was not made then. In 1960, Huston was planning again to make it, still with Clark Gable, and while he was agonizing over who to cast in the Bogie part, Clark Gable died. But Huston finally did make *The Man Who Would Be King* in 1975, starring Sean Connery and Michael Caine, a big Bogart fan, incidentally, who took his name from a marquee for my father's film *The Caine Mutiny*.)

There was one frightening setback while my father was

still in the hospital. One night he began coughing violently, and the spasms ripped open the stitches in his belly. Blood began pouring out of his abdomen. Fortunately, my mother was with him at the time and she was able to get help.

The morning of my father's return from Good Samaritan, Mother fussed around in their bedroom, fixing the bed, getting it in just the right place, making sure that his books and glasses and his chess set would all be within reach. She was nervous and excited. Leslie and I played indoors. Infected by Mother's mood, we were excited, too. It felt like Christmas. Finally, Mother heard the slam of a car door in the driveway.

"Kids, your father's home," she called. We gathered on the upstairs landing to wait for him, me on one side of my mother, little Leslie on the other. Dad was carried in on a stretcher by male attendants. He gazed up at us and smiled.

"You see," he said to the attendants, "this is why marriage is worth it." Then to Mother, "I've been trying to get it through these guys' thick skulls that it's a great thing to be married, that you can't beat having a wife and kids there to greet you when you get home from a nice relaxing vacation at the Good Samaritan."

The attendants took the ribbing and helped Bogie to his bed. Later that day Mother told Leslie and me the rules for the fiftieth time.

"No jumping on your father."

"If you're going to be noisy play outside."

"Don't let the dogs jump on your father."

A few weeks later my father began radiation treatments. Five days a week for eight weeks he had to drive to Los Angeles and get zapped by x rays. No one was saying that he still had cancer, just that they were targeting the places where it was most likely to recur. More and more I got the feeling that there were things going on that I didn't know about.

During the weeks of the radiation treatments Bogie ate little, though my mother would always set a tray of food in front of him by the fireplace. He felt nauseous from the x rays. Now and then he would take a few bites, or even ask for a particular food, and Mother would be filled with optimism. But later he would be weak and tired and nauseous, and she would be deflated. Sometimes at night when Leslie and I sat with him watching television, he would make sounds as if he was in pain, and then he would close his eyes and pretend to be sleeping, so that we would think he was just having a bad dream.

My father's first setback was emotional. Early in the radiation treatments he lost his friend Louis Bromfield the novelist. Bromfield, the man who had hosted the Bogart and Bacall wedding on his Ohio farm, died suddenly at the age of sixty.

But Dad was buoyed up by other friends. David Niven visited. And Nunnally Johnson, and Tracy and Hepburn, and Mike Romanoff, and so many others. Frank Sinatra came by almost every night. And Swifty Lazar, fighting a constantly terrible phobia about germs and sickness, came by often. During this time Bogie's friends thought they were visiting a man who was recovering from surgery, not a man who was sick.

My father took great delight in telling his friends the details of his surgery. He was fascinated by the medical procedures and, apparently, was able to look at his illness as if it belonged to someone else.

Raymond Massey, who was an acclaimed movie actor long before most of us got to know him as Dr. Gillespie on *Dr. Kildare,* said, "I didn't know what to expect when I was ushered into the sick room, but there was Bogart, sitting in a chair, looking as good as ever, sipping scotch and soda, waiting for me. I was just beginning on the small talk when he cut in. 'I'll tell you what happened to me down there,' he said. 'It was awful!' And he told me. And the sicker I got from the story, the healthier he became. Then we spent a marvelous afternoon reminiscing about our adventures together."

Throughout the ordeal my father joked as always, quipped, needled, and expressed his appreciation for the visits in that flippant way of his. "Jesus," he told one set of friends, "how am I supposed to get any rest with the likes of you coming every day?"

Though my father tended to hide many of his feelings behind joking, as I often do, there were those serious introspective moments, too. One day Bogie told Alistair Cooke that having money, the Jaguar, the great house, the boat, no longer was any comfort to him now that he was sick.

But Dad remained optimistic. He cheerfully told people that he was getting better, and he believed it was true. "Just losing a little weight, that's all," he said. "If I could put on a few pounds I would be fine."

Certainly he took what pleasure he could from life during this period. He continued to drink, though his drinking had been reduced considerably since he'd married my mother. And he continued to smoke, switching now to filtered cigarettes. This was somewhat reckless, I suppose, since drinking and smoking were almost certainly responsible for his cancer. But Bogie was, after all, Bogie. He had eating problems, of course, but eating had never been one of his great pleasures anyhow. Bogie ate for sustenance, not for entertainment. Another similarity between father and son.

So he had his books and his booze, and he had letters to

write. I remember that the phone rang often, and sometimes that scared me because I had a constant sense that something bad could happen, though I didn't know exactly what. But the phone calls were his friends mostly. They were always concerned, and always offering to help in any way they could. And many of those calls were from the press, checking into rumors that Bogie was dying. My father would get on the phone.

"It appears to me that I am not dead," he would say. "And I'm not dying. I'm fine. Just a little underweight."

The debilitating effects of the radiation lasted long after the treatments had ended, but by August my father was starting to feel better. He weighed himself daily, and the big excitement came one day when Daddy finally gained a single pound. Mother practically danced around the house. This was the sign that everybody had been waiting for, the proof that everything would be all right.

My mother, whose career had come to a halt, began work on *Designing Woman* with Gregory Peck. My father told Aurelio to take the Thunderbird down and have it serviced. "I'm going to take Stephen to Newport for a cruise again," he said.

And he did. But now he was too weak to do much and Pete, the skipper, had to handle the boat. I don't remember the cruise. But I remember standing on the deck with my dad, the feel of his hand on my shoulder. "Someday I'm going to teach you how to sail, Steve," he said. "I think you have the makings of a fine yachtsman. And then we can go off, you and me and Pete, on trips. Just the men will go." He laughed. "We'll leave the women behind."

And he made other visits to the boat, not to sail, but just

to be on it. For a while it seemed that the dark cloud had passed.

But it hadn't. My father began to feel pain in his left shoulder. The doctors told him it was nerve damage, common after surgery. But when they got him into the hospital they broke the terrible news to my mother: the cancer had returned.

At the hospital they began something called nitrogen mustard treatments, which then was the last hope for cancer treatment. Bogie was not told that cancer had returned. They told him they were working on the nerve damage. In an odd way, my father was relieved to be back in the hospital for a few days because he despised the feeling of being a burden to everybody at home.

When he returned from the hospital this time he was terribly weak. One night he collapsed in the living room. Mother was terrified. How could the indomitable Bogie have fallen?

She got him a male nurse, someone who could carry him up and down stairs. But that didn't work. Finally, as it became more and more difficult for Humphrey Bogart to walk, Aurelio got the wheelchair and rigged the dumbwaiter as my father's elevator.

Now all of Bogie's friends, who had been treated to a period of hope, had to one by one give up the belief that Bogie "just needed to gain a little weight," and face the fact. Bogie was dying.

What was I feeling, I wonder now. Was I thinking, Daddy is dying. Was I afraid? I don't know for sure. The emotions that moved through me then are mostly forgotten. But I don't think that I believed my father was dying, because my father himself didn't believe it. Or if he did, he protected us all from his fears.

Bogie acted like a man who intended to go on living for a long time. For example, he continued to work on his career, making plans for films, even with the notorious Harry Cohn.

Harry Cohn, the most feared and hated man in Hollywood, was the head of Columbia Pictures then. He was known for his vulgarity and his ruthlessness and such antics as spying on his employees with secret microphones and informers. He was a complex man who trumpeted his evil deeds and kept his acts of kindness secret.

Despite his reputation as a heartless son of a bitch, Cohn seemed to have had a fondness for my father. Bogie had made films at Columbia on loan from Warner Brothers, and he had even sold his production company, Santana Productions, to Columbia for a million bucks. In fact, my father's last picture, *The Harder They Fall*, was for Columbia.

Now, with Bogie losing weight at a horrifying rate and spending most of his time in bed, Cohn frequently announced in the press that my father would star in *The Good Shepherd*, a movie to be based on C. S. Forester's best-selling novel. Cohn used to call my father almost weekly telling him, "The part's great, we want to get rolling, so get your ass over here."

Bogart told a friend, "I'll tell you why I think I'm going to beat this rap. It's Harry Cohn. He keeps calling me about going to work. Now you know that tough old bastard wouldn't call if he thought I wasn't going to make it. Perhaps he's not such a bastard after all."

Even my mother was touched by what Cohn was doing.

"Harry Cohn knew Bogie wasn't going to make it," she says. "But he kept the act going."

The friends continued to come for cocktail hour, though by now my mother was insisting on no more than two visitors at a time, and asking people to call ahead and schedule. Judy Garland came, and Truman Capote, and Adlai Stevenson, and Richard Burton, and David and Jennifer Selznick. Even Jack Warner, who had been my father's nemesis through much of his career. And, of course, the inner circle of people who did not have to make appointments: Sinatra, Niven, Hepburn, Tracy, Lazar, and John Huston, who amused my father with stories about the filming of *Moby-Dick*, which he had just finished.

And when they came, they did not sit weeping by Bogie's bedside. Instead he came to them, down the dumbwaiter, into the wheelchair and into the study, where they all drank and laughed and said clever things. They did not ask my father how he felt. He hated to be asked. In fact, throughout his illness there was an air of denial. Bogie and his friends conspired to con each other into the belief that he would be fine.

John Huston said, "One night Betty, Bogie's doctor, Morgan Maree [my father's business manager], and I were all sitting around in his living room when Bogie said, 'Look, give me the lowdown. You aren't kidding me, are you?' I took a deep breath and held it. The doctor finally assured Bogie that it was the treatments he had undergone that were making him feel sick and lose weight. Now that he was off the treatments, he should improve rapidly. Then we all chimed in, compounding the falsehood. He seemed to accept it."

My mother says they did not talk about his illness as if it were a possibly deadly cancer, but rather as if it were a virus he would shake off. "When it's somebody else's illness you have to take your cue from them," she told me recently. "If they choose to pretend it's a cold, then you go along with that. You don't force them to say it's more than a cold. But deep down he knew."

And Father clung to the belief that if he could just make another film, everything would be okay. "If I could just work," he would say to his friends. "If I could just work, I'd be okay."

For these cocktail hours Mom was the hostess, laughing, pouring drinks, joining in, but always keeping an eye on my father. Was he comfortable? Was he being included? Was he getting tired? She was fiercely protective of him and she sternly warned anyone who wanted to visit that if they were going to fall apart they should not come. She insisted that everybody be upbeat. This was not a death watch.

When Clifton Webb came to visit he was shocked to see how emaciated my father had become, but Webb held together through the visit, probably out of fear of Bacall. When he left the room he broke down, sobbing.

Spencer Tracy was another one who had to fight constantly against what he was feeling. "Spence was shattered before and after each visit," Kate Hepburn told me.

There were a few friends who did not come to visit, and my mother was extremely angry about that. The late director Richard Brooks was one she singled out. But she says there were others.

When she complained about this to my father, he told her, "They're afraid of death and they don't want to be reminded of it. I don't like to be around sick people myself. I'm not sure I would come and visit me."

It is poignant that these friendships were the center of

my father's life during his final weeks, because my father had never thought of himself as a well-liked man. These friends meant everything to my father during his illness. I remember that my mother had a small black notebook and in it she would write the names of everybody who came to visit him, or sent him flowers or cards.

In time my father's wise-guy protestation of "I'm just losing a little weight, that's all," gave way to a promise that he would win what he, reluctantly, acknowledged was a battle with death. "I'm going to beat it," he told Swifty Lazar. "I feel in my heart I'm going to make it."

Still, while he eventually admitted that the enemy was death, he never admitted that he was losing the battle. Everyone I talked to has said the same thing. Bogie never acknowledged that he was dying.

In the movies my father had died many times, particularly in the early days. By 1942 he had made forty-five films. In them he was electrocuted or hanged eight times, and shot to death twelve times. He had also been sentenced to life in prison nine times. But in reality, Bogie had an incredible will to live and he was nowhere near ready to die.

My mother says, "There were only two times when I heard Bogie even come close to saying it. Once was when we were on our way to the hospital for his surgery. He said to me, 'I never had to go to doctors before. Now, I suppose, I'll be seeing them for the rest of my life.' The other time was very near the end when Dr. Brandsma came to see him. Bogie told Brandsma he was worried and he said, 'So, Doc, are things going pretty much the way you expect?' 'Yes,' Brandsma said. By this time it was clear that what Brandsma expected was that Bogie would die. Aside from those two moments Bogie never talked about dying of the cancer. And I never really thought: my husband's going to die. You just get into a routine way of life. Doctors come. Nurses come. It becomes somewhat normal, and you think it is always going to be that way. He'll be sick, but he won't die."

Alistair Cooke told me, "Your father never said he was dying. And he was resolved to rouse himself for two hours a day to relax with friends until the end came. He managed to convince everyone that he was only sometimes uncomfortable, though in fact he was in terrible pain."

Other friends of my father say the same thing: he never acknowledged that he was in pain. He wouldn't even admit it to his doctor.

One afternoon Samuel Goldwyn and William Wyler came by to visit. My father was incredibly weak by this time, and said little. Still, Mother handed him his martini, and he did his best to be amusing. Even at his worst, he was able to brighten up for company.

At one point a nurse walked into the room. It was time for Dad's morphine shot.

Bogie looked at her and then at his company. He had never taken an injection in front of company before. But now the pain was too much, even for him.

He lifted his pajama leg. By now my father's leg was only skin and bones. Goldwyn was shocked. He looked away while the nurse injected the needle. When it was over, my father, somewhat embarrassed that he had upset Goldwyn, smiled weakly. "For the pain," he said, then, "sorry." He never took another injection in front of company. He forced himself to have a high threshold of pain.

One thing my father did not have a high threshold for was the press. At first, the newspapers were good to him. They didn't hound him much. They didn't say he had cancer.

But as the weeks went by and he was no longer being seen at Romanoff's, no longer making movies, the rumors became too much to ignore.

Carolyn Morris says, "The reporters would call and your father would end up yelling at them. He threatened to sue them for saying he was in a coma. Then he would bang the phone down, coughing."

When one editor called to see if his reporter had really talked to Bogart, my father told him, "If you don't trust your reporters then fire them."

My father exploded when Dorothy Kilgallen, whom he despised, printed a story that said Bogie was on the eighth floor of Los Angeles Memorial Hospital, and that he was near death.

What was funny about the story was that the Los Angeles Memorial Hospital did not exist. But my father, a man who found almost everything amusing, was temporarily humorless. He called Kilgallen's paper, screaming and yelling about "the stupid bitch."

When he was relatively calm he called Joe Hyams, and asked Joe to print a statement from him. Obviously, by the time he wrote it, Bogie's sense of humor had returned.

"I have been greatly disturbed lately at the many unchecked and baseless rumors being tossed among you regarding the state of my health," he wrote. "Just to set the record straight, as they say in Washington (and I have as much right to say this as anybody in Washington has), a great deal of what has been printed has had nothing to do with the true facts. It may be even necessary for me to send out a truth team to follow you all around.

"I have read that both lungs have been removed, that I

couldn't live for another half hour, that I was fighting for my life in some hospital which doesn't exist out here, that my heart had been removed and replaced by an old gasoline pump salvaged from a defunct Standard Oil station. I have been on the way to practically every cemetery, you name 'em, from here to the Mississippi, including several where I'm certain they only accept dogs. All the above upsets my friends, not to mention the insurance companies . . . so, as they also say in Washington, let's get the facts to the American people—and here they are.

"I had a slight malignancy in the esophagus. So that some of you won't have to go to the research department, it's the pipe that runs from your throat to your stomach. The operation for the removal of the malignancy was successful, although it was touch and go for a while whether the malignancy or I would survive.

"As they also say in Washington, I'm a better man than I ever was and all I need now is about thirty pounds in weight, which I'm sure some of you could spare. Possibly we could start something like a Weight Bank for Bogart, and, believe me, I'm not particular from which portion of your anatomies it comes from.

"In closing, any time you want to run a little medical bulletin on me, just pick up the phone, and as they say in the old country, I'm in the book!"

The reporters did call. But the distressing stories kept coming: BOGIE WAGES A BATTLE FOR LIFE. DOWN TO 80 LBS., BOGART FIGHTS FOR LIFE AGAINST THROAT CANCER.

By December there was no denying the truth.

Christmas came and went. Leslie and I got lots of presents. It was Dad's fifty-seventh birthday. Then my birthday came two weeks later. My mother had a party for me, with lots of my friends.

Everybody knew the end was coming. By this time Dad was having trouble breathing and they had brought in oxygen tanks for him. I remember them, two big green tanks, one for upstairs and one for downstairs.

Soon friends were making final visits.

One of the people I talked to about my father's last days was Phil Stern. Stern is a top Hollywood photographer, who has taken shots of celebrities for *Look, Life,* and *The Saturday Evening Post.* At seventy-five, he is still very active in Hollywood.

He remembers Mapleton Drive, the beautiful house, the patio, the pool. And he remembers his last visit with my father.

"It really was a good-bye," he says. "I was just one of many, hundreds who came . . . a 'cast of thousands.' I remember Bacall greeting me at the door and saying, 'You've come to see the great man.' I went in and Bogart was lying on the couch. He had wasted away. At this time I had just had a book of photos published. Bogie had the book. He looked up at me and smiled and said, 'You did a great job, kid.' "

Phil Gersh says, "Near the end I went upstairs, the last time I saw him. He must have been eighty-five pounds.

" 'Hey, kid,' he said, 'where are the scripts?'

" 'They're in the car,' I said. This was a running bit with us, dialogue we had many times at Romanoff's.

" 'Well, who are they for?'

"I gave him some names. 'Hal Wallis wants you,' I said, or Joe Pasternak, or Stanley Kramer.

" 'Are they holding the jobs open for me?'

"I said, 'Absolutely, Bogie.' He was smoking. It didn't make any difference by this point, I guess."

My father's last visitors were Kate Hepburn and Spencer Tracy. For these last weeks of his life, Tracy and Hepburn had gone to see him every night at 8:30. Tracy would sit in a chair by the bed, and Kate would sit on the floor beside him. Tracy would tell jokes.

My father and Tracy had been friends for thirty years. There had been a time when they were the closest of friends, seeing each other every day and carousing together at night. Tracy, like my father, was a world-class drinker. Then there was a period of many years when they saw little of each other, and they seemed to find each other again after both became major movie stars. It was a good pairing then; Bogie was a talker and Tracy was a listener. Though they had separate social groups, they were always close. And more than that, there was enormous professional admiration. My father said that Spencer Tracy was our best screen actor. He said that with Tracy you didn't see the mechanism at work. "He covers it up," Bogie said, "never overacts, never gives the impression that he is acting at all. I try to do it, and I succeed, but not the way Spence does. He has direct contact with an audience he never sees."

This particular night, Tracy needed all of his acting skills, because he was a wreck.

Kate Hepburn described the last visit to me this way. "I was with Spencer. We spent time with your father. Before we left I kissed him good night, the way I always did, and Spencer put a hand on Bogie's shoulder. Bogie gave him one of those great Bogart smiles, you know, and he said, 'Good-bye,

Spence,' but those words, Stephen, they were so filled with meaning. You knew Bogie meant it as a final good-bye, because your father had always said good night in the past, not good-bye. We got downstairs in that lovely house they had, and Spence looked at me. He was terribly sad and he said to me, 'You know Bogie's going to die.' He meant that Bogie would die very soon."

Though my father almost never talked about dying during his illness, it seems that toward the end he knew. Even his doctor said that on his last visit Bogie said good-bye and thanked him for all that he had done. "I'm sure that night he knew he was going to die," Brandsma says.

After Tracy and Hepburn left that night, my mother and father watched *Anchors Away*, the film starring Gene Kelly and Frank Sinatra. Lately, my mother had been sleeping in another bed, so as not to disturb Bogie's sleep. But on this particular night he asked her to stay with him. The night was a horror for both of them. Dad suffered through the night in a claustrophobic nightmare, constantly picking at his body, clutching his chest, struggling, it seemed, to leave his body. I can only imagine what my mother went through, lying there helplessly beside him. Later she learned that this was a common phenomenon just before death.

In the morning Dad seemed a little better, as he usually did when day arrived. It was a Sunday, and Mother took Leslie and me to Sunday school at the All Saints Episcopal Church. When she came back she and Dad talked for a while and when she left to pick us up at Sunday school he said to her, "Good-bye, kid." These were his last words to her, and later the press would make something of it, filling the words with meaning, as if Bogie knew they were the last words. But my mother says no, he said, "Good-bye, kid," just the way he always said it.

When Mother brought us home from Sunday school my father was in a coma.

Dr. Brandsma came over. He told my mother that Bogie could come out of the coma, but that, more likely, this was the end. "He has fought harder than anyone," Brandsma told her. "He lived longer than we had a right to expect. He should have died four months ago, but he didn't because his will was so strong."

My mother was shaking. "What about Steve?" she said. "How do you tell an eight-year-old boy that his father is dying?" She asked Brandsma if he would talk to me.

Then she called me into the butternut room. "Steve, Dr. Brandsma wants to talk to you."

Mother asked me to sit. I must have known that something bad was going to happen because I remember sitting on the edge of the chair. Brandsma sat across from me.

"Stephen," he said, "you know your daddy has been very sick."

"Yes."

"And I've been trying everything I could to make him better," the doctor said. "But that's not enough."

I nodded.

"Stephen, your dad is sleeping now. He may go into a deeper sleep. And he might not wake up. Do you know what I'm trying to say to you?"

I nodded. My mother had her arm around me. "Stephen, do you understand what the doctor is saying?"

I ran out of the room.

Later my mother found me. "Daddy is in a deep sleep,"

she said. "Come and see him." We walked into that room, with its awful smell of sickness and decay. We sat on the bed. Mother was more frightened than me. I moved closer. We both took Bogie's hand, and sat there not talking to each other, just thinking our own thoughts, feeling our own feelings. After a moment I leaned over and kissed my father's cheek. Mother did the same.

Later that day she found me again in the bedroom, standing by my sleeping father. She asked me why I had come back. "Because I wanted to," I said.

That's what happened. I know from talking to my mother and from my own small fragments of memories. But for most of my life I could only guess at what I felt: fear, anger, loss. I could recall only some of the scene, as if I had glimpsed it quickly from a safe hiding place. And I recalled none of the feelings. Lately, they have been returning—glimpses, whispers, sensations of regret so poignantly felt that I have no words to describe them.

That night the nurse came to my mother. "Mrs. Bogart," she said, "Mr. Bogart has died." My mother sobbed all through the night. Because of their game, their pretense that it was all a passing virus, their insistence that Bogie was always on the road back to good health, Mom had had to hold so much in. And now, with him gone, all those trapped emotions came pouring out for her. She could let herself feel what she had been trying not to feel for months. I sometimes wonder if these memories I am having in bits and pieces are enough, or if I also need to have such a moment.

At dawn she came into my room.

"Darling, I'm sorry to have to tell you that your father died early this morning."

She says I lay there, rubbing my eyes with my fists. My eyes were wet and red, she says, but I did not cry.

"Is he in heaven?" I asked.

"Yes, he's in heaven," she said. "And he is watching over us, so you must be brave and strong. He was so proud of you. And he loved you very much."

Then she got Leslie and brought her in and told her. I do remember that Leslie kept playing while Mother told her, and because I was feeling sad while Leslie was still playing, I somehow thought that made me better than Leslie. Of course, Leslie kept playing. She was only four years old.

So I lost my father when I was eight, and within a year I would lose my home, my school, and my friends. All of those losses that I remember would be troubling, of course. But something happened during those final weeks that has troubled me even more all of my life. I was in my father's room one day. I don't know if I was talking to him or just playing there. And I don't know whether it was days before he died, or weeks before he died. But after I was gone, my father told my mother not to let me or Leslie in there anymore.

I'm forty-five now and I can perhaps gather some of what my father must have felt, the emotions that would make him say such a thing. The pain of having his children see him so impotent, so small and pathetic, must have been unbearable. He must have cried to think he would never see us grow up. It must have been more excruciating than the cancer for Bogie to look at his little boy and his little girl playing in the sunlight that streamed through his bedroom window, knowing that the light would go out much too soon.

But that's big Steve Bogart sizing things up with his adult brain. I was eight years old. And what I have held on to most of my life is that feeling of not being allowed to see him, of being somehow left out, of being rejected by my father during his final days. The memory of that feeling has stayed with me always. Perhaps it explains, in part, why until now I have been unwilling to talk about my father's life.

Mother and I stand outside of the house. We stare into the swimming pool.

"It wasn't here when we moved in," she explains. "I had it installed for you kids."

She points to the spot where Leslie and I left our small footprints in the cement four decades ago. Both somewhat stunned by our memories, we stand by the edge of the glistening water, as if our own feet are anchored in the cement. Our visit to the Mapleton Drive house is over, but we are not quite ready to leave. There is a slight breeze and I hear the soft play of the water as it slaps against the edges of the swimming pool. I replay a memory that I have replayed many times.

I am with my father on the boat, sailing to Catalina. Then I am on the shore. My father is offshore, on the boat. He is sending Pete in the skiff to pick me up. But I don't want to be picked up. I want to swim out to Dad, show him I can swim well. I wave to him. "I'll swim to you," I shout. He shouts something to Pete, telling Pete to let me swim but to keep an eye on me. I begin to swim.

The water is cold around me and the surface bobs at me, now and then splashing my face. I keep my mouth closed, afraid of swallowing water. I kick my feet the way I've been taught. My arms swing forward wildly, pulling me along through the water. I can swim good, I think.

My father is standing on the foredeck watching me. He holds his hands to the brim of his fisherman's cap, to keep the sun out of his eyes. He is rooting me on as if it is *a race and I am his favorite. "Come on, Steve, my boy!" I keep swimming. I want to get there. I don't want to fail.*

I swim onward, but the boat seems farther away than it did when I began. I begin to feel a burning in my chest. I am tired, but I am determined, and I flail my arms forward, wildly scooping the water behind me. Dad is cheering me on. The Santana *is bobbing in the water. "Good going, Steve," my father is shouting. Pete stays near me in the skiff. I keep swimming. Finally, the boat is getting closer. I'm going to make it, I think. I swim harder, I breathe faster. I'm going to make it. I'm feeling so good. Almost there, I find one last burst of energy, and rip through the remaining water. I did it, I think, I swam to the boat. I begin to climb the ladder. My father, excited, dashes over to help me aboard. I get to the top rung. He lifts me in his arms and swings me around. He is smiling. "Great going, kid," he says. "I'm so proud of you."*

The memories are coming rapidly now, and as the Santana *of my memory sails away, and Mother and I begin, at last, to leave the house I am suddenly aware of another memory, an incident that happened just a few weeks before this trip to California.*

I am at home, looking at videos of old home movies. There is my father swinging me upside down in the yard. There is Leslie and me, splashing in the pool. There is my dog Harvey loping across the lawn. There is the young Bacall with her Bogie. Suddenly a picture of me as an adult has flashed on the screen. I am confused.

"How did a picture of me get on this tape?" I say to Barbara.

She looks at me strangely. "Steve," she says, "that's not you. That's your father."

I look again. Barbara is right. For the first time I am seeing myself completely in my father's face. More and more lately I have been seeing pieces of my father in me. I have become preoccupied with questions that have never before bothered me. Am I my father's son? How are we alike? How are we different?

Now, when my mother and I walk around to the front of the Mapleton Drive house the morning seems very bright, like the mornings of my childhood. The smell of the grass and the trees rush into me as if for the first time. I feel as if I have come to the end of two journeys that all men must take, one way or the other. One journey, I began a decade ago when my wife told me, "Find out about your father." The other, a journey of self knowledge, which can last a lifetime, or a year, or even just the time it takes to walk through a house you once lived in.

Your *search is over, I think. The words just come to me suddenly, as if carried on the breeze. Though I have spent most of my life running away from the shadow of my father, I have come now to see what Barbara has told me, that just because I don't want to live life as "Bogie's son," I don't have to ignore him. "Bogie or not, he was still your father," she has told me.*

If I didn't know it before, I know it now, standing in the yard of my childhood home, that this search is all about looking at my own life and at my father's and trying to fig-ure out what, if anything, they have to do with each other. I feel as if I have, in a very real sense, come home. I want to embrace my father, not run from him. I know now that the words will come easier. Not just the words I write about my father, but also the words I speak to my children when they ask about their grandfather, the words I speak to strangers when they say, "So you're Bogie's boy, huh?" My mother and I are quiet with each other as we drive away from the Mapleton Drive house that morning. I love her. She is still my mother, and even when she is driving my sister and me nuts, she is loving us. We are on our way to visit some more old friends of Humphrey Bogart. I am anxious to see these people, to ask more questions. But I am anxious, too, to be done with this trip, and to get on a plane back to my home in New Jersey. I miss my kids.

Filmography

BROADWAY'S LIKE THAT. (Short). 1930. Vitaphone Corporation. Director: Murray Roth. With Ruth Etting, Joan Blondell.

A DEVIL WITH WOMEN. 1930. Fox. Director: Irving Cummings. With Victor McLaglen, Mona Maris, Luana Alcaniz, Michael Vavitch.

UP THE RIVER. 1930. Fox. Director: John Ford. With Spencer Tracy, Claire Luce, Warren Hymer, William Collier, Sr., Joan Marie Lawes, George MacFarlane, Gaylord Pendleton, Sharon Lynn.

BODY AND SOUL. 1930. Fox. Director: Alfred Santell. With Charles Farrell, Elissa Landi, Myrna Loy, Donald Dillaway, Craufurd Kent, Pat Somerset, Ian MacLaren, Dennis D'Auburn.

BAD SISTER. 1931. Universal. Director: Hobart Henley. With Conrad Nagel, Sidney Fox, Bette Davis, ZaSu Pitts, Slim

Summerville, Charles Winninger, Emma Dunn, Bert Roach.

WOMEN OF ALL NATIONS. 1931. Fox. Director: Raoul Walsh. With Victor McLaglen, Edmund Lowe, Greta Nissen, El Brendel, Fifi Dorsay, Marjorie White, T. Roy Barnes, Bela Lugosi.

A HOLY TERROR. 1931. Fox. Director: Irving Cummings. With George O'Brien, Sally Eilers, Rita LaRoy, James Kirkwood, Robert Warwick, Richard Tucker, Stanley Fields.

LOVE AFFAIR. 1932. Columbia. Director: Thornton Freeland. With Dorothy MacKaill, Jack Kennedy, Barbara Leonard.

BIG CITY BLUES. 1932. Warner Brothers. Director: Mervyn LeRoy. With Joan Blondell, Eric Linden, Inez Courtney, Evalyn Knapp, Guy Kibbee, Lyle Talbot, Gloria Shea, Walter Catlett, Jobyna Howland.

THREE ON A MATCH. 1932. First National–Warner Brothers. Director: Mervyn LeRoy. With Joan Blondell, Warren William, Ann Dvorak, Bette Davis, Lyle Talbot, Patricia Ellis, Glenda Farrell, Frankie Darro, Edward Arnold.

MIDNIGHT. 1934. All-Star/Universal. Director: Chester Erskine. With Sidney Fox, O. P. Heggie, Henry Hull, Margaret Wycherly, Lynne Overman, Katherine Wilson, Richard Whorf, Henry O'Neill.

THE PETRIFIED FOREST. 1936. Warner Brothers. Director: Archie Mayo. With Leslie Howard, Bette Davis, Genevieve Tobin, Dick Foran, Joseph Sawyer, Porter Hall, Charley Grapewin, Paul Harvey, Eddie Acuff, Adrian Morris, Nina Campana, Slim Thompson.

BULLETS OR BALLOTS. 1936. First National–Warner Brothers. Director: William Keighley. With Edward G. Robinson, Joan Blondell, Barton MacLane, Frank McHugh, Joseph King, Richard Purcell.

TWO AGAINST THE WORLD. (GB: THE CASE OF MRS PEMBROOK). 1936. First National–Warner Brothers. Director: William McGann. With Beverly Roberts, Helen MacKellar, Carlyle Moore, Jr., Henry O'Neill, Linda Perry, Virginia Brissac, Claire Dodd.

CHINA CLIPPER. 1936. First National–Warner Brothers. Director: Ray Enright. With Pat O'Brien, Beverly Roberts, Ross Alexander, Marie Wilson, Henry B. Walthall, Joseph Crehan, Joseph King.

ISLE OF FURY. 1936. Warner Brothers. Director: Frank McDonald. With Margaret Lindsay, Donald Woods, Paul Graetz, Gordon Hart, E. E. Clive.

BLACK LEGION. 1937. Warner Brothers. Director: Archie Mayo. With Dick Foran, Erin O'Brien-Moore, Ann Sheridan, Robert Barrat, Helen Flint, Joseph Sawyer, Addison Richards, Eddie Acuff, Clifford Soubier, Dickie Jones, Henry Brandon.

THE GREAT O'MALLEY. 1937. Warner Brothers. Director: William Dieterle. With Pat O'Brien, Sybil Jason, Ann Sheridan, Frieda Inescort, Donald Crisp, Henry O'Neill, Craig Reynolds, Gordon Hart.

MARKED WOMAN. 1937. First National–Warner Brothers. Director: Lloyd Bacon. With Bette Davis, Lola Lane, Isabel Jewell, Eduardo Ciannelli, Rosalind Marquis, Mayo Methot, Jane Bryan, Allen Jenkins.

KID GALAHAD. 1937. Warner Brothers. Director: Michael Curtiz. With Edward G. Robinson, Bette Davis, Wayne Morris, Jane Bryan, Harry Carey, William Haade, Soledad Cunningham, Veda Ann Borg, Ben Welden.

SAN QUENTIN. 1937. First National–Warner Brothers. Director: Lloyd Bacon. With Pat O'Brien, Ann Sheridan, Barton

MacLane, Joseph Sawyer, Veda Ann Borg, James Robbins, Marc Lawrence, Joseph King.

DEAD END. 1937. Sam Goldwyn/United Artists. Director: William Wyler. With Sylvia Sidney, Joel McCrea, Wendy Barrie, Claire Trevor, Allen Jenkins, Marjorie Main, Billy Halop, Huntz Hall, Bobby Jordan, Leo Gorcey, Gabriel Dell, Bernard Punsley, Ward Bond.

STAND-IN. 1937. Walter Wanger/United Artists. Director: Tay Garnett. With Leslie Howard, Joan Blondell, Alan Mowbray, Marla Shelton, C. Henry Gordon, Jack Carson.

SWING YOUR LADY. 1938. Warner Brothers. Director: Ray Enright. With Frank McHugh, Louise Fazenda, Nat Pendleton, Penny Singleton, Allen Jenkins, Ronald Reagan, Leon Weaver, Frank Weaver, Sue Moore.

CRIME SCHOOL. 1938. First National–Warner Brothers. Director: Lewis Seiler. With Gale Page, Billy Halop, Bobby Jordan, Huntz Hall, Leo Gorcey, Bernard Punsley, Gabriel Dell, Charles Trowbridge.

MEN ARE SUCH FOOLS. 1938. Warner Brothers. Director: Busby Berkeley. With Priscilla Lane, Wayne Morris, Hugh Herbert, Penny Singleton.

THE AMAZING DOCTOR CLITTERHOUSE. 1938. First National–Warner Brothers. Director: Anatole Litvak. With Edward G. Robinson, Claire Trevor, Allen Jenkins, Donald Crisp, Gale Page, Maxie Rosenbloom, John Litel.

RACKET BUSTERS. 1938. Warner Brothers–Cosmopolitan. Director: Lloyd Bacon. With George Brent, Gloria Dickson, Allen Jenkins, Walter Abel, Henry O'Neill, Penny Singleton.

ANGELS WITH DIRTY FACES. 1938. First National–Warner Brothers. Director: Michael Curtiz. With James Cagney, Pat O'Brien, Ann Sheridan, George Bancroft, Billy Halop,

Bobby Jordan, Leo Gorcey, Gabriel Dell, Huntz Hall, Bernard Punsley, Joseph Downing, Edward Pawley.

KING OF THE UNDERWORLD. 1939. Warner Brothers. Director: Lewis Seiler. With Kay Francis, James Stephenson, John Eldredge, Jessie Busley.

THE OKLAHOMA KID. 1939. Warner Brothers. Director: Lloyd Bacon. With James Cagney, Rosemary Lane, Donald Crisp, Harvey Stephens, Hugh Sothern, Charles Middleton, Edward Pawley, Ward Bond.

DARK VICTORY. 1939. First National–Warner Brothers. Director: Edmund Goulding. With Bette Davis, George Brent, Geraldine Fitzgerald, Ronald Reagan, Henry Travers, Cora Witherspoon, Dorothy Peterson.

YOU CAN'T GET AWAY WITH MURDER. 1939. First National–Warner Brothers. Director: Lewis Seiler. With Billy Halop, Gale Page, John Litel, Henry Travers, Harvey Stephens, Harold Huber, Joseph Sawyer.

THE ROARING TWENTIES. 1939. Warner Brothers–First National. Director: Raoul Walsh. With James Cagney, Priscilla Lane, Gladys George, Jeffrey Lynn, Frank McHugh, Paul Kelly, Elisabeth Risdon, Joseph Sawyer.

THE RETURN OF DOCTOR X. 1939. First National–Warner Brothers. Director: Vincent Sherman. With Wayne Morris, Rosemary Lane, Dennis Morgan, John Litel, Lya Lys, Huntz Hall, Charles Wilson, Vera Lewis.

INVISIBLE STRIPES. 1939. Warner Brothers–First National. Director: Lloyd Bacon. With George Raft, Jane Bryan, William Holden, Flora Robson, Paul Kelly, Lee Patrick, Henry O'Neill, Marc Lawrence, Moroni Olsen, Tully Marshall.

VIRGINIA CITY. 1940. Warner Brothers–First National. Director: Michael Curtiz. With Errol Flynn, Miriam Hopkins,

Randolph Scott, Frank McHugh, Alan Hale, Guinn Williams, Douglass Dumbrille, John Litel.

IT ALL CAME TRUE. 1940. Warner Brothers–First National. Director: Lewis Seiler. With Ann Sheridan, Jeffrey Lynn, ZaSu Pitts, Una O'Connor, Jessie Busley, John Litel, Grant Mitchell, Felix Bressart.

BROTHER ORCHID. 1940. Warner Brothers–First National. Director: Lloyd Bacon. With Edward G. Robinson, Ann Sothern, Donald Crisp, Ralph Bellamy, Allen Jenkins, Cecil Kellaway, Morgan Conway.

THEY DRIVE BY NIGHT. (GB: THE ROAD TO FRISCO). 1940. Warner Brothers–First National. Director: Raoul Walsh. With George Raft, Ann Sheridan, Ida Lupino, Gale Page, Alan Hale, Roscoe Karns, John Litel, George Tobias, Paul Hurst.

HIGH SIERRA. 1941. Warner Brothers–First National. Director: Raoul Walsh. With Ida Lupino, Alan Curtis, Arthur Kennedy, Joan Leslie, Henry Hull, Henry Travers, Jerome Cowan, Minna Gombell, Barton MacLane, Cornel Wilde.

THE WAGONS ROLL AT NIGHT. 1941. Warner Brothers–First National. Director: Ray Enright. With Sylvia Sidney, Eddie Albert, Joan Leslie, Sig Ruman, Cliff Clark, Charley Foy, Frank Wilcox, John Ridgeley.

THE MALTESE FALCON. 1941. Warner Brothers–First National. Director: John Huston. With Mary Astor, Gladys George, Peter Lorre, Barton MacLane, Lee Patrick, Sydney Greenstreet, Ward Bond, Jerome Cowan, Elisha Cook, Jr., James Burke, Murray Alper, Walter Huston.

ALL THROUGH THE NIGHT. 1942. Warner Brothers–First National. Director: Vincent Sherman. With Conrad Veidt, Kaaren Verne, Jane Darwell, Frank McHugh, Peter Lorre, Judith Anderson, William Demarest, Jackie Gleason, Phil Silvers, Barton MacLane, Martin Kosleck.

THE BIG SHOT. 1942. Warner Brothers–First National. Director: Lewis Seiler. With Irene Manning, Richard Travis, Susan Peters, Stanley Ridges, Minor Watson, Howard da Silva, Joseph Downing, Chick Chandler.

ACROSS THE PACIFIC. 1942. Warner Brothers–First National. Director: John Huston. With Mary Astor, Sydney Greenstreet, Charles Halton, Victor Sen Yung, Roland Got, Lee Tung Foo, Keye Luke, Frank Wilcox, Richard Loo.

CASABLANCA. 1942. Warner Brothers–First National. Director: Michael Curtiz. With Ingrid Bergman, Paul Henreid, Claude Rains, Conrad Veidt, Sydney Greenstreet, Peter Lorre, S. Z. Sakall, Madeleine LeBeau, Dooley Wilson, Joy Page, John Qualen, Leonid Kinsky, Helmut Dantine, Curt Bois, Marcel Dalio, Corinna Mura, Dan Seymour.

ACTION IN THE NORTH ATLANTIC. 1943. Warner Brothers–First National. Director: Lloyd Bacon. With Raymond Massey, Alan Hale, Julie Bishop, Ruth Gordon, Sam Levene, Dane Clark, Peter Whitney, Dick Hogan.

THANK YOUR LUCKY STARS. 1943. Warner Brothers–First National. Director: David Butler. With Eddie Cantor, Bette Davis, Olivia de Havilland, Errol Flynn, John Garfield, Joan Leslie, Ida Lupino, Dennis Morgan, Ann Sheridan, Dinah Shore, Alexis Smith, Jack Carson, Alan Hale, George Tobias, Edward Everett Horton, S. Z. Sakall.

SAHARA. 1943. Columbia. Director: Zoltan Korda. With Bruce Bennett, J. Carrol Naish, Lloyd Bridges, Rex Ingram, Richard Nugent, Dan Duryea, Carl Harbord, Patrick O'Moore, Kurt Krueger.

PASSAGE TO MARSEILLE. 1944. Warner Brothers–First National. Director: Michael Curtiz. With Claude Rains, Michele

Morgan, Philip Dorn, Sydney Greenstreet, Peter Lorre, George Tobias, Helmut Dantine, John Loder, Victor Francen, Vladimir Sokoloff, Eduardo Ciannelli, Hans Conried.

REPORT FROM THE FRONT. 1944. Red Cross Drive Committee of the Motion Picture Industry. Trailer featuring Bogart and Mayo Methot in clips from their North African tour in December 1943.

TO HAVE AND HAVE NOT. 1945. Warner Brothers–First National. Director: Howard Hawks. With Lauren Bacall, Walter Brennan, Dolores Moran, Hoagy Carmichael, Walter Molnar, Sheldon Leonard, Dan Seymour, Marcel Dalio.

CONFLICT. 1945. Warner Brothers–First National. Director: Curtis Bernhardt. With Alexis Smith, Sydney Greenstreet, Rose Hobart, Charles Drake, Grant Mitchell, Patrick O'Moore, Ann Shoemaker.

HOLLYWOOD VICTORY CARAVAN. 1945. Paramount for the War Activities Committee and the Treasury Department. Director: William Russell. With numerous Hollywood stars and the US Maritime Service Training Station Choir. 20-minute movie about a war hero's sister's efforts to join a train carrying stars to Washington in which Bogart appealed for Victory Loan Bonds.

TWO GUYS FROM MILWAUKEE. 1946. Warner Brothers–First National. Director: David Butler. With Dennis Morgan, Jack Carson, Joan Leslie, Janis Paige, S. Z. Sakall, Patti Brady. Cameos by Bogart and Lauren Bacall.

THE BIG SLEEP. 1946. Warner Brothers–First National. Director: Howard Hawks. With Lauren Bacall, John Ridgely, Martha Vickers, Dorothy Malone, Peggy Knudsen, Regis Toomey, Charles Waldron, Elisha Cook, Jr., Charles D. Brown, Louis Jean Heydt, Sonia Darrin, Bob Steele.

DEAD RECKONING. 1947. Columbia. Director: John Cromwell. With Lizabeth Scott, Morris Carnovsky, Charles Cane, William Prince, Marvin Miller, Wallace Ford, James Bell.

THE TWO MRS. CARROLLS. 1947. Warner Brothers–First National. Director: Peter Godfrey. With Barbara Stanwyck, Alexis Smith, Nigel Bruce, Isobel Elsom, Patrick O'Moore, Ann Carter, Anita Bolster.

DARK PASSAGE. 1947. Warner Brothers–First National. Director: Delmer Daves. With Lauren Bacall, Bruce Bennett, Agnes Moorehead, Tom D'Andrea, Clifton Young, Douglas Kennedy, Rory Mallinson.

ALWAYS TOGETHER. 1948. Warner Brothers–First National. Director: Frederick de Cordova. With Robert Hutton, Joyce Reynolds, Cecil Kellaway, Ernest Truex. Cameo by Bogart.

THE TREASURE OF THE SIERRA MADRE. 1948. Warner Brothers–First National. Director: John Huston. With Walter Huston, Tim Holt, Bruce Bennett, Barton MacLane, Alfonso Bedoya, John Huston, Jack Holt, Robert Blake.

KEY LARGO. 1948. Warner Brothers–First National. Director: John Huston. With Edward G. Robinson, Lauren Bacall, Lionel Barrymore, Claire Trevor, Thomas Gomez, Harry Lewis, Marc Lawrence, Monte Blue, Jay Silverheels, Dan Seymour.

KNOCK ON ANY DOOR. 1949. Santana–Columbia. Director: Nicholas Ray. With John Derek, George Macready, Allene Roberts, Susan Perry, Mickey Knox, Barry Kelley, Cara Williams, Jimmy Conlin.

TOKYO JOE. 1949. Santana–Columbia. Director: Stuart Heisler. With Alexander Knox, Florence Marley, Sessue Hayakawa, Jerome Courtland, Gordon Jones, Teru Shimada, Hideo Mori.

CHAIN LIGHTNING. 1950. Warner Brothers–First National. Director: Stuart Heisler. With Eleanor Parker, Raymond Massey, Richard Whorf, James Brown, Roy Roberts, Morris Ankrum, Fay Baker.

IN A LONELY PLACE. 1950. Santana–Columbia. Director: Nicholas Ray. With Gloria Grahame, Frank Lovejoy, Carl Benton Reid, Art Smith, Jeff Donnell, Martha Stewart, Robert Warwick.

THE ENFORCER (GB: MURDER INC.). 1951. Warner Brothers. Director: Bretaigne Windust. With Zero Mostel, Ted de Corsia, Everett Sloane, Roy Roberts, Lawrence Tolan, King Donovan.

SIROCCO. 1951. Santana–Columbia. Director: Curtis Bernhardt. With Marta Toren, Lee J. Cobb, Everett Sloane, Gerald Mohr, Zero Mostel, Nick Dennis, Onslow Stevens, Ludwig Donath, Harry Guardino.

THE AFRICAN QUEEN. 1951. Horizon–Romulus–United Artists. Director: John Huston. With Katharine Hepburn, Robert Morley, Peter Bull, Theodore Bikel, Walter Gotell, Gerald Onn.

DEADLINE U.S.A. (GB: DEADLINE). 1952. Twentieth Century–Fox. Director: Richard Brooks. With Ethel Barrymore, Kim Hunter, Ed Begley, Warren Stevens, Paul Stewart, Martin Gabel, Joe De Santis, Audrey Christie, Jim Backus.

BATTLE CIRCUS. 1953. MGM. Director: Richard Brooks. With June Allyson, Keenan Wynn, Robert Keith, William Campbell, Perry Sheehan, Jonathan Cott, Adele Longmire, Ann Morrison, Philip Ahn.

BEAT THE DEVIL. 1954. Santana–Romulus–United Artists. Director: John Huston. With Jennifer Jones, Gina Lollobrigida, Robert Morley, Peter Lorre, Edward Underdown, Ivor Barnard.

THE CAINE MUTINY. 1954. Stanley Kramer–Columbia. Director: Edward Dmytryk. With Jose Ferrer, Van Johnson, Fred MacMurray, Robert Francis, May Wynn, Tom Tully, E. G. Marshall, Lee Marvin, Claude Akins.

SABRINA (GB: SABRINA FAIR). 1954. Paramount. Director: Billy Wilder. With Audrey Hepburn, William Holden, Walter Hampden, John Williams, Martha Hyer, Joan Vohs, Marcel Dalio, Francis X. Bushman, Nancy Kulp.

THE BAREFOOT CONTESSA. 1954. Figaro Incorporated. Director: Joseph L. Mankiewicz. With Ava Gardner, Edmond O'Brien, Marius Goring, Valentina Cortesa, Rossano Brazzi, Elizabeth Sellars, Warren Stevens, Bessie Love.

WE'RE NO ANGELS. 1955. Paramount. Director: Michael Curtiz. With Aldo Ray, Peter Ustinov, Joan Bennett, Basil Rathbone, Leo G. Carroll, John Baer, Gloria Talbott, Lea Penman, John Smith.

THE LEFT HAND OF GOD. 1955. Twentieth Century-Fox. Director: Edward Dmytryk. With Gene Tierney, Lee J. Cobb, Agnes Moorehead, E. G. Marshall, Jean Porter, Carl Benton Reid, Victor Sen Yung, Benson Fong.

THE DESPERATE HOURS. 1955. Paramount. Director: William Wyler. With Fredric March, Arthur Kennedy, Martha Scott, Dewey Martin, Gig Young, Mary Murphy, Richard Eyer, Robert Middleton.

THE HARDER THEY FALL. 1956. Columbia. Director: Mark Robson. With Rod Steiger, Jan Sterling, Mike Lane, Max Baer, Jersey Joe Walcott, Edward Andrews, Harold J. Stone, Nehemiah Persoff.

Index

Index